Introducing Applied Linguistics

Introducing Applied Linguistics provides in-depth coverage of key areas in the subject, as well as introducing the essential study skills needed for academic success in the field.

Introducing Applied Linguistics:

- is organised into two sections: the first introducing key concepts in applied linguistics; and the second devoted to the study skills students need to succeed.

- features specially commissioned chapters from key authorities who address core areas of applied linguistics, including both traditional and more cutting edge topics, such as: grammar, vocabulary, language in the media, forensic linguistics, and much more.

- contains a study skills section offering guidance on a range of skills, such as: how to structure and organise an essay, the conventions of referencing, how to design research projects, plus many more.

- is supported by a lively companion website, which includes interactive exercises, information about the contributors and why they've written the book, and annotated weblinks to help facilitate further independent learning.

Ideal for advanced undergraduate and postgraduate students of applied linguistics and TEFL/TESOL, *Introducing Applied Linguistics* not only presents selected key concepts in depth, but also initiates the student into the discourse of applied linguistics.

To explore a wealth of extra online learning material that accompanies this book, go to www.routledge.com/textbooks/9780415447676

Susan Hunston is Professor of English Language and Head of the School of English, Drama, and American & Canadian Studies, at the University of Birmingham, UK.

David Oakey is an Assistant Professor in the Applied Linguistics Program at Iowa State University, USA.

Contributing authors: Svenja Adolphs, Aileen Bloomer, Zoltán Dörnyei, Adrian Holliday, Alison Johnson, Chris Kennedy, Almut Koester, Ruby Macksoud, Kirsten Malmkjær, Kieran O'Halloran, David Oakey, Juup Stelma, Joan Swann, Geoff Thompson, Dave Willis, Jane Willis, and David Woolls.

'This book does an excellent job of providing students new to applied linguistics or TESOL with a very accessible and stimulating introduction to the field. It offers an innovative design, core concepts are clearly defined and exemplified and the chapters draw insightfully on a wide range of current research. There is every possibility that this will become a standard text for students studying applied linguistics for the first time.'

Ken Hyland, *Institute of Education, University of London*

'For those of us involved in teaching postgraduate students where resources are limited, this is an ideal book to have at hand. The topics are varied and presented in such a way as to stimulate discussion in a very thought-provoking way. I teach postgraduate courses in Thailand, Vietnam and China and this book will be "a must" on my reading list.'

Joseph Foley, *Graduate School of English, Assumption University, Thailand*

Introducing Applied Linguistics

Concepts and Skills

Susan Hunston and David Oakey

Routledge
Taylor & Francis Group

LONDON AND NEW YORK

First published 2010
by Routledge
2 Park Square, Milton Park, Abingdon, Oxon OX14 4RN

Simultaneously published in the USA and Canada
by Routledge
270 Madison Ave, New York, NY 10016

Routledge is an imprint of the Taylor & Francis Group, an informa business

Typeset in Minion by M Rules
Printed and bound in Great Britain by MPG Books Group, UK

British Library Cataloguing in Publication Data
A catalogue record for this book is available from the British Library

Library of Congress Cataloging-in-Publication Data
Hunston, Susan, 1953–
Introducing applied linguistics: concepts and skills / Susan Hunston and David Oakey.
p. cm.
1. Applied linguistics. I. Oakey, David.
II. Title.
P129.H86 2010
418–dc22
2009003472

ISBN 10: 0-415-44768-2 (hbk)
ISBN 10: 0-415-44767-4 (pbk)
ISBN 10: 0-203-87572-9 (ebk)
ISBN 13: 978-0-415-44768-3 (hbk)
ISBN 13: 978-0-415-44767-6 (pbk)
ISBN 13: 978-0-203-87572-8 (ebk)

Contents

SECTION 1: KEY CONCEPTS IN APPLIED LINGUISTICS

SECTION 2: STUDY SKILLS FOR APPLIED LINGUISTICS STUDENTS

Figures and tables

Notes on contributors

Svenja Adolphs is Associate Professor in Applied Linguistics at the University of Nottingham. She specializes in the analysis of spoken corpora and multimodal corpora.

Aileen Bloomer specializes in teaching EFL, TEFL and intercultural communication. She was formerly a lecturer at York St John University.

Zoltán Dörnyei is Professor of Psycholinguistics at the University of Nottingham. He is well known for his research and publications in second language acquisition.

Adrian Holliday is Professor of Applied Linguistics at Canterbury Christ Church University. He has published widely in the critical sociology of TESOL, qualitative research methodology and intercultural communication.

Alison Johnson is Lecturer in Modern English Language at the University of Leeds. She specializes in forensic linguistics and institutional interaction.

Chris Kennedy is Associate Professor and Director of the Centre for English Language Studies at the University of Birmingham. He also works extensively as a project advisor and consultant.

Almut Koester is Senior Lecturer and Director of the Centre for Academic and Professional English at the University of Birmingham. She is an expert in business communication and the language of the workplace.

Ruby Macksoud has taught English as a foreign and second language in Canada, Japan, the UK, Puerto Rico, and the US. She is a faculty member in the department of English at Arizona State University, USA. In addition, she works as a technical writing editor and instructional design consultant in the private sector.

Kirsten Malmkjær is Professor of Translation Studies at Middlesex University in London. She has published widely in translation theory, semantics and pragmatics.

David Oakey is an Assistant Professor in the Applied Linguistics Program at Iowa State University, USA. He has taught English in Japan, Korea and Turkey and researches the phraseology of written academic English.

Kieran O'Halloran is Senior Lecturer in Linguistics at the Open University. His speciality is the application of corpus linguistics to critical discourse analysis.

Juup Stelma is Lecturer in TESOL at the University of Manchester. His main research interests are teaching languages to young learners and classroom interaction.

Joan Swann is Senior Lecturer in Education and Director of the Centre for Language and Communication at the Open University. She specializes in sociolinguistics and language and creativity.

Geoff Thompson is Senior Lecturer in Applied Linguistics at the University of Liverpool. He is an authority on systemic-functional linguistics.

Dave Willis is well known as a writer and consultant on English Language Teaching. He was formerly Senior Lecturer in Applied Linguistics at the University of Birmingham.

Jane Willis is widely known a writer and consultant on English Language Teaching. She was formerly Lecturer in Applied Linguistics at the University of Aston in Birmingham.

David Woolls is a software developer with a particular interest in language, especially forensic linguistics and translation.

Acknowledgements

The editors and publishers wish to thank the following for permission to use copyright material.

Canagarajah, A. S. (2000) 'Constructing hybrid postcolonial subjects: Codeswitching in Jaffna classrooms' from *Voices of Authority: Education and linguistic difference*, M. Heller and M. Martin-Jones (eds) © 2001 Monica Heller and Marilyn Martin-Jones. Reproduced with permission of Greenwood Publishing Group, Inc., Westport, CT.

Dam, L. and Lentz, J. (1998) *It's Up to Yourself if You Want to Learn: Autonomous language learning at intermediate level* (video and print), Copenhagen: DLH. Reproduced by kind permission of Leni Dam.

Davies, J. A. (2000) *Expressions of Gender: An enquiry into the way gender impacts on the discourse styles of pupils involved in small group talk during GCSE English lesson, with particular reference to the underachievement of boys*. Sheffield: unpublished PhD Thesis, University of Sheffield. Reprinted by kind permission of the author.

The Guardian 4 August 1976 (headline and first paragraph – 40 words)

Jewitt, C. and Kress, G. (2003) 'A multimodal approach to research in education', in Goodman, S., Lillis, T., Maybin, J. and Mercer, N. (eds) *Language, Literacy and Education: A reader*. Stoke-on-Trent: Trentham Books in association with the Open University.

Maybin, J. (2006) *Children's Voices: Talk, Knowledge and Identity*. Basingstoke, Hamps/New York: Palgrave Macmillan, reproduced with permission of Palgrave Macmillan.

Maybin, J. and Swann, J. (2007) 'Everyday creativity in language: textuality, contextuality and critique', in J. Swann and J. Maybin (eds) Special Issue of *Applied Linguistics* on *Language Creativity in Everyday Contexts*, 28 (4): 497–517, by permission of Oxford University Press.

Mercer, N., Dawes, L., Wegerif, R. and Sams, C. (2004) 'Reasoning as a scientist: ways of helping children to use language to learn science', *British Educational Research Journal*, 30 (3): 359–377. Taylor & Francis Ltd, http://www.informaworld.com, reprinted by permission of the publisher and author.

Norris, S. © 2004 from *Analyzing Multimodal Interaction: A methodological framework*, London: Routledge. Reproduced by permission of Taylor & Francis Books UK.

O'Halloran, Kieran (2007) Adaptation of parts of (3,000 words) *Applied Linguistics* 28 (1): 1–24. Oxford University Press. Reproduced by kind permission of the author.

Rampton, B. (2005, 2nd edn) *Crossing: language and ethnicity among adolescents*. Manchester: St Jerome Press. Reproduced by permission of the publisher.

Swann, J. (1989) 'Talk control? An illustration from the classroom of problems in analysing male dominance of conversation', in Coates, J. and Cameron, D. (eds) *Women in their Speech Communities*, London: Longman. Reprinted by permission of Pearson Education.

Uys, Stanley (1976) 'Police open fire as Soweto erupts again', 4 August, the *Guardian*. Copyright Guardian News & Media Ltd 1976. Reproduced with permission.

Willis, Jane and Willis, Dave 'Applying linguistics to task-based learning: six propositions in search of a methodology', publicados en *La Lingüística Aplicada a finales del siglo XX*. Ensayos y propuestas. Tomo 1. Editores: Isabel de la Cruz Cabanillas, Carmen Santamaría García, Cristina Tejedor Martínez, Carmen Valero Garcés. Servicio de publicaciones de la Universidad de Alcalá. 2001. ISBN: 84813847275. Reprinted by permission of Universidad de Alcala.

Wray, A. M. and Bloomer, A. M. (2006) *Projects in Linguistics* (2nd edn) London: Hodder Arnold. © 2006 Alison Wray and Aileen Bloomer. Reproduced by permission of Edward Arnold Publishers Ltd.

This publication has made use of the Cambridge and Nottingham Corpus of Discourse in English (CANCODE). CANCODE was funded by Cambridge University Press and is a five-million word computerized corpus of spoken English, made up of recordings from a variety of settings in the countries of the United Kingdom and Ireland. The corpus is designed with a substantial organized database giving information on participants, settings and conversational goals. CANCODE was built by Cambridge University Press and the University of Nottingham and it forms part of the Cambridge International Corpus (CIC). It provides insights into language use, and offers a resource to supplement what is already known about English from other, non-corpus based research, thereby providing valuable and accurate information for researchers and those preparing teaching materials. Sole copyright of the corpus resides with Cambridge University Press from whom all permission to reproduce material must be obtained.

Every effort has been made to trace the copyright holders but if any have been inadvertently overlooked, the publishers will be pleased to make the necessary arrangements at the first opportunity.

About this book

Susan Hunston and David Oakey

This book prepares you for studying Applied Linguistics or courses with titles such as TEFL, TESL or TESOL. The first four sections of the book will familiarize you with key topics in the area. They will also give you practice in reading books and articles that are similar to those you will need to read as part of a course in TEFL or Applied Linguistics. Sections 5–7 of the book contain advice and practice in looking at the way English is used in writing about Applied Linguistics. They will be helpful to you in becoming more skilled at reading academic material and in writing essays.

You and this book

As editors of this book, we have made a number of guesses about you, the reader, and we have organized the book accordingly.

- **You speak English (if you did not you could not read this introduction!).**
  English may be your first, second or third language, but you have an interest in how English works. The first four chapters of the book are about English, though much of what they say would apply to other languages too. Chapters 1 and 3 are about grammar; chapter 2 is about vocabulary; chapter 4 is about spoken discourse.

- **You are a language teacher or planning to become one.**
  Chapters 5–8 cover key topics in the teaching and learning of languages. Chapters 5 and 6 are about language teaching methodology; chapter 7 is about how languages are learned; and chapter 8 deals with one of the social aspects of language learning.

- **You have interests in language and linguistics that lie beyond teaching, whether or not you are a language teacher.**
  The next four chapters cover a variety of topics in Applied Linguistics that are not primarily related to education. Chapter 9 looks at how a study of language can be applied to an interpretation of how newspaper texts influence our thinking. Chapter 10 applies linguistic concepts and skills to the investigation of dishonesty in writing. The remaining chapters in this section look at languages and speakers in contact with each other. Chapter 11 is about translation and how translators work. Chapter 12 examines ideas about cultures and the experience of relating to people from a different culture to your own.

- **You expect to carry out your own research in Applied Linguistics, either for coursework or as a research project.**
  The next four chapters of the book offer advice on different ways of doing research, that is, using questionnaires (chapter 13) and interviews (chapter 14), transcribing spoken language (chapter 15) and using a corpus (chapter 16).

- **You want to improve your skills in reading books and articles and in writing essays, all in the area of Applied Linguistics.**

  The final six chapters of the book introduce 'skills' as well as 'concepts'. They are not a complete course in academic skills but they deal with a number of issues that from experience we know are important to students. Chapters 17 and 18 concern aspects of English that sometimes cause problems in reading: long noun phrases and reporting verbs. Chapters 19 and 20 focus on skills that are important when you are writing essays: knowing how to express agreement or disagreement with particular ideas, and organizing your essay. The final two chapters of the book deal with more mechanical matters: setting out a bibliography and editing or proofreading your work. You will find that all the examples, and a lot of the information, in these six chapters come from the other chapters in this book. All the long noun phrases shown in chapter 17, for example, are taken from chapters 1 to 16. This means that you can be confident that all the examples are genuine and have been used by real Applied Linguists in their writing. In addition you should find it easier to understand the examples because you have already 'met' them in their original context. The reverse is true also: the final six chapters will help you to interpret the more difficult parts of the other chapters.

Using this book

So, how should you go about reading this book? We suggest you start with the chapters that most interest you – you do not need to start the book at the beginning and finish at the end. If you are a teacher, you will probably find the 'teaching and learning a language' chapters the most accessible as they relate to topics you are already familiar with. If you are planning to carry out research, section 4 will probably interest you most. Each chapter has an introduction written by us, the editors. The aim is to introduce the main ideas of the chapter as simply as possible, and to give any background information that you will need to understand the chapter. If you find any chapter difficult, you may want to go back to its introduction and read it again.

Remember that what you are reading has been written by researchers for an academic audience. The writers have not simplified their ideas; they talk to you as a fellow academic. Their aim is to pass on their experience of doing Applied Linguistics, describe their research and express their own opinions. Each of the writers has his or her own style – we have not told them to write in a particular way. Because of this, you will find that the chapters are somewhat different from each other and that some are easier to read than others are. All this is quite deliberate, as it gives you practice in dealing with the range of material you will meet when studying Applied Linguistics. We suggest that you start with the chapters that are most familiar to you; as your skill and knowledge develop you will find that you are able to tackle even the 'difficult' chapters with confidence. The advantage of this book is that when you start your course, you will know something about many of the issues that you are asked to study and you will be skilled in reading the discourse of Applied Linguistics.

SECTION 1

KEY CONCEPTS IN APPLIED LINGUISTICS

I Describing English

Introduction to chapter 1

This chapter takes us into the area of pedagogic grammar, a field that concerns how the grammar of a language might best be described for learners, and how it might best be taught to learners. In this chapter, Dave Willis considers both these questions and also how they relate to what is known about how learners learn. The key concepts introduced in this chapter are: the link between grammar and context (the grammar of orientation); the link between grammar and meaning (pattern grammar); and the relationship between what is taught and what is learnt.

The background to this chapter

In other publications, Willis has talked about three aspects of English grammar. The first aspect – the grammar of structure – is very familiar. It deals with aspects of grammar such as how questions are formed, or the fact that in English adjectives usually come before nouns, not the other way round. If a learner writes *What time you went home?* instead of *What time did you go home?*, we could say that the learner has not mastered the grammar of structure. Most grammar coursebooks deal very fully with the grammar of structure.

The second aspect – the grammar of class – is less familiar and most coursebooks pay little or no attention to it. It deals with the fact that whether a structure is correct or not often depends on a particular choice of word. So if a learner writes *He advised me to go to the dentist*, this is correct, whereas *He suggested me to go to the dentist* is not. This is because *advise* is used with the pattern 'verb + noun + to-infinitive' but *suggest* is not used with this pattern. In Willis's terms, *advise* belongs to the class of verbs used in this way and *suggest* does not. It is very difficult for learners to become familiar with the grammar of class because there is such a lot to learn – each item of vocabulary (such as *advise* or *suggest*) belongs to its own class. In this chapter, Willis uses the term 'pattern grammar' to talk about the grammar of class, and he makes some suggestions as to how learners may be encouraged to develop their competence in this area.

The third aspect that Willis talks about is what he calls the grammar of orientation. This covers some fairly familiar ground, such as choice of tense, and use of *a* or *the*. However, it relates these things to much more than just the sentence the word is used in. A learner may produce what appears to be a perfectly correct sentence, such as *Did you go to a conference last year?*, that is nonetheless wrong because the speakers have been talking about a specific annual conference, and this speaker is asking about that event. The correct sentence would be *Did you go to **the** conference last year?* As Willis points out in this chapter, it is almost impossible for a teacher to give learners all the information they need to make the correct choice in every case, so this is another very difficult area.

In this chapter, Willis links these ideas about grammar to a very different area of research – Second Language Acquisition. Some researchers in this area argue that **acquiring** a language (that is, being able to speak, write and understand it) is a very different process from **learning** a language (that is, knowing its rules). There is debate about the exact relationship between acquiring a language and learning it, but most researchers agree that when learners produce language spontaneously, they are drawing on what they have acquired (subconsciously, as it were) rather than on the rules they have consciously learnt. It follows that teachers should spend most of their time making acquisition (of grammar) possible, rather than teaching rules (of grammar). In this chapter, Willis uses his ideas about grammar to suggest an explanation as to why there is no direct link between acquisition and learning.

Focusing on the argument

In this chapter, Willis brings together two ideas: he makes descriptions of English grammar relevant to theories about how languages are learnt. Most of the chapter is about two aspects of the grammar of English – the grammar of orientation and pattern grammar – but these are expressed as answers to a question: Why are teaching and learning not directly linked? Willis then adds a further answer, citing Widdowson, relating to what learners are doing when they speak English. So the three answers to the question are:

- Teaching is not linked directly to learning because some parts of the language system are too complex to be taught explicitly. This applies in particular to the grammar of orientation.
- Teaching is not linked directly to learning because some parts of the language system are too extensive to be taught within a reasonable time limit. This applies particularly to pattern grammar.
- Teaching is not linked directly to learning because we teach <u>how</u> to say things (we teach 'wordings' or expression) whereas learners are concerned with <u>what</u> they are saying (with 'meaning' or content). This applies to all areas of grammar, but helps to explain why elements of the grammar, which seem relatively simple and straightforward, are still difficult to acquire. Willis cites the formation of *do*-questions and past tense forms.

The chapter illustrates the importance of finding the right question to answer; identifying a new and interesting question enables Willis to bring together very diverse ideas and to present an original argument.

A language tip

In the section 'Complexity and the grammar of orientation', Willis uses one word, *article*, with two different meanings:

1   the words *the* and *a*;
2   a piece of text in a newspaper.

Here are some sentences from that section:

The question is: which is the original *article*? The answer is that the first *article* is genuine, the second is doctored. But both are perfectly grammatical – even though the *article* use is quite different.

In this extract, the first two uses of *article* are meaning 2 and the third use is meaning 1.

In the same section, Willis also uses another term, *determiner*, to refer to words such as *the* and *a*.

To think about

1   Do you have experience, either as a teacher or as a learner of a language, of knowing a grammatical point in theory but being unable to apply it in practice?

2   Think of a language that you speak other than English. Can the concepts of 'grammar of class' and 'grammar of orientation' be applied to that language too?

3   Do you agree with Willis that the grammar of English is too complex to be taught directly to learners? Are there any aspects of grammar that can be taught directly, in your opinion?

CHAPTER 1

Three reasons why

Dave Willis

Language teaching and learning aim at practical outcomes in the real world, not simply at classroom outcomes. If we want to show that a feature of language has been taught or learned it is not enough to show that a learner can produce it under artificial conditions, in a grammar test for example, or as a controlled response to a teacher's question. We need to see that it has become a consistent part of the learner's language repertoire, that the learner can use it consistently as part of an act of communication. If we take this as the yardstick, then the findings of research into second language acquisition suggest that there is no direct link between teaching and learning (see, for example, Skehan 1998: 94–95). Learners may, for example, have a conceptual understanding of the use of past tense forms when their attention is focused on producing the required form but, at the same time, they may fail to produce these forms when they are using language spontaneously. The conclusion from the research is that we should recognize that the relationship between teaching and learning is indirect. Even if a form is understood and produced under controlled circumstances this does not guarantee that learners will be able to use it.

It is, however, comfortable for teachers and teacher educators, and for the writers and publishers of teaching materials, to maintain that there is a direct relationship between teaching and learning. For teachers and teacher educators this belief offers security. It suggests that we know exactly what we are doing and where we are going. We can plan lessons and recommend methodologies with confidence. For writers and publishers it means that they can make clear, unqualified claims in terms of teaching and learning for the materials they produce. There is, then, built in resistance to the notion that learning is, at best, indirect. The inconvenient arguments from second language acquisition (SLA) are rejected on the grounds that they are unscientific, or that the work on which they rest is carried out under experimental rather than classroom conditions, or that one study often contradicts another with respect to the details, or that they are too diffuse to offer a firm basis for a teaching programme. But the fact that almost all the research points in the same direction casts doubt on these criticisms.

For my part I believe that the overall findings of SLA research are convincing. They reinforce my experience in the classroom. I am horribly familiar with the situation in which learners can produce a language form under controlled conditions, but cannot produce the same form spontaneously. In this chapter I will argue, taking language description as a starting point, that there are two good reasons why we should recognize that the link between teaching and learning is bound to be indirect. I will then go on to cite Widdowson (1979) to suggest a third reason for this phenomenon.

Complexity and the grammar of orientation

There is an important aspect of the grammar of English that shows, among other things, how elements in the message are related to one another in space and time, and whether or not a participant in a text is identifiable by the receiver. I will call this the grammar of *orientation* (see Willis 2003). In part this is carried by systems often referred to as *deictic*, in particular the tense system and the determiner system. Beyond this we have grammatical devices and conventions such as the passive voice and cleft forms which enable us to build coherent text. Such devices enable us to mark which elements of a text are given and which are new and how the propositions carried in the clauses and sentences in the text relate to one another logically.

From the teaching and learning point of view the problem with these grammatical devices is that they are extremely complex. Hughes and McCarthy (1998), for example, cite a generally accepted pedagogic generalization 'that the past perfect tense is used for an event that happened in past time before another past time'. This may or may not be a useful generalization. It is certainly one that most teachers will have used at some stage, but it is most certainly an oversimplification. Hughes and McCarthy point out that the rule will enable learners to produce the well-formed sentences *I spoke to Lisa Knox yesterday for the first time. I had met her 10 years ago but had not spoken to her.* But they then go on to point out that this rule does not show 'that the two sentences would be equally well formed if the second were in the past simple'. It does not, in other words, show learners that they often have to choose between the two forms according to subtle differences in the intended meaning.

There is a further complication that Hughes and McCarthy do not point out. A careful application of the rule would lead learners to produce some forms such as *I opened the door when the postman had knocked,* which are distinctly odd, if not ungrammatical. It is virtually impossible to frame a rule which will enable learners to make an appropriate choice between the past simple and present perfect in all contexts. Hughes and McCarthy go on to draw the conclusion that:

> The rule, therefore . . . does not offer sufficiently precise guidelines to generate the choice when appropriate. In situations such as this our proposal is to look at the choices that real speakers and writers have made in real contexts and consider the contextual features that apparently motivated one choice or the other.
>
> (Hughes and McCarthy 1998: 268)

Contextual features and speaker's choice tend to be rather more subtle than hard and fast rules. Let us look briefly at the use of the definite and indefinite articles for example. The usual pedagogic generalization is that when something is first mentioned it is preceded by the indefinite article. Subsequent mentions are preceded by the definite article. Look at the following texts:

> **A:** Police were last night searching for ***the*** eight-year-old who attempted to hold up a sweet shop with a pistol.
> ***A*** boy, wearing a balaclava, threw a carrier bag at ***a*** shop keeper at a corner store in Ashton-under-Lyme, and ordered her to fill it up.

B: The Police were last night searching for *an* eight-year-old who attempted to hold up a sweet shop with a pistol.

The boy, wearing a balaclava, threw a carrier bag at *the* shop keeper at a corner store in Ashton-under-Lyme, and ordered her to fill it up.

One of these is a bona fide newspaper article taken from the upmarket *Guardian* newspaper of 22 February 1994. The other has been doctored, replacing *the* with *a* in certain places and vice versa. The question is: which is the original article? The answer is that the first article is genuine, the second is doctored. But both are perfectly grammatical – even though the article use is quite different. The reason is that the two paragraphs exploit the article system in different ways. The first article shifts unusually from referring to *the eight-year-old* in the first sentence to referring to *a boy* in the second sentence, just the opposite of what one would normally expect. The writer has chosen to think of the eight-year-old as defined by the post-modifying clause *who attempted to hold up a sweet shop* and has therefore gone for the definite article. By choosing the indefinite article in the second sentence the writer is announcing that he is about to commence a narrative, taking this as a new starting point. The second text adopts the more usual strategy of using *a* for the first mention of the boy and *the* for the second mention. In this text *the shopkeeper* is seen as defined by the post-modifying phrase *at a corner store*.

What this shows us is that we cannot give hard and fast rules about the uses of the articles. We can make useful generalizations about first and second mentions. For example the opening sentence *Police were last night searching for the eight-year-old who attempted to hold up **the** sweet shop with **the** pistol* would almost certainly be regarded as ungrammatical. But hard and fast rules may simply get in the way of learners acquiring the ability to exploit the meaning potential of the system to its full. Rules are only a starting point in the learning process. Learners must go beyond the rules to an understanding of how the system is exploited to create text. Rules do not exist to distinguish grammatical from ungrammatical sentences. They are there to be exploited in the creation of meaning.

Pattern grammar: extent and coverage

Francis et al. (1996, 1998) and Hunston and Francis (2000) explore the phenomenon of pattern grammar. Pattern grammar points to a predictable relationship between words and meanings. The preposition *about*, for example, has three basic meanings:

1   Concerning a particular subject: *Think **about** it; I read a book **about** that recently.*
2   Approximately: *It takes **about** two hours to drive to London; It'll cost **about** a hundred quid.*
3   To indicate spatial orientation: *We spent the morning walking **about** town; I'm just looking **about**.*

Each of these meanings is likely to be found in association with particular sets of words. Meaning 1 is associated with verbs of speaking and thinking such as *read, think, talk* and *forget*. The preposition *about* also goes with nouns denoting items which communicate such as *book, article, story* and *programme* and acts of communication such as *advice, agreement* and *opinion*. We also find adjectives which describe attitudes towards information, states or events, such as *happy, pleased* or *sorry*. With meaning 2 we find numbers such as *a hundred* and measurements such as *a kilometre, an hour* or *four litres*. With meaning 3 we have phrases such as *hanging about, waiting about* and *sitting about*.

Francis et al. (1996) list around 30 prepositions (*about, as, at, between, by, for* etc.) which feature in patterns with verbs. They list around 25 similar words as featuring with nouns and 15 with adjectives. They also list a number of patterns with verbs, nouns or adjectives followed by *that* or *wh*-words.

There are then a limited number of words around which a very large number of patterns are built. If we think of the first meaning of *about*, for example, Francis et al. (1996) list over 120 words associated with this meaning, ranging from very frequent words such as *ask, know, talk* and *think*, which would be found in any elementary course, through to words such as *quibble* and *whinge*, which might not be found even at the most advanced level.

Some prepositions are much less predictable in their patterning than the word *about*. Francis et al. (1996) identify 20 semantic groups of verbs followed by the preposition *for*. These cover, for example, THE 'PLAN' GROUP (*plan, arrange, provide* etc.); THE 'COMPENSATE' GROUP (*compensate, pay, apologize* etc.); THE 'SEARCH' GROUP (*search, look, hunt, shop, listen* etc.). Further examples are THE 'WORK' GROUP (*act, fight, play, speak* etc.); THE 'ARGUE' GROUP (*pray, speak, vote*) and THE 'CARE' GROUP (*feel, grieve* etc.). So *for* is more complex in its relationships than *about*, but it is still possible to make useful generalizations about the verbs followed by *for*.

Although the 20 semantic categories identified by Francis et al. represent useful generalizations they are, perhaps, more precise than we need for an initial pedagogic exploration. For example the PLAN, COMPENSATE and SEARCH groups might all be seen as answering the question *why?* If someone apologizes for lateness or plans for an emergency, the noun *lateness* or *emergency* explains the reason for the apology or the planning. The nouns following the WORK, ARGUE and CARE groups can all be seen as answering the question *Who benefits?* or *Who wants or needs . . .?* – who needs praying for or fighting for or grieving for? The important point is that it is possible to make useful generalizations about the verbs followed by *for* by grouping them semantically.

We can then begin at an elementary level by exploring the basic meanings of the preposition *for*:

Why? *She was waiting for a friend. What are they for? For example . . . Look for more ideas.*
Who wants or needs? *Can you spell your name for me? I'll do that for you. This is for you.*

and also:

Time: *He paused for a moment. They are out for the afternoon.*
Distance: *We walked for three miles.*

We can then at a later stage show how these meanings relate systematically to groups of verbs, nouns and adjectives, and we can design teaching activities to focus on these systems. But in doing these things we need to recognize that we are doing no more than giving useful guidelines. It still remains for learners to sort out these categories for themselves. They may, for example, have quite different ways of categorizing *for,* taking account of their first language.

The important point to recognize here is that the extent of this learning task is such that we can never cover all the words that are likely to be found in a particular pattern. We can simply give useful starting points and encourage learners to look at the language for themselves, to process critically the text that they come across and to draw useful conclusions from it.

Building a meaning system

So far I have cited two reasons why learning is not directly related to teaching. First, I have argued that some aspects of the grammar, such as the tense and the article systems, are simply too subtle to explain. We can offer useful generalizations, but we must also rely on learners exploring the language for themselves. And we must take care that we do not shackle that exploration by offering hard and fast rules which are in danger of inhibiting learner exploration. Second, I have argued, giving pattern grammar as an example, that some systems are so extensive that it is impossible to offer complete coverage. Again we can offer useful hints, but must then depend on learners exploring language for themselves.

There is a third reason for the gap between learning and teaching. If we see learning as being measured by the ability to produce more and more of the sentences sanctioned by the target language, then perhaps we should not be surprised if learners do not always reproduce faithfully what they have been taught. As soon as learners begin to use the language, they are concerned with operating a meaning system. Widdowson (1979: 197) argues that:

> [Errors] take place because the learner attempts to adjust the language he is learning to make it an effective instrument of communication . . . Errors are the result of the learner's attempt to convert his linguistic usage into communicative use.

Widdowson refers here to the gap between linguistic usage (the learner's knowledge of language forms) and communicative use (the learner's ability to deploy the language in communication). An example would be where the learner is aware of the form of *do-*questions but under the pressure of producing language in real time fails to incorporate them into spontaneous production. The same applies initially to past tense forms. They are 'known' but not used. It takes time before learners can incorporate newly encountered forms within their spontaneous production. As they are working towards this they operate a simplified system, one which they can deploy in real time.

Conclusions

We have then two necessary characteristics of the language learning process relating to the nature of language as system:

- Some language systems are so complex that they cannot be taught or consciously learned. They must be acquired by contact with the language in use.

• Some language systems are so extensive that it is impossible to offer anything like complete coverage of them. We can simply offer learners useful starting points and leave them to flesh out the systems from exploratory contact with the language.

Third, we have the necessity of seeing the language in the learner's terms as a meaning system rather than a system of wordings. Taking these together we have three reasons why we need to accept that learning a language is a complex process which cannot be controlled by the teacher, and cannot be consciously controlled by the learner.

As teachers we can offer learners useful generalizations about language, but we need to recognize that all we are doing is equipping the learner to explore the language more productively. The language system is so complex and so extensive and varied that we can never offer a full pedagogic description. This means that we need to offer learners ample exposure to language. Only through this exposure can they find opportunities to sift through the complexities and the extent of the language system. At the same time we need to offer learners ample opportunities to use the language. Wordings are a means to an end, not an end in itself. Only by wide experience of language in use can learners refine their meaning system. And only by refining their meaning system do they create the need for more precise wordings and so find reasons to develop their grammar.

There are, then, three good reasons why exposure to language and opportunities for language use are absolutely central to language learning. Teaching is preparatory and supplementary, but is necessarily subordinate to the natural processes by which the learner develops a meaning system.

References

Francis G., Hunston S. and Manning E. 1996. *Grammar Patterns 1: Verbs*. London: HarperCollins.

—— 1998. *Grammar Patterns 2: Nouns and Adjectives*. London: HarperCollins.

Hughes R. and McCarthy M. 1998. From sentence to discourse: Discourse Grammar and English Language Teaching. *TESOL Quarterly 32/2*.

Hunston S. and Francis G. 2000. *Pattern Grammar*. Amsterdam: John Benjamins.

Skehan P. 1998. *A Cognitive Approach to Language Teaching*. Oxford: OUP.

Widdowson H. 1979. *Explorations in Applied Linguistics*. Oxford: OUP.

Willis D. 2003. *Rules, Patterns and Words: Grammar and Lexis in English Language Teaching*. Cambridge: CUP.

Introduction to chapter 2

This chapter is one of four that deals with different aspects of describing language – in this case, describing the vocabulary or lexis of English, and in particular the aspect of vocabulary study that is known as 'collocation'. In this chapter David Oakey (one of the editors of this book) explains what collocation is and why it matters. Using particular collocations can make English sound very 'native-like' or quite 'non-native-like', and Oakey raises questions about this in those English language learning contexts in which learners might not be aiming to sound like native speakers. The key concept introduced in this chapter is collocation, and terminology associated with it, such as 'span', 'creativity' and 'lexical unit'.

The background to this chapter

As Oakey points out in this chapter, the word 'collocation' has a number of uses. Some people use 'collocation' to refer to words which are associated in terms of meaning. For example, we might say that the words *night* and *dark* are connected to each other, because we know that 'nights' are 'dark' and that 'dark' is the condition of 'night-time'. Nowadays, however, 'collocation' is usually used to talk about two words that often occur together. A computer can count the number of times *night* and *dark* are used close to each other (e.g. *the night was very dark, it was a dark and stormy night* and so on). The computer can compare the number of times the words occur together in two different sets of texts (or 'corpora'). For example, in the Fiction corpus of the BNC (the British National Corpus), there are 79 occurrences of *dark* occurring close to *night* (including examples such as *dark night, the dark of night, down a dark alley at night, standing dark against the night sky*). In the Academic corpus, there are only five such examples.

One of the fascinating features about collocation is its association with meaning. A simple way to explain this is to say that if a word has more than one meaning, each meaning will be associated with a different set of collocates. For example the word *head* collocates with these other words (among others): *shook, turned, lifted, injury,* and with *office, state, department, appointed.* The first four of these occur when *head* is used to refer to a part of the body (*I shook my head* and so on), while the second four occur when *head* is used to mean 'chief' or 'in charge' (*head of department* and so on). Another way to think about this is to say that *head* by itself does not really have a meaning, but that the meaning belongs to the whole phrase: 'shake one's head', 'department head' and so on.

Focusing on the argument

It has been recognized for a long time that in English some words 'sound right' together and others do not. For example, *absolutely delighted* sounds right but *absolutely pleased* does not. In the British National Corpus there are examples of the first of these but not the second; what 'sounds right' tends also to be what is frequent. Oakey makes this point but also raises two problem issues. First, some writers (especially literary writers) may wish to avoid what is frequent on the grounds that they want to be more creative, to work harder to achieve their effects. Should student writers be encouraged to be creative in this way, or to use what is frequent? Second, 'what sounds right' means 'what sounds right to a native speaker of English'. But English does not belong only to native speakers. Does it matter if a learner of English uses a collocation (e.g. *absolutely pleased*) that might sound strange to a native speaker but not to many other speakers of English? These are important issues for teachers to consider.

A language tip

There are some important technical terms in this topic area, but they can be confusing to use. *Collocation* is mostly thought of as an uncountable noun, but it can also be a countable noun (*a collocation, collocations*). *Collocate* can be a noun or a verb. Here are some examples:

- 'the research literature which is relevant to collocation' (from this chapter). Here *collocation* is an uncountable, abstract noun referring to the concept or phenomenon of words occurring together. Other examples include *insights into collocation.*
- 'one method of discovering more about a word's collocations', 'If a native speaker decides that a particular collocation is unacceptable' (from this chapter). Here *collocation* is a countable noun referring to the connection between one specific word and another one or more.
- 'the collocates of *purse*', '*rummage* is the second most frequent collocate after *fumble*' (from this chapter). Here *collocate* is a countable noun referring to the words with co-occur with another word.
- '*rummage* collocates with *purse*' (invented example). Here *collocate* is a verb. Notice that it is used with the word *with*.

To think about

1 How important do you think it is that learners of English use collocations that sound natural to native speakers of English? If you are a learner of English, do you want to use native-like collocations? If you are a teacher of English, do you want your students to do so? Or do you think that this is an area that is not important to learners? Do you think that collocation in International English is so flexible that we do not need to pay attention to it?

2 Look at the English dictionary that you usually use. What information does it contain about collocation? How useful is it?

3 Do you agree with Oakey that a corpus is a better source of information about collocation than intuition is?

CHAPTER 2

English vocabulary and collocation

David Oakey

One goal of applied linguistics is to improve the decisions made by dictionary writers and syllabus designers when systematically presenting English vocabulary to users or learners of the language. The area of English vocabulary most studied by applied linguists over the past 25 years has been collocation. Depending on the theoretical approach adopted, collocation is a semantic, textual, or statistical property (Partington 1998) which involves words being used together more frequently than might otherwise be expected, or being used together very rarely. In the research literature which is relevant to collocation there is little agreement as to exactly how and why this 'togetherness' is motivated or restricted. This is principally because much of this literature has been produced as a result of work in other areas such as lexicography and dictionary design (Sinclair 1991; Moon 2007), English language teaching (Nattinger and DeCarrico 1992; Lewis 2000; Willis 2003), and language acquisition (Pawley and Syder 1983; Wray 2002).

The use of the term *collocation* consequently varies depending on the writer's research priorities. It is used by some writers to refer to one type of word combination and exclude others (Aisenstadt 1981), while others adopt it as a broadly inclusive term (Nesselhauf 2005). Some researchers maintain that collocation is central to language production (Sinclair 1991; Hunston and Francis 2000), while others regard it as a peripheral, albeit useful, aspect of lexical knowledge (Nation 2001: 27). As a result, the term *collocation* can refer to a combination of two or more words, such as an adjective or a verb which tends to be used with a limited number of nouns, or the term can be extended to include longer, more complex combinations such as phrases, idioms and proverbs, which can be made up of a fixed or variable number of grammatical and/or lexical words.

The term *collocation* in this chapter refers to the phenomenon as a whole, *collocations* are frequently co-occurring lexical items of one or more words, and *collocational relations* are the semantic, textual or statistical connections between their constituent words. This chapter describes the insights into collocation which can be obtained using two different methodological approaches, and then discusses where collocation may sit between the conflicting demands of creativity and conformity in English language use, first as a native language and then as an international lingua franca.

Intuitive and empirical approaches to collocation

The following section describes two methodological approaches to investigating collocation using the verb and noun forms of *purse*. *Purse* is an ergative verb, that is, it has both a transitive form, in which the Subject does something, as in Example 1 below, and an intransitive form, as in Example 2 below (Hunston and Francis 2000: 183). The distinguishing feature of ergative verbs is that the object of the transitive form can also function as subject of the intransitive form.

Example 1 <u>Richard pursed his lips</u> in a long, slow whistle.

Example 2 William deals. He picks up his cards and <u>his lips purse</u>.

According to the *Collins English Dictionary* (Butterfield 2003: 1317) *purse* means 'to contract (the mouth, lips, etc.) into a small rounded shape'. By specifying *mouth* and *lips* as part of the definition of *purse*, the dictionary shows that there are restrictions on what can be pursed in the real world. If there is a restriction on what can be pursed, then it follows that there will be restrictions on the words that an English language user can use *purse* with, and therefore these words which can be used with *purse* will be used with it more frequently than other words. The dictionary definition, however, cannot fully state where the collocational restrictions on the use of this verb end; indeed, the *New Shorter Oxford English Dictionary* (Brown 1994: 2422) in its definition of *purse* specifies a collocation with *brow* rather than with *mouth*, and refers to the final shape of something that has been pursed as 'wrinkles or puckers' rather than 'rounded'. The English language user or learner seeking guidance from either dictionary is from this point on their own, and so insights from applied linguistics are needed: more information about the uses and meanings of words and other vocabulary items will enable English language users and learners to make more appropriate word choices.

One method of discovering more about a word's collocations is used in the field of lexical semantics, which investigates and describes lexical relations such as synonymy. A set of verbs with individually similar meanings can be juxtaposed with a set of nouns with individually similar meanings, and a native speaker can then be asked to judge their acceptability as collocations. If a native speaker decides that a particular collocation is unacceptable, perhaps by saying 'you could say this, but you probably wouldn't as it somehow sounds odd,' then the researcher could conclude that there is a restriction on the collocability of the two words. Table 2.1 illustrates this approach by showing the acceptability (or not) of different verb–noun collocations. Collocations marked with a '+' are judged as acceptable, those with '–' as unacceptable, and those as '?' as questionable (cf. Cruse 1986: 281).

Table 2.1 Collocational relationships of *purse* and its near-synonyms

	lips	*mouth*	*brow*	*forehead*
purse	+	?	–	–
pucker	+	+	–	–
furrow	–	–	+	?
knit	–	–	+	?

Table 2.1 suggests the existence of what Cruse (ibid.) calls 'semi-systematic collocational restrictions' which act on *purse* and other near-synonyms. Part of the meanings of *purse* and *pucker* is that they form a person's lips and mouth into a rounded shape, but not their brow or forehead. The semantic motivation behind these restrictions might be physical: mouths and lips are able to assume rounded shapes, unlike brows and foreheads which, being wider, can only assume linear shapes. This information

would be useful for a lexicographer in improving the definition of *purse,* and creating an entry for *purse* in a dictionary of collocations (cf. Benson et al. 1997).

The problem with using such intuition-based data to learn more about collocation, however, is that intuition reflects a user's knowledge of only those collocational relationships which they have encountered in their experience of life. Some users might judge some collocations acceptable whereas other users might not. Examples of acceptable collocations elicited directly from a native speaker's intuition are similarly unreliable, as such collocations tend be memorable or salient in some way, rather than frequent (Fox 1987: 146).

Empirical methods of investigating collocation, by contrast, use language data from a corpus instead of eliciting from native-speaker intuition. A corpus is a large collection of language use, in the form of written texts or transcripts of speech, usually stored on a computer and often designed to be a representation of the way a language is used. When data from a corpus is examined, the object of study becomes the language system itself, rather than individual users' intuitive knowledge of the language system, and frequently occurring collocations used by many users can be identified.

The empirical notion of 'togetherness', that is, when a word can be considered to be used together with *purse,* is necessarily linear, since computers deal with English language as characters and spaces from left to right. There are differing ideas over how far to the left and right of a word its collocational relations extend. In corpus linguistics, following Sinclair (1991), the area of togetherness is generally a 'span' of around four or five words to the left or right of the node word, in this case *purse.* Other corpus linguists regard each word as having its own unique span (Mason 1999), while in text linguistics the span can include the whole text in which the word is found (Hoey 1991: 219).

Figure 2.1

Ten concordance lines for *purse* in the Bank of English, left-sorted

```
1   elbarrow full of money to buy a     purse   full of goods. Political Leaders
2   eted us with a wave of the coin      purse   ! This young man had found my add
3   ready brought a coin out of her      purse   and was preparing to pay. I pick
4   tab was picked up by the public      purse   -- which was funded by the peasa
5   was ever returned to the public      purse   . The funds were used to acquire
6   facture a sow's ear from a silk      purse   . Bristol may have recruited hand
7   et prayer, and opened her small      purse   . She turned slowly, still more a
8   asy when the Treasury holds the      purse   strings. Know what I mean?' I th
9   also had her pin number in the       purse   . Sun spot 10 September 2001 isn'
10  chance to use the power of the       purse   and shop for a fairer world.
```

Figure 2.1 shows ten examples of *purse* from the Bank of English (2005), a 450-million word electronic corpus, displayed in concordance lines with the four-word span highlighted in bold for each example. The lines are sorted so that the words to the left of *purse* are arranged in alphabetical order.

In an empirical approach to collocation, any word within the span is seen as a collocation of *purse,* in this case grammatical words such as *a, the* and *her,* and lexical words such as *public, silk* and *strings.* In Figure 2.1 it can also be seen that when *purse* is at the end of a sentence, the span includes the first few words of the next sentence, so that empirical collocational relations between words extend across sentence boundaries.

Ten examples of a word will not give the researcher enough information about which words occur most frequently in the span. Modern corpora such as the Collins Word Web (2007), to which the Bank of English belongs, contain several billion running words, and it would be impossible to look at the span for *purse* line by line. Instead, the number of occurrences of each word in each position in the span can be counted, and calculations can be made to identify words whose occurrence together with *purse* is statistically significant.

Lexical words which occur with *purse* in this way in the Bank of English are *public, strings, money, Darren, silk, million, control, power* and *privy*. A lexicographer would use this information to decide whether the collocational relationship between *public* and *purse* and between *purse* and *strings* is so strong that *public purse* and *purse strings* should each be treated as a single choice, or unit of meaning. In the *COBUILD Advanced Learner's Dictionary* (Sinclair 2006), *public purse* is given as an example of a sense of *purse* – part of the meaning of *purse* comes from its collocation with *public* – but *purse strings* is listed as a separate, multi-word lexical item. The collocation of *Darren* and *purse* is motivated by real-world facts: *Darren Purse* is the name of a former player with Birmingham City Football Club, and his name is frequently mentioned in newspaper reports of football matches collected as part of the corpus.

The collocation of *purse* with *silk* arises from their use in an idiom. The meanings of idioms are often very different from the meanings of their constituent words, and, while this makes them an interesting feature of English vocabulary, they are consequently more difficult for learners to understand and use than for a native speaker who has acquired them by repeated exposure to their contextualized use. While the *COBUILD Dictionary of Idioms* lists the canonical or base form of this idiom as *you can't make a silk purse out of a sow's ear*, corpus evidence confirms, as in Examples 3 to 8 below from the Bank of English, how varied the actual form of this idiom can become while still containing the words *silk* and *purse*:

Example 3 Washington wagered billions of dollars in its attempt to <u>convert a sow's ear into a silk purse</u>.

Example 4 Spinning Jenny goes merrily on her way, picking up trophies and <u>manufacturing a silk purse</u> from a career that had all the characteristics of a <u>sow's ear</u>.

Example 5 . . . a director who managed to <u>transform</u> an artistic <u>sow's ear into</u> a theatrical <u>silk purse</u> with the cringe-making *Napoleon* . . .

Example 6 Crest Homes aims to <u>turn the sow's ear</u> of a 53-acre industrial site <u>into a silk purse</u> with houses in various styles . . .

Example 7 The tourist industry is a good example of perestroika's unerring ability to <u>make a pig's ear out of a silk purse</u>

Example 8 They've <u>made a sow's ear</u> of any reform plan that would hit them in the <u>silk purse</u>.

The empirical approach to English collocation has led to the view that it is more helpful to see each word as having its own lexico-grammatical patterning (Hunston and Francis 2000) and to view meaning at ever more abstract levels, such as that of the 'extended lexical unit' (Stubbs 2001: 87). Language use is seen as resulting from the interplay between the collocation of these patterns and the individual language user's creativity in communicating with others in different social situations.

Collocation, creativity and cliché

In many social situations there are phrases which are seen as being particularly appropriate to the occasion. Knowledge of the collocations which make up these phrases therefore comprises part of a language user's communicative competence (Hymes 1971). Through repeated exposure, use and feedback, the collocations used in successful communication in these situations are internalized by language users, so that in effect these collocations constitute a single choice, a formula which the user knows will contribute to the success of a social interaction. Collocations like these are often referred to as *formulaic* or *pre-fabricated* language. One example of a highly specialized social interaction involving formulaic language is in a diplomatic exchange between two countries. At the end of a diplomatic Note, the formula shown in Example 9 is used:

Example 9   The Embassy of [country A] avails itself of this opportunity to renew to the Ministry of Foreign Affairs of [country B] the assurances of its highest consideration.

Apart from the variation permitted with the insertion of the names of the countries involved in the exchange, this phrase is completely fixed: these words are always used in exactly this order and 'lend a degree of gravity to the content that would perhaps be missing if the same message was passed in a letter' (Protocol Division of the Foreign and Commonwealth Office, Personal Communication). At this point in the communication there is little use for linguistic creativity. Regardless of the actual content of the Note, the omission of this formula by the writer, or the slightest variation – intentional or not – from the collocations of which it is composed could have serious diplomatic consequences. The use of collocations in certain communicative situations is therefore mandated by the weight of convention and precedent established by previous users of the language, and by the expectations of current members of the discourse community.

However, while empirical linguists observe and describe the role of collocations in particular communicative situations, language users themselves often make value judgements about such phrases, which appear to be neither creative nor original. Some collocations are seen as *clichés*, which are felt to have lost their force through over-use (Howarth 1996: 13). Where the empirical linguist observes 'a large number of semi-preconstructed phrases that constitute single choices' (Sinclair 1991: 110), the language user sees 'phrases tacked together like the sections of a prefabricated hen-house' (Orwell 1946: 3; cf. Parris 2007). There is consequently an apparent tension between creativity and collocation in certain communicative situations:

what we value most in language – creativity, expressiveness [. . .] – allows us to succeed less well in having others understand us than the largely prefabricated phrases we use to say almost the same thing over and over again. Paradoxically, language is at its best when it matters least; at its worst when it matters most.

(Moore and Carling 1988, quoted in Howarth 1996: 13)

There is a difference between *perceived* and *observed* frequent use however; a collocation which appears to be used repetitively may not in fact be used repeatedly. Empirical work on collocation has revealed that clichés and idioms are rare in the use of English as a whole (Moon 1998), and that they only appear to be over-used by speakers in particular domains or genres.

This tension between creativity and collocation is more apparent in English literature, when writers deliberately try to break collocational relations between words in order to say something new:

the prose writer or the poet strives, over a larger or smaller stretch of text, to convey something which he cannot achieve by normal means, and he thereby sets us a problem in which we can lean on no experience of directly relevant instances.

(McIntosh 1961: 336)

Literary authors go to great lengths to avoid using language which appears to them to be unoriginal and lacking creativity. Smith (2007), for example, is highly self-critical when she describes when she has been unable to break collocational relations successfully:

in each of my novels somebody 'rummages in their purse' for something because I was too lazy and thoughtless and unawake to separate 'purse' from its old, persistent friend 'rummage'. To rummage through a purse is to sleepwalk through a sentence – a small enough betrayal of self, but a betrayal all the same.

(Smith 2007: 3)

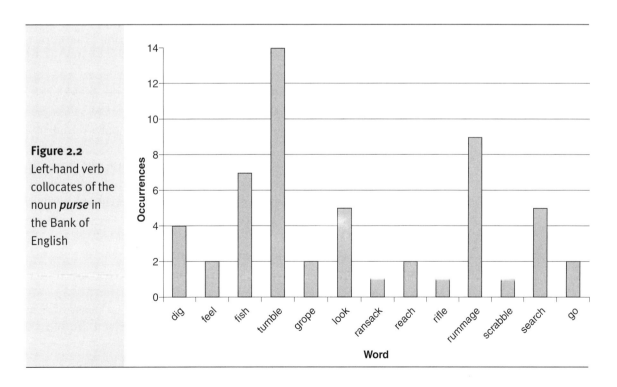

Figure 2.2
Left-hand verb collocates of the noun *purse* in the Bank of English

Figure 2.2 shows empirical evidence from the Bank of English of the collocates of *purse* in the sense Smith describes above. Without distinguishing between the British sense of *purse* (in American English a *change purse*) or the American sense (in British English a *handbag*), it can be seen that *rummage* is the second most frequent collocate after *fumble*.

To find a more original collocation in an attempt to convey a more profound literary meaning, the writer would need to choose a verb with a conceivably similar meaning to *rummage*, *fumble* and so on, but which the reader is unlikely to have encountered before in connection with *purse*.

Collocation and English as a lingua franca

Both the approaches to English collocation outlined above rely on the native speaker as a data source: intuitive descriptions of collocational relations rely on a native speaker's judgement, while most corpora traditionally contain texts and spoken data produced by native speakers, and so the collocational tendencies identified normally reflect native speaker usage. These approaches to collocation need to be re-assessed in the light of the unique status of English both as a language with different standard versions around the world (Kachru 1985) and as a lingua franca in which most communication worldwide now involves one or more non-native speakers (Crystal 2003).

The main area of uncertainty for applied linguists is the place of native speaker varieties of English in English language teaching and learning. If a minority of the users of a language speak it as a mother tongue, then it is not clear which variety of the language should continue to be taught to its learners. The variety of English chosen as the model for learning will ultimately depend on the communicative situations in which learners intend, or will be obliged, to use it. Some learners will prefer to learn English the way native speakers use it (Timmis 2002) since 'being perceived as a member of a certain linguistic group that speaks the L2 natively . . . is also important to certain learners of a language' (Nesselhauf 2005: 2). On the other hand, some learners might be suspicious of the ideological assumptions behind a native speaker model. Several writers (Phillipson 1988; Pennycook 1994; Canagarajah 1999) have warned that politically and economically powerful native English-speaking countries seek to perpetuate and extend their dominance by disseminating, through the 'imperial troopers' (Edge 2003: 10) of the global English language teaching industry, a native English-speaking view of the world.

It may be difficult to predict the possible effects of releasing English, and thereby its collocations, from the obligation to be acceptable to native speakers. Johns (1996: 1) identifies a 'slight oddity' arising from a learner's collocation of *present* and *insight* in Example 10:

Example 10   The variation of these ratios presents some insight about the financial intermediary role of banks.

After referring to corpus data, Johns suggests that the sentence could be improved using *present* with its more frequent collocate *findings* or by using *offer* with its frequent collocate *insights*. Users of English as a lingua franca may come to have higher tolerances of formerly odd-sounding collocations, since by definition these will no longer sound 'odd'. Alternatively, lingua franca users might insist upon continued restrictions on collocability.

Applied linguistics must inform this debate over the vocabulary of English as a lingua franca by empirically establishing its collocational norms, if any. Data can be collected on English use by lingua franca speakers in specific contexts, although defining a suitable lingua franca speaker is not straightforward (Prodromou 2006). Initial moves towards identifying new and continued tendencies of words to co-occur have already been made, with the VOICE corpus (Seidlhofer 2001) and descriptions of lingua franca collocational patterning (Mauranen 2004) which suggest that non-native speaker use continues at times to approximate to native speaker use.

Conclusion

This chapter has briefly discussed two approaches to investigating the role of collocation in English vocabulary. The terms collocation, collocations, and collocational relations have all been used to illustrate the different aspects of the phenomenon and how it is relevant to the work of lexicographers and language teachers. The possible effects on collocation of the use of English as a lingua franca have also been discussed, with the implication that descriptions of collocation will become more context-dependent.

References

Aisenstadt, E. (1981) 'Restricted collocations in English lexicology and lexicography', *ITL (Instituut voor Toegepaste Linguistiek) Review of Applied Linguistics*, 53: 53–61.

Bank of English. (2005) Corpus jointly owned by HarperCollins Publishers and the University of Birmingham.

Benson, M., Benson, E., and Ilson, R. (eds) (1997) *The BBI Dictionary of English Word Combinations*, Amsterdam: John Benjamins.

Brown, L. (ed.) (1994) *New Shorter Oxford English Dictionary*, Oxford: Oxford University Press.

Butterfield, J. (ed.) (2003) *Collins English Dictionary*, 6th edn, Glasgow: HarperCollins.

Canagarajah, S. (1999) *Resisting Linguistic Imperialism in English Teaching*, Oxford: Oxford University Press.

Collins Word Web (2007) Online. Available HTTP: http://www.collins.co.uk/books.aspx?group=180 (accessed 1 January 2008).

Cruse, D. A. (1986) *Lexical Semantics*, Cambridge: Cambridge University Press.

Crystal, D. (2003) *English as a Global Language*, 2nd edn, Cambridge: Cambridge University Press.

Edge, J. (2003) 'TEFL and international politics: a personal narrative', *IATEFL Issues*, 175: 10–11.

Fox, G. (1987) 'The case for examples', in J. McH. Sinclair (ed.) *Looking Up: an account of the COBUILD project in lexical computing*, London: Collins ELT.

Hoey, M. (1991) *Patterns of Lexis in Text*, Oxford: Oxford University Press.

Howarth, P. A. (1996) *Phraseology in English Academic Writing*, Tübingen: Max Niemeyer.

Hunston, S., and Francis, G. (2000) *Pattern Grammar*, Amsterdam: John Benjamins.

Hymes, D. H. (1971) *On Communicative Competence*, Philadelphia: University of Pennsylvania Press.

Johns, T. F. (1996) *Kibbitzer 12, Offering Insights*, Online. Available HTTP:

http://www.eisu2.bham.ac.uk/Webmaterials/kibbitzers/kibbitzer12.htm (accessed 1 January 2008).

Kachru, B. B. (1985) 'Standards, codification and sociolinguistic realism: the English language in the outer circle', in R. Quirk and H. G. Widdowson (eds) *English in the World: teaching and learning the language and literatures*, Cambridge: Cambridge University Press, pp. 11–30.

Lewis, M. (ed.) (2000) *Teaching Collocation: further developments in the Lexical Approach*, Hove: Language Teaching Publications.

Mason, O. (1999) 'Parameters of collocation: the word in the centre of gravity', in J. M. Kirk (ed.) *Corpora Galore: analyses and techniques in describing English*, Amsterdam: Rodopi.

Mauranen, A. (2004) 'Formulaic sequences in lingua franca English', paper presented at the 37th BAAL Conference, Kings College, London, September.

McIntosh, A. (1961) 'Patterns and ranges', *Language*, 37: 325–37.

Moon, R. (1998) *Fixed Expressions and Idioms in English: A corpus based approach*, Oxford: Clarendon Press.

Moon, R. (2007) 'Sinclair, lexicography, and the Cobuild project: the application of theory', *International Journal of Corpus Linguistics*, 12: 159–81.

Moore, T., and Carling, C. (1988) *The Limitations of Language*, London: Macmillan.

Nation, I. S. P. (2001) *Learning Vocabulary in Another Language*, Cambridge: Cambridge University Press.

Nattinger, J. R., and DeCarrico, J. (1992) *Lexical Phrases and Language Teaching*, Oxford: Oxford University Press.

Nesselhauf, N. (2005) *Collocations in a Learner Corpus*, Amsterdam: John Benjamins.

Orwell, G. (1946) 'Politics and the English Language', *Horizon*, April.

Parris, M. (2007) 'Not my words, Mr Speaker', *The Sunday Supplement*, BBC Radio 4, Online. Available HTTP: http://news.bbc.co.uk/1/hi/programmes/the_westminster_hour/6991605.stm (accessed 1 January 2008).

Partington, A. (1998) *Patterns and Meanings: using corpora for English language research and teaching*, Amsterdam: John Benjamins.

Pawley, A., and Syder, F. H. (1983) 'Two puzzles for linguistic theory: nativelike selection and nativelike fluency', in J. C. Richards and R. W. Schmidt (eds), *Language and Communication*, London: Longman.

Pennycook, A. (1994) *The Cultural Politics of English as an International Language*, London: Longman.

Phillipson, R. (1988) *Linguistic Imperialism*, Oxford: Oxford University Press.

Prodromou, L. (2006) 'Defining the "successful bilingual speaker" of English', in R. Rubdy and M. Saraceni (eds), *English in the World: global rules, global roles*, London: Continuum.

Seidlhofer, B. (2001) *Vienna-Oxford International Corpus of English*, Online. Available HTTP: http://www.univie.ac.at/voice/ (accessed 1 January 2008).

Sinclair, J. McH. (1991) *Corpus, Concordance, Collocation*, Oxford: Oxford University Press.

Sinclair, J. McH. (ed.) (2006) *Collins COBUILD Advanced Learner's English Dictionary*, 5th edn, Glasgow: HarperCollins.

Smith, Z. (2007) 'Fail better', *The Guardian*, 13 January.

Stubbs, M. (2001) *Words and Phrases: corpus studies of lexical semantics*, Oxford: Blackwell.

Timmis, I. (2002) 'Native-speaker norms and international English: a classroom view', *English Language Teaching Journal*, 56: 240–9.

Willis, D. (2003) *Rules, Patterns and Words: grammar and lexis in English language teaching*, Cambridge: Cambridge University Press.

Wray, A. (2002) *Formulaic Language and the Lexicon*, Cambridge: Cambridge University Press.

Introduction to chapter 3

This is one of four chapters in this book about how English can be described. The chapter introduces an interesting concept – grammatical metaphor – from the approach to grammar known as Systemic-Functional Grammar. The name most associated with Systemic-Functional Grammar is that of Michael Halliday. In this chapter, Geoff Thompson explains what grammatical metaphor is and then uses the concept to report a research project comparing dissertations written by students in the area of Applied Linguistics. The key concepts introduced in this chapter are: grammatical metaphor, nominalization and academic writing. The chapter is also a useful example of how research of this kind is carried out and interpreted.

The background to this chapter

Systemic-Functional Grammar (SFG) is a complex theory of how language can be described that links the detail of how something is expressed (the 'wording') with aspects of the situation such as who is talking to whom, or what ideology lies behind what is said. The ideas in SFG are often used by researchers investigating the language of newspapers, or the way that politicians speak, or the language of novels or poetry. SFG has also been used extensively in describing the language of classrooms, of textbooks, and of children's writing. It is not routinely used in second language teaching, but because it is used so much in language studies it is an important area of knowledge for Applied Linguists.

One of the key ideas in SFG is that a clause can be described in terms of the **process** (the action, activity, or 'doing') it expresses, and the **participants** (people and things) involved in that process. This means that any text can be analysed in terms of the processes and participants in it. The examples below all come from *An Introduction to Functional Grammar* (3rd edition) by M. A. K. Halliday and C. M. Matthiessen (Arnold, 2004):

1 *The lion caught the tourist*
   The process is Material (representing the physical world).
   The participants are Actor (*the lion*) and Goal (*the tourist*).
2 *I hate cockroaches*
   The process is Mental (representing the world of the mind).
   The participants are Senser (*I*) and Phenomenon (*cockroaches*).
3 *John became a plumber*
   The process is Relational (representing the relationship between the participants).
   The participants are Carrier (*John*) and Attribute (*a plumber*).

These examples are what Halliday calls 'congruent' – people and things are represented by nouns (*lion, tourist*) while actions are represented by verbs (*caught*). English allows other forms of expression, however. For example, we might see *The lion's attack startled the onlookers*. This clause is Mental process rather than Material process, and the action (*attack*) is expressed as a noun rather than as a verb. Using *attack* as a noun rather than as a verb is an example of 'nominalization' or 'grammatical metaphor'.

Halliday suggests that written language is more likely to have a large amount of grammatical metaphor in it than spoken language; conversely, something with a large amount of grammatical metaphor will sound 'like writing' even if it spoken. Nominalization in particular is also associated with academic disciplines, especially science disciplines. So anyone learning to read or write texts in an academic subject will need to become familiar with nominalizations.

Focusing on the argument

It is worth reading the 'Findings' section of this chapter in some detail to see how Thompson constructs his argument. Notice that he starts with purely numerical information – how many nominalizations there were in each set of dissertations – then goes on to a more detailed breakdown – how many nominalizations in each category – and ends with a discussion of particular examples. This progression is used to build up an argument that has the most significant points at the end:

- There are differences in the number of nominalizations in each set of dissertations, but these differences do not tell us much that is useful . . .
- It is more useful if we divide the nominalizations into types . . .
- We then have to sub-divide the types . . .
- And this gives us the main differences between the two sets.

In this section of the chapter Thompson gives us information, but he also sets that information in the context of how we as readers might react to it: he warns us how the figures should not be interpreted (e.g. *some caution is needed* . . .); he points out how the figures do not meet our expectations in some cases (e.g. *this apparent discrepancy*); and he indicates when an interpretation is obvious or interesting (e.g. *perhaps more revealing . . . throw light on . . . most obvious difference*).

A language tip

Thompson mentions that he has 'normalized' the figures used in his study:

In order to allow comparisons between the two sets of dissertations, the figures *were then normalized* to give the frequency of nominalizations per 1000 words.

Let's take a look at how this works. Suppose you are looking at two essays, one of 3,000 words and the other of 4,000 words. Each essay uses the word *explanation* 12 times. Obviously, although the word is used in each essay the same number of times, it is proportionally more frequent in the shorter essay than in the longer one. We can demonstrate that this is the case by normalizing the figures. That is, we say that if a word is used 12 times in 3,000 words, then it is used on average four times in each thousand words (dividing 12 by 3); but if a word is used 12 times in 4,000 words it is used on average three times in each thousand words (dividing 12 by 4). So rather than saying that *explanation* is used 12 times in each essay, we can say that it is used four times per thousand words (ptw) in one essay and three times ptw in the other essay.

To think about

1 These phrases all contain nominalizations (underlined); can you rewrite them so that the noun underlined is expressed as a verb?

Further <u>investigation</u> revealed that . . .

There has been a considerable amount of <u>discussion</u> about . . .

These problems have been caused by excessive <u>consumption</u> of resources . . .

2   Look at something you have written yourself in English, such as an essay or a letter. Can you find any examples of nominalization? If not, can you find any places where nominalization would have helped the argument?

3   Thompson warns us that the 'good' essay writers in his experiment did not only use more nominalizations, but also used them more effectively. What do you think are the dangers of simply deciding as a writer to use nominalizations often?

CHAPTER 3

Grammatical metaphor and success in academic writing

Geoff Thompson

CONTENTS

The concept of grammatical metaphor was introduced into linguistics by Halliday (1985), and it is increasingly recognized that this is a key mechanism by which the resources for the making of meaning in a language can be greatly expanded (see, for example, Ravelli 1988, Martin 1992, Halliday and Martin 1993, Simon-Vandenbergen et al. 2003). It has also been argued that one kind of grammatical metaphor, nominalization, plays a crucial role in the construction of knowledge and thus in education: success in education is seen as, to large extent, being associated with the ability to understand and use this type of grammatical metaphor (Christie and Martin 1997).

In this chapter I will explore one aspect of this phenomenon, by investigating to what extent mastery of nominalization is associated with academic success in dissertations written by students on MAs in Applied Linguistics and TESOL whose first language is not English. I will look both at the frequency of nominalizations in a small corpus of high-rated dissertations (HRDs) and low-rated dissertations (LRDs), and at the types of nominalizations used. The working hypothesis, based on previous research, is that better dissertations will show higher frequencies of nominalizations, but also, and perhaps more importantly, a more varied range of uses.

Grammatical metaphor

Grammatical metaphor may be simply defined as the use of a grammatical form to express a meaning which is different from the meaning that the form originally evolved to express.[1] For example, the traditional account describes nouns as referring to things, and verbs as expressing actions and events. That description is based on an intuitive sense of how these word classes are normally used, and clearly has a degree of validity; but, equally clearly, it does not apply easily in the following example from an academic article on economics:

Example 1   Increased sugar production meant a greater use of temporary labour.

Here, the writer talks about two actions – [people – presumably sugar companies] *produce* [sugar] and [people] *use* [temporary labour]; but these actions are expressed as nouns, that is, *production* and *use* are both nominalizations. At the same time, the verb *meant* does not refer to an action but expresses a causal relationship between the two actions which would more naturally be expressed by a conjunction such as *because*. In some respects, the example could be more simply phrased as (1a):

Example 1a   Sugar companies used temporary labour more because they were producing more sugar.

It is important to stress that the paraphrase in Example 1a is not straightforwardly equivalent in meaning to the original version in Example 1. That is, the two versions would not be interchangeable: the original is appropriate to the formal text from which it was taken, whereas the paraphrase would be more suitable for a less formal text, perhaps aimed at younger readers. In the original, the information is expressed in a more condensed way: whereas the paraphrase consists of two clauses, the original is a single clause in which the 'doer' of the actions is left non-explicit (though in this case easily recoverable). Beyond that, the way in which the world is represented in the two versions is different. The paraphrase represents a concrete world in which people act on objects and other people around them, and it clearly corresponds more closely to a 'common-sense' description of the state of affairs in the world that is being represented. The original, on the other hand, construes a world in which concepts enter into causal relations with each other, and it is therefore 'distanced' from the events into a generalized domain of abstraction (see Thompson 2004: 229–30 for a fuller account of the effects of nominalization).

The kind of condensed, abstract wordings that result from nominalization are particularly characteristic of formal written text: starting in scientific writing (Halliday 1988), such wordings have spread into nearly all other areas of academic writing. A good deal of research has shown that school students need to learn how to understand and use the resources of nominalization (see e.g. Martin 1991); and that the ability to do this competently is strongly associated with academic success. Much of the research has focused on students reading and writing in their mother tongue, but there have been some studies of writers of English as a Second Language (e.g. Schleppegrell 2004, Chen and Foley 2004). These latter have demonstrated that there is a similar link between higher proficiency in the use of nominalization in the L2 and academic success. In this study I aim to explore patterns in the ways in which the resource of nominalization is deployed in advanced L2 academic writing that appear to be characteristic of higher-rated dissertations.

Materials and methods

The findings presented below are based on the analysis of parts of ten MA dissertations, all written by non-native speakers of English. Five of the dissertations were classed as high-rated, that is, they were awarded marks in the 70+ (Distinction) range. The other five were classed as low-rated, and were awarded marks between 53 per cent and 56 per cent. The pass mark is 50 per cent, so these 'low-rated' dissertations are still safely of passable standard, and reflect the fact that the writers have a competent level of English proficiency. I did not use dissertations at the pass–fail borderline because they typically showed basic language problems which at times made it difficult to be certain what the writer was trying to say. Where the dissertations analysed had language errors or infelicities, I ignored these unless they involved nominalizations; in the latter cases, I categorized them according to the intended use.

I analysed the same parts of each dissertation: the whole of the introduction, methodology and conclusion chapters, and 20 pages of the chapter (which was given various titles) in which the findings of the study were presented and discussed. I omitted the literature review, because that frequently contained extensive quotations or close paraphrases from other authors, and I wished to focus on the writers' own language (for the same reason, I also omitted any quoted material that occurred in the parts that I analysed).

Identification of nominalizations is not always straightforward. One formal criterion for identifying a nominalization is that the nominal form is derived from a verb; but this is only the first step. With nominals derived from verbs, there is a cline from most 'noun-like' to most 'verb-like'. For instance, a noun such as *administration* is derived from the verb *administer*, but there is a clear difference between examples such as 2 and 3:

Example 2   At the same time, the *administration* has failed to take decisive action.
Example 3   One week was left between the last teaching session and the *administration* of the questionnaire.

In Example 2, the noun refers to a body of people and has little, if any, sense of an event being represented, whereas in Example 3 it refers to the process of administering. Only the second of these counts as a nominalization in the sense in which I am interested. A further criterion, therefore, is whether an instance allows a paraphrase with 'the process of X–ing'.[2]

Since there is no simple automatic way of identifying all cases of nominalization in a text, the analysis was done manually. This was the main reason why the corpus was small: just over 42,000 words in all. The first step was a simple count of all cases that matched the criteria above, keeping a running record of types and tokens in each dissertation (e.g. the nominalization *administration [of the questionnaire]* was used three times in one of the dissertations, which therefore counted as one type and three tokens). In order to allow comparisons between the two sets of dissertations, the figures were then normalized to give the frequency of nominalizations per 1000 words.

Findings

As expected, the basic frequencies in the use of nominalizations show differences between the high- and low-rated dissertations – see Table 3.1.

	High-rated dissertations	Low-rated dissertations
Average number of tokens	71.2	54.6
Average number of types	31.9	15.1
Type:token ratio	0.45	0.28

Table 3.1
Frequencies of nominalizations (per 1000 words)

In terms of tokens, the HRDs used an average of 30 per cent more nominalizations per 1000 words than the LRDs. However, some caution is needed in interpreting this difference, because the averages mask some large differences between individual dissertations within each group. For example, the frequency in the dissertation which had the highest number in the LRD group (87.5 per thousand), was only just below that in the dissertation with the highest number in the HRD group (90.1 per thousand).

Perhaps more revealing is the fact that the HRDs also used a greater variety of nominalizations, as shown by the type:token ratio. This is calculated by dividing the number of different nominalizations by the total number of nominalizations. For HRDs the figure is 0.45, and for LRDs it is 0.28 (to put that simply, it means that on average each nominalization in the HRDs was used just over twice per thousand words, whereas in LRDs each was used between three and four times). Thus, the writers of the LRDs tended to use fewer nominalizations more often. The most extreme case of this is the writer in the LRD group mentioned above who used the highest number of tokens in her group: in terms of type, she ranked very low, using only 16.3 types per thousand. This gives a type:token ratio of 0.19 (that is, on average she used each nominalization five times per thousand words).

When we examine the kinds of nominalizations that were used, further, more important, differences emerge. The nominalizations in the data can be broadly grouped into three categories: those which relate to the topic being investigated (e.g. *teaching, repetition, use [of literature], selection [of activities]*), where the understood 'doer' is typically learners or teachers; those which relate to the research being carried out (e.g. *investigation, limitation, assumption, conclusion*), where the understood 'doer' is the researcher and/or other researchers (including the reader); and those which have a primarily textual cohesive function. This latter type partly cuts across the two other groupings: it occurs when some event or state described in a clause is subsequently picked up in a nominalized form which refers back to what has just been said. Here is a very simple example from a high-rated dissertation:

Example 4   Through the repetition of input, the taught language is reinforced, and this *reinforcement* is considered to be essential in the learning process.

Reinforcement here would normally be included in the first group, but it is categorized as having a textual cohesive function because it encapsulates the preceding clause *the taught language is reinforced* in a condensed form and, as Halliday and Matthiessen (2004: 642) point out, it can function as the subject of the clause in which it appears, thus supporting the step-by-step development of an argument (the use of *this* is a typical signal of such cases).

	High-rated dissertations	Low-rated dissertations
Topic-related	34.7	38.3
Research-related	33.9	16.3
Cohesive	2.6	0.0
Total	71.2	54.6

Table 3.2 Frequencies of different types of nominalizations (per 1000 words)

When the frequencies of tokens in each of these three categories are calculated, the picture is somewhat altered and clarified – see Table 3.2.

Table 3.2 shows that the frequencies of topic-related nominalizations do not correlate with differences in the rating – in fact, contrary to what might be expected, the LRDs have a higher average frequency than the HRDs in this category. Examination of individual dissertations reveals a possible reason for this apparent discrepancy. I mentioned earlier that there are large differences in frequencies between individual dissertations in the same group. It turns out that most of this variation arises from a very great variation in the frequency of nominalizations in the first category, topic-related terms: within the HRD group, the range is from 60.7 per thousand words in the dissertation which uses this category most, to 5.2 in the dissertation which uses them least; and within the LRD group, it is from 66.3 per thousand words to 8.5. It therefore seems that the major factor in the use of this kind of nominalization may be the topic of the dissertation rather than anything else.

However, within this category, more delicate distinctions can be made which throw light on how LRDs and HRDs differ. There are nominalized forms that are standard technical terms associated with different areas of Applied Linguistics which even the less successful writers use comfortably – indeed, it would be difficult to write about certain topics without using these terms. Example 5, from a LRD, illustrates this:

Example 5   It is widely acknowledged by most teachers and learners that *reading* plays an essential part in language *learning*. Particularly in universities in China, *reading* seems to occupy the most important position compared with the three other language skills: *listening, speaking* and *writing*. In the university which I investigated, according to the *teaching* program, teachers should spend ¾ of the *teaching* time on *reading*.

While the extract certainly has a high density of these nominalizations, the overall effect is not particularly sophisticated, partly because all of the nominalizations are ready-made terms which would be familiar even to non-specialists. It is hard to think of ways in which full clauses (e.g. '[when readers] *read*', '[when listeners] *listen*') could have been used instead of nominalizations without making the text unacceptably clumsy. On the other hand, many nominalizations in the topic-related category are less 'ready-made'. In Example 6, from a high-rated dissertation, the nominalizations, while still topic-related and relatively non-specialized, suggest that the writer has chosen to express the ideas in the form of nominalizations rather than of clauses:

Example 6   They may be utilized for the *selection* of literary texts in the EFL classroom, as well as the *design* or *evaluation* of the tasks accompanying them.

One factor in making the nominalizations in Example 6 appear more carefully 'tailored' for the particular context is that they are post-modified and thus encapsulate specific clauses, such as '[when teachers] *select literary texts in the EFL classroom*' – as this wording suggests, the writer could equally well have used a clause to express the idea instead. Although the distinction between 'tailored' vs. 'ready-made' nominalizations is a fuzzy one and it is therefore impossible to calculate exact frequencies, a rough count of the cases which fall definitely into one or other of these categories indicates that tailored nominalizations are markedly more characteristic of HRDs than LRDs. The fact that a writer shows awareness of the option of using a nominalization rather than a clause in such cases might well be taken by dissertation assessors to indicate that s/he has a more secure grasp of the field – or at least of the way in which experts write about the field.

Returning to the broader categories, the most obvious difference between the HRDs and LRDs in Table 3.2 is in the second category, research-related nominalizations. Not only do the HRDs use this type twice as often as the LRDs on average, but the results here are more consistent. There is a narrower range within each group, and the results for the two groups do not overlap: the highest frequency in a low-rated dissertation (21.2 per thousand) is lower than the lowest frequency in a high-rated dissertation (26.7 per thousand). Example 7 illustrates the way in which this type of nominalization is typically used in a high-rated dissertation (it is also worth noting that nearly all the cases in the example are 'tailored'):

Example 7   The main criterion for *inclusion* in the corpus was length . . . No *attempt* was made to include only articles written by native speakers of English. In the *absence* of direct *collaboration* with journal editors, it was impossible to obtain information on the writers' native language. In addition, *segregation* of authors into native speakers and non-native speakers would have been counter to the purposes of this study.

What seems to happen here is that successful writers show more convincingly, through the nominalized terms which they use (as well as through other means, of course), that they are able to talk about the process of research in the approved academic style. This is highly prized by dissertation assessors, since it generally suggests that students have developed the ability to stand back and see what they have done in collecting and interpreting data in terms of abstract research concepts. It is evidence that a writer may be making the difficult transition from student to researcher.

The final category, nominalizations with a textual cohesive function, was very little used, even in the HRDs (and did not occur at all in the LRDs); and I will therefore comment on it only briefly.[3] Use of this type of nominalization seems to indicate, more directly than the other types, an advanced level of proficiency in English, in that it reflects an awareness of the need to control the flow of information and to provide appropriate signalling of relations between steps in the argument. As with the second category, it is therefore possible to see reasons why the ability to deploy this resource might be associated with higher grades.

Conclusion   It should be stressed that this study has not, of course, shown a direct causal link between better mastery of nominalization and higher grades. It is quite possible that a larger corpus would have thrown up cases where a high-rated dissertation used relatively little nominalization or where a low-rated dissertation used a great deal. It is certainly true that – as with any linguistic resource – overuse and/or inappropriate use of nominalization may be counter-productive. There will be many factors which assessors use in deciding on a grade for a dissertation, most of which have no direct relation to the use or non-use of nominalization.

What I have aimed to show, however, is that the resource of nominalization is more fully used, in particular ways, in higher-rated dissertations; and that connections can be made between, on the one hand, the general characteristics that are valued by dissertation assessors, and, on the other, the abilities that seem to be reflected in the deployment of nominalization – particularly an intellectual sense of research as a generalized process into which the student is being initiated, and a linguistic capacity to go beyond the use of ready-made nominalizations and to condense clauses into 'tailored' nominalized forms.

Notes

1   In what follows, I focus only on nominalization. Grammatical metaphor, however, is a wider phenomenon, which includes interpersonal forms of metaphor – see Halliday and Matthiessen 2004 for a full account.

2   There is a further grouping which also counts as nominalizations: nouns derived from adjectives. The test here is slightly different: whether they can be paraphrased as 'the state of being X'. For example, *authenticity* can be paraphrased as 'the state of being authentic'.

3   A note of caution is required here. A quick check of a small sample of applied linguistics articles published in academic journals showed that this category is generally very infrequent even in the writing of experts: just over one occurrence per thousand words. The very small numbers involved mean that any comparisons and conclusions can therefore only be very tentative.

References

Chen, Y.P. and Foley, J.A. (2004) 'Problems with metaphorical reconstrual of meaning in Chinese EFL learners' expositions', in L.J. Ravelli and R.A. Ellis (eds).

Christie, F. and Martin, J.R. (eds) (1997) *Genre and Institutions: social processes in the workplace and school*, London: Cassell.

Halliday, M.A.K. (1985) *An Introduction to Functional Grammar*, London: Edward Arnold.

—— (1988) 'On the language of physical science', in M. Ghadessy (ed.) *Registers of Written English*, London and New York: Pinter. Reprinted in M.A.K. Halliday and J.R. Martin, 1993.

Halliday, M.A.K. and Martin, J.R. (1993) *Writing Science: literacy and discursive power*, London: The Falmer Press.

Halliday, M.A.K. and Matthiessen, C.M.I.M. (2004) *An Introduction to Functional Grammar*, 3rd edn, London: Arnold.

Martin, J.R. (1991) 'Nominalization in science and humanities: distilling knowledge and scaffolding text', in E. Ventola (ed.) *Functional and Systemic Linguistics: approaches and uses*, Berlin: Mouton de Gruyter.

—— (1992) *English Text: system and structure*, Amsterdam and Philadelphia: John Benjamins.

Ravelli, L.J. (1988) 'Grammatical metaphor: an initial analysis', in E.H. Steiner and R. Veltman (eds) *Pragmatics, Discourse and Text: some systemically-inspired approaches*, London and New York: Pinter.

Ravelli, L.J. and Ellis, R.A (eds) (2004) *Analysing Academic Writing: contextualized frameworks*, London and New York: Continuum.

Schleppegrell, M.J. (2004) 'Technical writing in a second language: the role of grammatical metaphor', in L.J. Ravelli and R.A. Ellis (eds).

Simon-Vandenbergen, A.-M., Taverniers, M. and Ravelli, L.J. (eds) (2003) *Grammatical Metaphor: views from Systemic Functional Linguistics*, Amsterdam and Philadelphia: John Benjamins.

Thompson, G. (2004) *Introducing Functional Grammar*, 2nd edn, London: Arnold.

Introduction to chapter 4

The background to this chapter

This chapter is one of the series describing different aspects of English, in this case the structure of spoken interaction. Specifically, it focuses on one approach to this structure, called Conversation Analysis or CA. The chapter also relates CA to teaching oral skills in English. The key concepts in this chapter are those associated with Conversation Analysis, including turn-taking, adjacency pairs, and opening and closing sequences.

Almut Koester herself presents an informative overview of Conversation Analysis and its key ideas. She points out that it was initially developed by sociologists rather than by linguists, and that it argued for the importance of attention to the details of how people interacted and the assumptions they made.

Koester makes a strong argument for language teachers and materials writers to focus on the findings of CA. In fact, there are two arguments. One is that materials for learners will be improved if the dialogues presented in coursebooks accord with the features of naturally occurring conversation as demonstrated by CA. The second is that learners can be explicitly taught what conversation in English is like and how to participate in it.

This raises the question of why language teachers have not more routinely taken up the CA ideas and used them in teaching. One reason may be that, particularly in the early days, Conversation Analysts focused on interactions that were extremely informal, usually between people who knew each other well and who were chatting about inconsequential matters. It could be argued that few learners of English are likely to find themselves in such situations. Another argument sometimes made is that mechanisms such as turn-taking do not need to be taught, as anybody taking part in a conversation will use them automatically. More recent developments present the case in favour of incorporating insights from CA in language teaching. One of these is the extensive work, including that by Koester herself, on a CA approach to language in institutional settings such as hospitals, law courts, offices and classrooms. This has the effect of making CA more relevant to learners. In addition, comparative work on interaction in a number of languages has shown that practices such as turn-taking are not the same in all languages and that explicit teaching is therefore warranted.

Focusing on the argument

This chapter is one of several in this book that combines approaches to language with approaches to language teaching (compare this with Dave Willis's chapter, for example). It is also one of several that present information (in this case, information about what CA does) in the service of an argument or the answer to a question (in this case, how can speaking skills best be taught?). The reader is presented not just with information but with an 'angle' on that information. In this case, Koester presents us first with a problem – interactions between students that sound highly artificial – and then offers insights from CA as a possible solution to the problem. What is crucial here is the establishment of a question that suggests how the information might best be shaped so that the result is an argument as well as a set of facts.

A language tip   Koester needs to define or explain a number of technical terms in this chapter and she uses a number of linguistic devices to alert the reader that an explanation is present. Here are some examples:

* *CA takes an 'emic' (rather than 'etic') approach to analysis, which means that it tries to take the point of view of the participants in the interaction, rather than impose the analyst's view.*
  The terms 'emic' and 'etic' are defined using 'which means that'.
* *. . . 'repair', i.e. dealing with dysfluency or misunderstanding.*
  The term 'repair' is defined using 'i.e.'
* *Such initial turns are labelled 'first pair parts' and responding turns which fulfil the expectation set up by the first turn are called 'second pair parts'.*
  The terms 'first pair part' and 'second pair part' is defined using 'are labelled' and 'are called'.
* *A sequence of two such turns is an 'adjacency pair'.*
  The term 'adjacency pair' is defined using 'is'.
* *An acceptance would be a 'preferred second pair part' in CA terminology . . .*
  The term 'preferred' is defined using 'in CA terminology'. Notice also that here the definition is given by way of an example – an 'acceptance' is an example of a preferred second pair part, not a definition of it.

To think about

1   Are the conventions for turn-taking, or for opening or closing conversations, the same in other languages as in English? (Think about another language that you know well to answer this question.)

2   Look at a language teaching coursebook. Presumably it does not use words such as 'adjacency pairs' and 'preferred'. But can you identify where these concepts are used and taught using different names?

3   Koester talks about 'sensitizing' learners to how finding out information often involves more than just asking a question. Can you imagine in practice how this sensitization might be carried out?

CHAPTER 4

Conversation Analysis in the language classroom

Almut Koester

Among the many abilities and skills that language teachers aim to develop in their students, developing oral fluency is an increasingly important one. Most teachers would agree that one of the most important objectives of classes focusing on speaking skills is to prepare students to use the language outside the classroom in real-life situations, whether it be in everyday conversation or in service encounters, face to face or on the telephone. Nevertheless, while they may feel fairly confident teaching grammar and vocabulary, teachers may not always feel they are well-equipped to teach less clearly defined areas as 'oral fluency' or 'conversational skills'. Indeed, lessons designed to teach such skills often bear very little resemblance to real-life conversations outside the classroom. The following two examples illustrate such a discrepancy. The first is from a naturally occurring conversation between two colleagues greeting each other after the winter break and the second is from an English language lesson in which two students are doing a speaking activity in front of the class.

Example 1[1]

1	Gene	Hello Helga,
2	Helga	Hi.
3	Gene	Thank you for your card.
4	Helga	Oh. Happy new year.
5	Gene	I'm thinking of . . . writing out something with . . . a- a family newsletter to bring to you, with uh- but most o' the news you already know. You know about our new grandson?
6	Helga	Yes. That's uh really wonderful. How old is he now?
7	Gene	Well uh about . . . three weeks old, Hehehe
8	Helga	That's nice.

Example 2

Three Brazilian students have been asked 'to stand up and chat with each other about anything they wanted' (adapted from Hoey, 1991: 66). Initially, only two of the students speak:

1   A: Good morning.
2   B: Good morning.
3   A: I love Tina Turner.
4   B: Tina Turner?
5   A: Tina Turner is a famous singer.
[8 turns in which A and B talk about Tina Turner]
6   A: How's the weather?
7   B: It was cloudy.

8 B: Oh, what time is it?
9 A: It's twelve o'clock.
10 B: How are you?
11 A: Not bad.
[. . .]

Both conversations start with an initial greeting, but after that they progress very differently. The speakers in Example 1 develop a series of related topics (the New Year holiday, writing seasonal cards and newsletters, family news, the new grandson), whereas the two students in Example 2 switch abruptly between seemingly unrelated topics (the singer Tina Turner, the weather, the time, asking how the other person is). Gene and Helga in Example 1 are clearly engaging with one another, whereas the two students seem to be bringing up any topic that comes to mind simply to keep the conversation going. Part of the problem here is of course that the students are under pressure to perform in front of the class. In naturally occurring situations outside the classroom, people usually have something they want to say to one another, whereas the students have no particular motivation to talk except for the fact that they have been asked to by the teacher.

But a further problem may be that the students do not know how to structure and develop a conversation in the target language. In order to help students with such conversational skills, teachers need to have an understanding themselves of how conversations are structured. Conversation Analysis (CA) is an approach used to investigate how speakers collaboratively co-construct talk, and therefore can be a useful tool for analysing classroom discourse and for teaching oral skills. Hoey (1991) uses the example above to discuss eight 'properties of spoken discourse' and shows how these are lacking in the classroom interaction in Example 2. In doing this, he draws on CA as well as other methods of discourse analysis. Here only insights from CA will be considered.

Of course, teaching conversation is only one of the many pedagogical concerns of a language teacher; therefore one should not expect classroom interaction always to mirror conversation. In fact, Seedhouse (2004), who uses CA to investigate classroom language, argues that the classroom has its own 'interactional architecture' which differs from that of language outside the classroom. He argues that the turn-taking structure in the classroom is linked to pedagogical goals, and he identifies four types of classroom contexts, each with their own turn-taking structure: form-and-accuracy, meaning-and-fluency, task-oriented and procedural.

CA methods can therefore be used to investigate other types of interactions besides everyday conversation. In fact, it has been widely applied to 'institutional' contexts (see Drew and Heritage 1992), and classroom interaction must first and foremost be seen as a type of institutional discourse. Analysing classroom interaction is a further relevant application of CA to language teaching. CA can be used to identify the specific characteristics of this type of institutional discourse (e.g. Seedhouse 2004), and can also be used as a reflexive tool for teachers to evaluate their interactions with students. In addition, CA is increasingly being used in second language acquisition research and to investigate (and also challenge the notion of) non-native speaker discourse (Firth 1996,

Wong 2000).[2] These applications of CA will not be dealt with in this chapter, and the discussion will be limited to the application of CA to the teaching of speaking skills. The chapter thus has two aims: 1) to introduce the reader to some of the basics of Conversation Analysis; 2) to demonstrate the relevance of Conversation Analysis to teaching the spoken language in general and conversational skills in particular.

Background

Conversation Analysis refers to a specific approach to the study of spoken interaction first pioneered by the American sociologist Harvey Sacks and his collaborators Gail Jefferson and Emanuel Schegloff in the 1960s and 1970s. These sociologists were not interested in language as such, but in the organization of interaction. While CA remains a sub-discipline within Sociology, nowadays it is also used in a variety of disciplines concerned with the study of language, including Applied Linguistics.

CA takes a 'bottom up' approach to the study of spoken discourse in that it does not work with a priori models or categories. The method consists in recording and transcribing naturally occurring conversations and looking for recurring patterns and structures. CA takes an 'emic' (rather than 'etic') approach to analysis, which means that it tries to take the point of view of the participants in the interaction, rather than impose the analyst's view. Therefore the phenomena identified by a conversation analyst should be real to participants themselves, which does not mean that they are consciously aware of them, but that evidence can be found in the data that participants 'orient to' these phenomena. 'Evidence' is provided by the way in which participants respond to one another's turns and display their understanding of previous turns (see Hutchby and Wooffitt 1998: 1–9).

But although they avoid imposing categories on the interactions they study, conversation analysts do not reinvent the wheel every time they look at data. The large body of literature carried out using Conversation Analysis has identified a number of basic conversational structures and patterns which recur across a range of situations and speakers. These include turn-taking (Sacks et al. 1974), 'repair', that is, dealing with dysfluency or misunderstanding (Schegloff et al. 1977) and various types of turn-sequences such as adjacency pairs (Sacks 1992, vol. 2), opening and closing sequences (Schegloff 1968, Schegloff and Sacks 1973), side-sequences (Jefferson 1972) and pre-sequences (Schegloff 1980). As it will not be possible to deal with all of these within the scope of this chapter,[3] I will focus on just three types of phenomena: 1) adjacency pairs; 2) the related notion of preference; and 3) opening and closing sequences.

Adjacency pairs

One of the first noticeable patterns in looking at a transcript of a naturally occurring conversation is that some turns are more closely linked together than others. For instance turns 1–2 and 6–7 in Example 1:

1	Gene	Hello Helga,
2	Helga	Hi.
6	Helga	[. . .] How old is he now?
7	Gene	Well uh about . . . three weeks old, Hehehe

In turn 2 Helga responds to Gene's greeting, and in turn 7 Gene responds to a question posed by Helga. Turns 1 and 6 respectively set up the expectation that a certain type of next turn will occur, thus a greeting expects another greeting in return, and a question expects an answer. Such initial turns are labelled 'first pair parts' and responding turns which fulfil the expectation set up by the first turn are called 'second pair parts'. A sequence of two such turns is an 'adjacency pair'. If we turn to the language classroom, learners clearly need to be able to produce appropriate second pair parts in order to engage in spoken interaction. The classroom interaction in Example 2 shows that the two students are indeed capable of producing coherent adjacency pairs, for example:

1   A: Good morning.
2   B: Good morning.

6   A: How's the weather?
7   B: It was cloudy.

8   B: Oh, what time is it?
9   A: It's twelve o'clock.

As far as adjacency pairs are concerned, their interaction seems to be realistic. However, as we shall see, other aspects of their interaction deviate considerably from what happens in naturally occurring conversation, resulting in very unnatural and stilted-sounding discourse.

Preference organization

With many adjacency pairs, the addressee has two options for a second pair part; for example, if offered a cup of coffee, (s)he could accept or decline the offer. An acceptance would be a 'preferred second pair part' in CA terminology, whereas declining would be 'dispreferred' (Pomerantz 1984). Some common types of first pair parts and their preferred and dispreferred seconds are shown below:

First parts:	Offer/Invitation/Suggestion	Request	Assessment
Second parts:			
Preferred	Acceptance	Compliance	Agreement
Dispreferred	Declination/Rejection	Refusal	Disagreement

What CA researchers found from examining many interactions was that the two alternative types of second pair parts systematically have quite different structures and characteristics. Preferred seconds are structurally very simple: they are usually produced without any hesitations and are short and direct, for example:

Example 3 A: But you know maybe- maybe what I should do is . . .   → **Suggestion**
            is just write a little memo.
         B: That's not a bad idea,   → **Accept**

(From the Cambridge International Corpus, © Cambridge University Press.)

Dispreferred seconds, on the other hand, not only occur much less frequently, but are also longer and more complex, often having the following features (Levinson 1983: 332–345):

1 Delay and preface typically including:
   - discourse markers (e.g. *well, oh*)
   - token agreement (e.g. *Yes but . . .*)
   - appreciation (e.g. *that's very kind of you*)
   - apology
   - hesitation and pausing
   - hedges (*I don't know, I mean, you know*).
2 Declination component (refusal, rejection, disagreement).
3 Accounts: explanation.

Example 4 shows a dispreferred response in an extract taken from a workplace interaction in which two co-workers discuss how often to perform a task:

Example 4 A: So I can do 'em . . . Let's say weekly. or something like that from here on out.
     I don't think it pays to do it any more often than that.   → **Suggestion**
     B: Well weekly, I mean you have to do it . . . [1.5] ah . . . more often than that
     right now, for this week an' next week, 'cause we gotta- .hh . . . have 'em all
     entered into the system by a week on Friday.   → **Rejection**

Speaker B's response in Example 4 is much longer than in Example 3, and displays many of the typical features of dispreferred second pair parts: hesitations and pauses, a discourse marker (*well*), a hedge (*I mean*) and an account (or explanation) introduced by *'cause* . . . Note also that there is no overt declination component, but that speaker B simply says what he thinks should happen instead (*you have to do it . . . more often than that*).

   An important point here is that conversation analysts are not attempting to give a psychological explanation of why people might find it harder to say 'no' than 'yes', but are simply describing a structural phenomenon, that is, that second pair parts fall into these two groups which are consistently very different from one another across different situations and speakers.

   This finding is of utmost relevance to the teaching of spoken English, as students need to learn when and how to produce appropriate second pair parts, with dispreferred seconds such as disagreements and refusals posing a greater challenge, as they are structurally more complex. There is evidence that this difference between preferred and dispreferred seconds is not always reflected in course material or in learners' performance (see Pearson 1986 on agreeing/disagreeing). However, it would be relatively easy to teach, as the different types of second pair parts have systematically different characteristics that have been described in detail by conversation analysts.

Opening and closing sequences

As we have seen, adjacency pairs form the basic interactional units of conversation, and a very strong bond exists between first and second pair parts. When a first pair part has been produced, the expectation (known as 'conditional relevance') is that a second pair part will follow, even if it is not immediately forthcoming. There may be delays arising from misunderstanding, in which case a repair sequence ensues (see Hutchby and Wooffitt 1998: 59–69), or because some further questioning or discussion is needed in order to produce an appropriate second pair part, which results in a side sequence (Jefferson 1972). Therefore conversations do not consist solely of a series of adjacency pairs, but can be more complex, with longer sequences occurring. Looking again at Example 2 – the 'conversation' between two students – we can see that one reason it seems so unnatural is that it consists almost exclusively of simple adjacency pairs (turns 1–2, 6–7, 8–9, 10–11),[4] which makes it sound more like an interrogation than a conversation.

In addition to sequences caused by delayed second pair parts, beginnings and endings of conversations have routinized structures which have been described as opening and closing sequences.

Opening sequences

The following is a real example of an opening sequence that took place between colleagues in an office:

Example 5	1	Liz	Morning Ron
	2	Ron	Hello, how are you?
	3	Liz	Fine, thank you, how are you?
	4	Ron	Yeah all right, yeah,
	5	Liz	Good,
	6	Ron	hhh Can't be that machine [. . .]

Clearly there are several parts to this sequence: it begins with a greeting, (turns 1 and 2), then enquiry as to the other person's health (3–5), and then a 'first topic' is introduced in line 6 (Ron has in fact come in to use the photocopier and finds there is a problem). But opening sequences can contain other elements as well: conversation analysts have identified the following set of elements typically occurring in the order listed (Schegloff 1968; see also Hutchby and Wooffitt 1998: 122–126):

1 Summons/answer
2 Identification/recognition
3 Greetings
4 Initial enquiries
5 First topic

The 'first topic' is not actually part of the opening sequence, but occurs after completion of the opening sequence and often gives the reason for the encounter. The following (invented) beginning of a telephone conversation shows all five elements:

Example 6	1	[Ring]		Summons
	2	A:	Hello	Answering summons
	3	B:	Hello, Dan?	Identification
	4	A:	Yeah.	
	5	B:	This is Jenny.	Recognition
	6	A:	Oh hi Jenny.	Greeting
	7	B:	Hi,	
			how are you doing.	Initial enquiries
	8	B:	Pretty good. How 'bout you.	
	9	A:	I'm fine.	
	10	B:	The reason I called was to ask [. . .]	First topic

Note that the elements occur as adjacency pairs, e.g. 'summons – answering summons', or as sequences, e.g. 'initial enquiries', which consists of two reciprocal adjacency pairs. The first 'hello' in a telephone call is not actually a greeting, but answers the summons (the ringing of the phone). In face-to-face conversations, summons are not usually necessary, unless calling to attract the other person's attention. If speakers know each other (or, on the phone, recognize each others' voice or if the name of the caller appears on the display), a separate identification/recognition stage is not necessary either. So variation occurs in opening sequences in line with the CA notion of 'recipient design', that is, participants design their turns according to the assumed state of shared knowledge between them. For instance, in Examples 1 and 5, the opening sequence begins with a greeting pair, as speakers know each other, and in Example 1 there is a seasonal variation in the initial enquiries stage:

3	Gene	Thank you for your card.
4	Helga	Oh. Happy new year.

Knowing something about opening sequences now allows us to pinpoint what is wrong with the students' conversation in Example 2 (besides the overly simplistic adjacency pair structure). It contains a number of opening sequence elements scattered throughout the interaction: while a greeting pair occurs at the beginning (Good morning – Good morning), two candidates for initial enquiries occur much later (turns 6–7 and 10–11). On the other hand, a likely candidate for first topic (the singer Tina Turner) occurs immediately after the greeting pair (see also Hoey 1991). If students had been able to learn about and practise opening sequence structures, they might not have produced such a deviant conversation opening, even in this fairly contrived situation of performing in front of the class. However, textbook dialogues do not necessarily provide appropriate models of opening sequences. A study of telephone dialogues in a selection of English language textbooks (Wong 2002) revealed that the opening sequences bore little resemblance to those of natural conversations.

Closing sequences

Ending a conversation also follows a fairly routine pattern. Conversation analysts have shown that this involves much more than simply saying 'goodbye'; in fact three stages are necessary (Schegloff and Sacks 1973), as illustrated in the example below from the end of a workplace encounter:

Example 7

1 Becky   Okay 'cause I th- I wanted to just see who was → **Topic closing**
            doing what, an' I was gonna make some *calls* this afternoon, but
            I'll do it tomorrow.
2 Amy   ⌊Mhm, There-
3 Amy   Okay.   → **(poss.) pre-closing**
4 Becky   Okay.
            Then uh: good night,   → **Terminal exchange**
5 Amy   ⌊Uhm Good night.
6 Becky   We'll see you tomorrow morning,
7 Amy   Okay
[Becky leaves]

Becky moves towards closure by summarizing what the conversation was about (*I just wanted to see who was doing what*) and what action she will take as a result (*I was gonna make some calls ... I'll do it tomorrow*). This topic closing is followed by two lexically empty turns (*Okay – Okay*), whose function it is effectively to close down the conversation. It is a *possible* pre-closing, as this slot provides the opportunity for either speaker to introduce a further topic. Amy initially seems to have more to say, as she produces an incomplete utterance in turn 2 overlapping with Becky's turn 1, but she then moves to pre-closing in turn 3 (*Okay*), which Amy echoes in turn 4, thus confirming that both speakers are happy to end the conversation. The speakers can now move on to the terminal exchange, where they say 'goodbye' – typically an adjacency pair, but here expanded to two pairs (turns 4–7). As with opening sequences, exposure to and practice of the structure of closing sequences would be of practical value to language learners. Furthermore, initial evidence from classroom-based research shows that CA-based teaching material can be effective in developing learners' pragmatic ability in a second language (Huth and Taleghani-Nikazm 2006).

'Applying' CA to the classroom

Conversation Analysis has thus shown that speakers orient to a number of recurring conversational structures, including adjacency pairs, preference organization and different types of sequences. It is argued here that knowledge of these structures would be beneficial to teachers in developing their students' conversational skills. Armed with these insights from CA research, teachers could devise activities aimed at developing awareness of and practising these conversational structures.

The sample activity in Figure 4.1 shows the transcript of a real encounter in a university office between a student, who has a query, and an administrative member of staff.

Figure 4. 1

Beginning and ending a conversation

Getting information can sometimes be more complicated than simply asking a question. It is also important to know how to begin and end a conversation.

Look at the following real conversation which took place in a university office in the US. Karen, a student, goes into the office to ask Don, who works there, a question about her ID (her student identity card). Karen and Don know each other.

What happens in the conversation *before* Karen asks the question she wants answered? How do the speakers end the conversation?

1   Karen   Hello.
2   Don   Hiya
3   Karen   How are you?
4   Don   I'm all right.
5   Karen   Good. I have a quick question for you. I *hope* it's a quick question.
            Tell me *why* on my ID this year it says it expires on *June* thirtieth as
            opposed to September thirtieth.
6   Don   It always said June thirtieth as far as I know.
7   Karen   The last . . . I just checked the last two I had; the last two years, it said
            September thirtieth.
8   Don   Maybe- are you scheduled to graduate this June?
9   [Karen shakes head]
10 Don   I don't know. Talk to Helga.
11 Karen   Okay, thank you.
12 Don   You can go right in.
13 Karen   Okay.
[Karen goes into back office to talk to Helga and comes back out about 1 minute later]
14 Karen   Thank you, Don
15 Don   So it *was* a quick question and answer, huh?
16 Karen   Quick question, quick answer.
17 Don   All *right*!
18 Karen   Thanks.
19 Don   Yeah.

This activity is designed to sensitize students to the fact that making a query often involves much more than simply asking a question: the encounter needs to be opened and closed and the question may need to be prefaced in some way. The conversation has clear opening and closing sequences (turns 1–4 and 14–19 respectively) which students should easily be able to identify. It can also be used to raise awareness of the important role opening and closing sequences play in relationship-building. CA does not deal with this aspect of such sequences, but other research (e.g. Laver 1975) has shown that one of the key functions of 'phatic communion' at the beginning and end of encounters is relationship-building.

The transcript could also be used to illustrate other types of sequences which we have not had room to discuss here, such as pre-sequences and side sequences, that are common in everyday conversation, and therefore important for the development of conversational skills. An awareness-raising activity like the one shown in Figure 4.1 could be followed by activities which provide students the opportunity of practising these conversational structures, for example in a guided role play.

Conclusion

The aim of this chapter has been to demonstrate the relevance and application of findings from Conversation Analysis to the teaching of the spoken language in general and conversational skills in particular in the language classroom. CA analysis has demonstrated that everyday conversation is orderly and exhibits recurring structures and sequences. It thus provides valuable information for language teachers about the structure of talk which can be easily applied to the teaching of conversation. But it is important that this is not simply a mechanistic application of structural phenomena identified by CA. A central premise of CA is that participants in interaction do not simply 'apply' conversational rules, but design each turn specifically in relation to preceding talk and to the context (i.e. the other participants, the setting etc.) in which they are interacting. Therefore what kind of turn-taking is appropriate or 'natural' will depend on the specific interactional activities in which learners engage in the classroom.

Transcription conventions[5]

,	slightly rising in intonation at end of tone unit;
?	high rising intonation at end of tone unit;
.	falling intonation at end of tone unit;
!	animated intonation;
. . .	noticeable pause or break within a turn of less than 1 second;
-	sound abruptly cut off, e.g. false start;
italics	emphatic stress;
/ /	words between slashes show uncertain transcription;
/?/	indicates inaudible utterances: one ? for each syllable;
⌊	overlapping or simultaneous speech;
=	latching: no perceptible inter-turn pause;
[ ]	words in these brackets indicate non-linguistic information, e.g. pauses of 1 second or longer (the number of seconds is indicated), speakers' gestures or actions;
[. . .]	ellipsis marks between square brackets indicates that the speaker's turn continues, that the extract starts in the middle of a speaker turn, or that some turns have been omitted;
.hh	inhalation (intake of breath);
hhh	aspiration (releasing of breath);
'Hehehe'	indicates laughter, for each syllable laughed a 'he' is transcribed.

Notes

1   Unless otherwise stated, all extracts in the chapter are from the author's own data.
2   See Schegloff et al. (2002) for a useful overview of the relevance of CA to various areas of Applied Linguistics.
3   See Hutchby and Wooffitt 1998 for a good introduction to CA.
4   The full transcript shown in Hoey (1991: 66–67) also confirms this simple adjacency pair structure.
5   Adapted from, but not identical with, standard CA conventions developed by Gail Jefferson (see Hutchby and Wooffitt 1998: vi–vii).

References

Drew, P. and Heritage, J. (eds) (1992) *Talk at Work*, Cambridge: Cambridge University Press.

Firth, A. (1996) 'The discursive accomplishment of normality: On "lingua franca" English and conversation analysis', *Journal of Pragmatics* 26: 237–260.

Hoey, M.P. (1991) 'Some properties of spoken discourse', in R. Bowers and C. Brumfit (eds) *Applied Linguistics and English Language Teaching*: 65–84. Basingstoke: Macmillan/MEP.

Hutchby, I. and Wooffitt, R. (1998) *Conversation Analysis*, Cambridge: Polity Press.

Huth, T. and Taleghani-Nikazm, C. (2006) 'How can insights from conversation analysis be directly applied to teaching L2 pragmatics?', *Language Teaching Research* 10 (1): 53–79.

Jefferson, G. (1972) 'Side Sequences', in D. Sudnow (ed.), *Studies in Social Interaction*: 294–338, New York: Free Press.

Laver, J. (1975) 'Communicative functions of phatic communion', in A. Kendon, R. Harris and M. Key (eds), *The Organization of Behaviour in Face-to-Face Interaction*: 215–238. The Hague: Mouton.

Levinson, S. (1983) *Pragmatics*, Cambridge: Cambridge University Press.

Pearson, E. (1986) 'Agreement/Disagreement: An example of results of discourse analysis' applied to the oral English classroom', *International Review of Applied Linguistics* 74: 47–61.

Pomerantz, A. (1984) 'Agreeing and disagreeing with assessments: some features of preferred/dispreferred turn shapes', in Atkinson, J.M. and Heritage, J. (eds), *Structures of Social Action*: 57–102. Cambridge: Cambridge University Press.

Sacks, H. (1992) *Lectures on Conversation*, ed. G. Jefferson, 2 vols. Oxford: Blackwell.

Sacks, H., Schegloff, E.A. and Jefferson, G. (1974) 'A simplest systematics for the organisation of turn-taking for conversation', *Language* 50 (4): 696–735.

Schegloff, E.A. (1968) 'Sequencing in conversational openings', *American Anthropologist*, New Series 70 (6): 1075–1095.

—— (1980) 'Preliminaries to preliminaries: "Can I ask you a question?"', *Sociological Inquiry* 50 (3/4): 104–152.

Schegloff, E.A. and Sacks, H. (1973) 'Opening up closings', *Semiotica* 8 (4): 289–327.

Schegloff, E.A., Jefferson, G. and Sacks, H. (1977) 'The preference for self-correction in the organization of repair in conversation', *Language* 53: 361–382.

Schegloff, E.A., Koshik, I., Jacoby, S. and Olsher, D. (2002) 'Conversation analysis and applied linguistics', *Annual Review of Applied Linguistics* 22 (3): 2–31.

Seedhouse, P. (2004) *The Interactional Architecture of the Language Classroom: A conversation analysis perspective*, Oxford: Blackwell Publishing.

Wong, J. (2000) 'Delayed next turn repair initiation in native/nonnative speaker English conversation', *Applied Linguistics* 21: 274–297.

Wong, J. (2002) 'Applying' conversation analysis in applied linguistics: Evaluating dialogue in English as a second language textbooks, *International Review of Applied Linguistics* 40 (2): 37– 60.

II Teaching and learning a language

Introduction to chapter 5

This chapter is one of four that deals with how a language is taught and learnt; these are issues of central concern to teachers. Juup Stelma's chapter introduces a concept that has been important to English Language Teaching in particular since the 1970s: an approach to teaching known as Communicative Language Teaching (or CLT). It discusses three key issues: Communicative Competence, Communication used in classroom teaching, and controversies surrounding the introduction of CLT in non-Western countries.

The background to this chapter

Communicative Language Teaching was a new idea in the 1970s and was widely welcomed as the revolution that would transform language teaching. Like many revolutions, it arose out of a sense of dissatisfaction with the past. As Willis points out in chapter 1, many language teachers were frustrated by the fact that learners could master a grammar point when being drilled or tested but could not use the same item when speaking spontaneously. Learners were disappointed that having studied a language for many years, they still had difficulty managing day-to-day communication when they visited a country where that language was spoken. This was an age of growth for languages taught for specific purposes, and traditional syllabuses that proceeded through a language grammar point by grammar point were seen as far removed from the learners' immediate needs.

At the same time, views about how languages should best be described, and what it meant to know a language, were changing as well. Whereas traditional language studies focused on what went on in the mind of the individual speaker, prioritizing grammar, the new approaches saw language as a social phenomenon that varied according to the speakers and the situation. Language was studied as a tool for communication rather than as a system in the mind. As a consequence, for the learner it was not enough to know the grammar of a language – to speak a language it was necessary to have 'Communicative Competence', knowing how to use the language appropriately in different contexts.

These two developments came together to inspire Communicative Language Teaching, where communication was both the goal of teaching (learning a language in order to communicate) and the method of teaching (learning a language by communicating in it). The CLT revolution was hugely influential and eventually came to dominate the world of English Language Teaching. In spite of this (or maybe because of it), there is no real accepted definition of CLT, and no single methodology can claim to be the 'correct' version of CLT. In the early days it was often defined negatively – the CLT classroom did not focus on grammar; there was little or no teacher explanation; accuracy of language use was less important than fluency. As this chapter points out, however, CLT has in recent times become more focused and principled in terms of the classroom activities and teaching methods it encompasses.

Focusing on the argument

Some of the issues dealt with in this chapter are important to other chapters in this book. For example, Task-Based teaching methods (see chapter 6) are a form of Communicative Language Teaching. CLT recommends communication within the classroom; tasks are a way of motivating and managing that communication. As mentioned earlier, a criticism of CLT is that it tends to ignore things that are nonetheless important to learners, such as grammatical accuracy; the task cycle described by Jane and Dave Willis includes a language focus element designed to restore that balance.

You might also like to compare the views in this chapter with those expressed in chapter 12. In that chapter, Holliday argues that cultural stereotyping can have the effect of denigrating non-Western teachers of English. Communicative Language Teaching, developed in the West and (arguably) promoting Western concepts of what a classroom should be like, has often been recommended to teachers in non-Western countries as being necessarily better than the methods they might prefer. Stelma discusses a similar view and asks teachers simply to consider whether CLT is suitable for them and their students without insisting that it is better in all contexts.

A language tip

The third paragraph under the heading 'Communication as competence' discusses three 'challenges' to CLT. In this paragraph Stelma describes three ways in which CLT may be regarded as 'wrong'. In each case, a version of CLT appears to make an assumption which is incorrect. Stelma uses a variety of ways to indicate the assumption and the judgement that it is incorrect. Here is a paraphrase of Stelma's main points in the paragraph – try matching them up with what Stelma wrote:

1   Assumption: Language can be represented in a few abstract constructs.
    This is wrong because: Language use across varieties and situations is complex.
2   Assumption: Communicative competence can be defined as a fixed thing.
    This is wrong because: Societies and communication constantly change.
3   Assumption: It is possible to define learners' needs.
    This is wrong because: A group of learners may have very different sets of needs, or may have no clearly defined needs.

You will notice that the second set is expressed most clearly in the paragraph. In the first set, the assumption and its correction are combined in a single sentence. In the third set, the assumption is not expressed explicitly at all.

To think about

1   If you are a teacher, do you consciously use communicative teaching methods? If you are a learner, have you been taught using them?
2   To what extent do you agree with the argument that CLT is a 'Western' concept and should not be applied to other contexts?
3   Can you explain how the concept of 'negotiating meaning' is different from those of 'explaining' and 'understanding'?

CHAPTER 5

What is communicative language teaching?

Juup Stelma

The origins of Communicative Language Teaching (henceforth CLT) can be traced back to the late 1960s and early 1970s, when several influential applied linguists, writing in journals and speaking at conferences, argued that language learners, despite their often rigorous study of language as a system (essentially grammar and vocabulary) and extensive practice in language structures (through e.g. audio-lingual language teaching), were unable to use language effectively in real-world communicative situations. Since this time, a central aspect of CLT has been how to understand the concept of communication and how it should inform language teaching. For this reason, the present chapter explores how CLT might be understood when considering communication from a number of different perspectives.

While communication is arguably universal, what forms of communication we engage in, how we understand communication, how it is affected by changes in technology and society, and how it is intertwined with context and cultures is more complex. Here we will approach this complexity from three perspectives: communication as competence (generally regarded as the aim of CLT), communication as process (sometimes used to inform communicative methodology) and communication in context (addressing concerns about the 'Western' origins of CLT). Exploring CLT in this way is not meant to generate specific advice about communicative teaching techniques, or in any other way 'tell' teachers what or what not to do in the classroom. Rather, by exploring communication from these different perspectives, the chapter hopes to promote teachers' own reflection on whether and how CLT may be appropriate in their own particular practice.

Communication as competence

Describing communication as the goal of language teaching has, since the early 1970s, involved the development of increasingly refined definitions of communicative competence. Hence, understanding communicative competence is one way of understanding CLT.

Prior to the 1970s, the dominant view of language was structural, that is, language as consisting of discrete items (vocabulary) and rules (grammar). In the 1970s, a confluence of factors allowed applied linguistics to coalesce on a new view of language as communicative competence. Notable influences included Halliday's (1973) work on the semantic potential of language, Hymes' (1972) exploration of the relationship between language as a system and communication in social situations, and Wilkins' (1976) development of the analytical notional/functional syllabus. Another important factor was the development of (British) applied linguistics as a field generating ideas distinct from earlier structural and Chomskian theories. These various influences culminated in Canale and Swain's (1980) widely used 'standard' definition of communicative competence. According to these authors, and considering also Canale's (1983) later revision, communicative competence includes not only grammatical competence (in the Chomskian sense), it also includes sociolinguistic, discourse and strategic competence. This means that speakers draw on a range of competencies when using language for communication.

One challenge to the usefulness of any definition of communicative competence is that it attempts to represent 'in a few abstract constructs the complex realities of language use across an unforeseeable range of variation and situational contingency' (Lee 2006: 351). The range of variability extends not only to the real-time unfolding of situations, but also to variation in patterns of communication across and within both small cultures (cohesive groups of people in particular societal settings) and large national cultures. Another challenge to the definitions of communicative competence is that they are usually formulated to represent communicative competence as something quite fixed. This means that the aim of language teaching is fixed as well (because communicative competence is the aim of language teaching). In reality, societies and technologies constantly change, and ways of communicating therefore keep changing. Hence, the aim of language teaching is something that may constantly change. Recent research into intercultural and computer-mediated communication has established particularly good examples of how communication is changing along with changes in society and technology. A final challenge to defining an aim for language teaching is that learners, across contexts and within any single classroom, may have widely different, and in some cases no clearly defined, future communicative needs. Some forms of language teaching, such as English for Specific Purposes, establish future needs directly through Needs Analyses (West 1994), commonly used to design courses for relatively homogeneous groups of students. However, teachers of English for general purposes, such as secondary school teachers, might find it harder to identify the future communicative needs of their students. These teachers may feel that they are teaching English for no particular purpose (Abbott 1980), that students need English to pass examinations that test mainly grammatical and lexical knowledge (Hu 2002), or that students' future uses of English are for social mobility rather than any real communicative purposes (Yong and Campbell 1995).

The real-world dynamics that challenge a stable or context-free definition of communicative competence have given rise to a number of alternative views. For example, Alptekin (2002) argues that Canale and Swain's native speaker grammatical competence is an inappropriate aim in contexts where students are more likely to use English with other non-native speakers. Alptekin suggests that a more appropriate aim is the kind of linguistic competence developed by successful learners of English. Smith (2002) proposes that exploring patterns of communication in social networks can help define communicative competence for groups of individuals. Moreover, Leung suggests that we should go back to the ethnographic bases of Hymes' (1972) original formulation of communicative competence, arguing that language educators should 're-engage with the socially dynamic uses of English and continually re-work the contextual meaning of the concept' (Leung 2005: 138).

Finally, communicative competence, whether the standard definition or a more recent one, is not a recipe for what should happen in classrooms. It may be possible to argue that a de-contextualized focus on grammar and vocabulary is unlikely to result in learners developing sociolinguistic, discourse, strategic and/or intercultural communicative competence. However, focusing exclusively on language use in context, without any focus on grammar, has more recently also been challenged (cf. Swain 1995). A more cautious interpretation, then, is that because communicative competence includes grammatical, sociolinguistic, discourse and strategic (and if you like intercultural, computer-mediated and other) competence, language teaching should focus on all of these things. However, definitions of communicative competence do not help us decide how to focus on these things in actual classroom activity. As a perspective informing CLT, communicative competence may give us a sense of 'where' we are going; it does not tell us 'how' we get there.

Communication as process

To understand CLT methodology, or what should be happening in classrooms, the CLT literature has, more or less overtly, turned to models of the communication process. The implicitly held position is that you learn to use language through communicating. Hence, understanding what is involved in the process of communication is a second way of understanding CLT.

Maybe the most well-known model of the communication process is the linear model sometimes associated with the work of Claude Shannon, a US-based communication theorist active in the 1940s and 1950s. Broadly speaking, the Shannon model deals with the transmission of messages, with one person sending information through some sort of channel of communication and another person receiving this information. This early notion of the communication process continues to have tremendous influence on how many of us understand language teaching. For example, productive and receptive language skills mirror the model's focus on sending (producing) and receiving messages. We talk about (the) oral (channel of) communication with speaking as the productive and listening as the receptive skill, and (the) written (channel of) communication with writing as the productive and reading as the receptive skill. More particular to CLT, the communicative nature of various information transfer activities suggested in the literature can be understood using this transmission model. Take Johnson's (1982) five principles for communicative exercises: the information transfer principle, the information gap principle, the jigsaw principle, the task dependency principle and the correction for content principle. The first principle, that communicative exercises should encourage transfer of information from one participant to another, as well as the second principle (because it motivates information transfer), correspond directly to the transmission model. However, Johnson's principles also illustrate at what point the basic transmission model is no longer useful. The jigsaw principle, which states that information should flow not only from one learner to another, but also both ways, corresponds to an interactive model of the communication process. An interactive model sees communication as a two-way process between individuals that share a common environment. Finally, Johnson's correction for content principle implies that communication has to do with the meaning of messages rather than their form, further challenging the simple notion of transmitting information.

There are, then, potential correspondences between models of the communication process and what may be happening in language classrooms. However, as our understanding of communication processes changes, our understanding of what is communicative language teaching may change as well. Conversely, when what we understand to be communicative both inside and outside of the classroom changes, we may well change our understanding of the communication process. Take the following analogy for communication itself:

Communication is like dancing – at least the kind of dancing we do with partners. Like dancing, communication depends on the involvement of a partner. And like good dancing, successful communication can't depend just on the skill of one person. A great dancer who doesn't consider and adapt to the skill level of his or her partner can make both of them look bad.

(Adler et al. 1998: 13)

This analogy emphasizes the co-active nature of communication; it is something we do with people, not to people (ibid.). With a co-active view of the communication process, new and different ways of thinking about language teaching present themselves. For example, when both or all participants contribute to the success of the communication process it becomes less appropriate to speak of productive and receptive language skills. We have seen the emergence of several terms in the language teaching literature to describe this potentially co-active nature of classroom communication, including negotiation of meaning (Long 1983) and collaborative dialogue (Swain 1997).

To try to get at the underlying model of communication in popular applications of CLT it is useful to look at two treatments of CLT, both published around 1990, at a time when CLT had been developing for a number of years. The first is from Nunan (1989), who was concerned with developing communicative tasks. For him, such tasks should involve comprehending, manipulating, producing and interacting in the target language. These are comparatively 'concrete' things to do with language, and the term 'producing' implies some correspondence to the transmission model. By contrast, in a state-of-the-art article on CLT published around the same time, Savignon (1991) defined CLT as involving negotiation, interpretation and expression of meaning in the target language. There is an overlap with Nunan here, but also important differences. For example, while Nunan sees 'producing' as a communicative act, Savignon argues that the terms 'productive' and 'receptive' hinder an understanding of communication as negotiated, implying therefore a more co-active understanding of the communication process. Furthermore, Savignon's inclusion of interpretation and expression of meaning as part of CLT has somewhat different consequences for the language classroom. For example, to activate expressive and interpretive processes, teachers could design individual and/or group tasks that engage learners in making sense of cultural, social and/or political issues, expressing feelings, beliefs or opinions, and offering interpretations for comparison and feedback.

We have now moved quite far from our starting point, that is, Shannon's transmission model. It might even be possible, at this point in the discussion, to argue that simple information transfer activities are not communicative at all. In defence of Shannon: he never wrote anything about language teaching; all he tried to do was to offer a model of information transmission to aid the invention of the modern telephone and computers.

Finally, it is important to point out the limitations of understanding language teaching in terms of communication as process. Most importantly, models of the communication process are not theories of either pedagogy or learning. Recent dynamical explanations of the language learning process lend theoretical support to the position that you learn language by using it (in communication). However, this ignores empirical evidence showing that to develop particular aspects of communicative competence, pedagogic 'manipulation' of communicative activities may be needed. For example, communicative tasks need to encourage focus on form (not just meaning) in order to develop acceptable levels of grammatical competence (Swain 1995). In sum, although there are several apparent correspondences between communication processes and language teaching, there is also some empirical evidence that challenges the extent to which communication as process can inform language teaching.

Communication in context

There has been widespread uptake of CLT in language teaching worldwide. McKay criticizes this spread of CLT because its emphasis on 'democracy, individuality, creativity and social expression' (McKay 2002: 120–121) fails to respond to local teachers and students' needs and backgrounds.

McKay may well have a valid point. Focusing on the origins of the modern concept of communication can help make sense of this debate in a possibly novel way. In an attempt to establish who the most important communication theorists are, Beniger (1990) analysed the text references made by the 465 contributors to the *International Encyclopedia of Communications* (Barnouw 1989). When including all text references to people in the various articles of the encyclopaedia, the list of the 25 most frequently referenced individuals included Shakespeare, Hitler, Lenin, Gutenberg and Franklin Roosevelt. More importantly, when the analysis was limited to those text references used in support of the formulation of communication theory, Aristotle, Plato, Saussure, Chomsky and Kant topped the list. Furthermore, the top 41 individuals on this second list were all 'Western' (Shannon was thirty-second). Hence, when we talk about communication theory, terms such as 'expression, negotiation and interpretation of meaning' (Savignon's terms) and 'democracy, individuality, creativity and social expression' (McKay's terms) may indeed have a Western genesis. The increasing influence of English as the international language of academics serves to reinforce this Western genesis of ideas informing how communication is understood. For this reason, an uncritical adoption of CLT in non-Western contexts may therefore be inappropriate.

This Western origin of communication theory, and therefore also CLT (according to the present argument), has been used as part of an argument against exporting CLT to non-Western contexts. The other half of this argument is that communication, what it is and how we understand it, is something quite fixed: that CLT is something clearly defined with a fixed set of techniques. This means that when the fixed techniques of CLT are 'exported' to non-Western contexts they simply will not 'fit'. On this view it would indeed be inadvisable to use CLT in anything else than Western contexts. It might even be inadvisable to use CLT at all.

An alternative view is made possible by taking the starting point of this chapter seriously. That is, 'communication is universal; how we understand communication, how it is affected by changes in technology and society, and how it is intertwined with context and cultures, is more complex'. According to this more critical view, rejecting CLT for certain parts of the world because prevailing descriptions of communication are 'Western' would be to 'throw out the baby with the bathwater'. Rather, actual communication is a situational and cultural dynamic that cannot be ignored in any context. This view, then, constitutes an opportunity for, or a call to, language teaching professionals worldwide to explore what communication may or can be to them, in their own language teaching situations, and in their own small or large cultural contexts. The fact that CLT has 'Western' origins certainly adds to this challenge. However, we should be careful not to dismiss the capacity of language teaching professionals in all parts of the world to approach both communication and CLT in a critical manner.

Conclusion

This chapter has explored how three perspectives on communication seem to inform language teaching. This is by no means the only way to approach what CLT is or is not. However, it is a response to the question 'What is communicative language teaching?' that raises new and hopefully interesting questions. These new questions are ones that teachers may ask themselves when reflecting on whether and how CLT may be appropriate in their own practice. Possible questions for reflection include:

- What kind of communicative competence do my students need?
- What communicative processes might my students meaningfully engage in?
- Do my answers to the first two questions make sense when considering communication in the real world around us?

Responding to these questions would hopefully help determine the appropriateness, possible shape, as well as the limitations of CLT in context.

Acknowledgements

I would like to thank Julian Edge and the editors for reading and providing feedback on earlier versions of this chapter.

References

Abbott, G. (1980) 'ESP and TENOR', *ELT Documents*, 107: 122–124.

Adler, R.B., Rosenfeld, L.B., Towne, N. and Proctor II, R.F. (1998) *Interplay: the process of interpersonal communication*, Fort Worth, TX: Harcourt Brace.

Alptekin, C. (2002) 'Towards intercultural communicative competence in ELT', *ELT Journal*, 56(1): 57–64.

Barnouw, E. (1989) *International Encyclopedia of Communications*, Oxford: Oxford University Press.

Beniger, J.R. (1990) 'Who are the most important theorists of communication?', *Communication Research*, 17(5): 698–715.

Canale, M. (1983) 'On some dimensions of language proficiency', in J.W. Oller (ed.) *Issues in Language Testing Research*, Rowley, MA: Newbury House.

Canale, M. and Swain, M. (1980) 'Theoretical bases of communicative approaches to second language teaching and testing', *Applied Linguistics*, 1(1): 1–47.

Halliday, M.A.K. (1973) *Explorations in the Functions of Language*, London: Edward Arnold.

Hu, G. (2002) 'Recent important developments in secondary English-language teaching in the People's Republic of China', *Language, Culture and Curriculum*, 15(1): 30–49.

Hymes, D.H. (1972) 'On communicative competence', in J.B. Pride and J. Holmes (eds.) *Sociolinguistics*, Harmondsworth: Penguin.

Johnson, K. (1982) *Communicative Syllabus Design and Methodology*, Oxford: Pergamon.

Lee, Y-A. (2006) 'Towards respecification of communicative competence: condition of L2 instruction or its objective?', *Applied Linguistics*, 27(3): 349–376.

Leung, C. (2005) 'Convivial communication: recontextualizing communicative competence', *International Journal of Applied Linguistics*, 15(2): 119–144.

Long, M. (1983) 'Native speaker/non-native speaker conversation and the negotiation of comprehensible input', *Applied Linguistics*, 4(2): 126–141.

McKay, S. (2002) *Teaching English as an International Language.* Oxford: Oxford University Press.

Nunan, D. (1989) *Designing Tasks for the Communicative Classroom*, Cambridge: Cambridge University Press.

Savignon, S.J. (1991) 'Communicative language teaching: state of the art', *TESOL Quarterly*, 25(2): 261–277.

Smith, L.R. (2002) 'The social architecture of communicative competence: a methodology for social-network research in sociolinguistics', *International Journal of the Sociology of Language*, 153: 133–160.

Swain, M. (1995) 'Three functions of output in second language learning', in G. Cook and B. Seidlhofer (eds.) *Principle and Practice in Applied Linguistics: studies in honour of H.G. Widdowson*, Oxford: Oxford University Press.

Swain, M. (1997) 'Collaborative dialogue: its contribution to second language learning', *Revista Canaria de Estudios Ingleses*, 34: 115–132.

Yong, Z. and Campbell, K.P. (1995) 'English in China', *World Englishes*, 14(3): 377–390.

West, R. (1994) 'Needs analysis in language teaching', *Language Teaching*, 27(1): 1–19.

Wilkins, D.A. (1976) *Notional Syllabuses*, Oxford: Oxford University Press.

Introduction to chapter 6

The background to this chapter

This chapter is one of two that focuses on language teaching methodology. Chapter 5 considered Communicative Language Teaching in general. This chapter by Dave Willis and Jane Willis presents one specific approach within this tradition – task-based teaching (TBT). In the chapter you will find an account of what TBT consists of, and also a rationale for it based on a number of theories of how people learn languages.

Jane and Dave Willis have been writing about task-based learning (TBL) and task-based teaching (TBT) since the late 1980s (see J. Willis 1996, for example). A 'task' is a classroom activity with a focus on meaning. Essentially, it involves real communication between teacher and class, or two or more students communicating with each other, and producing something as a result. For example, one student might tell the other one how to draw something, and the drawing is the result, or a group of students might discuss and agree on a list of priorities, and the list is the result. A task can also be carried out in teacher-led mode with the whole class contributing. The point is that there is always an outcome to the task that exists separately from the language that has been used to produce it.

Tasks of this kind have been used in language classrooms for years, and in fact they were part of the very earliest experiments in Communicative Language Teaching. They have always been seen as having a number of drawbacks, however. For example, students may only use language that they are already comfortable with, and may not stretch themselves to try out more difficult language. Another possible objection is that a group of students may use very inaccurate English amongst themselves and may never worry about correcting themselves or each other. Dave and Jane Willis have addressed these problems by proposing that the task itself is embedded within a 'task cycle' which includes activities besides carrying out the task itself. These might include: listening to other people carrying out a similar task, and having attention drawn to some of the language they use; preparing a report of the task outcome for the whole class, where accuracy of language is important; and doing activities that focus on details of language use. The aim of the task cycle is to help learners develop their language, experiment with recently acquired language and improve the accuracy of the language they already use, but all within the context of motivated communication.

Focusing on the argument

In this chapter, Willis and Willis not only present ideas about doing tasks, they also give a justification for the task cycle from a variety of linguistic theories, including Halliday's model of language as meaning, Krashen's theories of language learning and acquisition, and work by sociolinguistics such as Labov on language variation. It is quite unusual to have such a wide spread of work brought together in this way, but the range allows Willis and Willis to give strong arguments in favour of their approach. For example, they see a parallel between Halliday's focus on meaning (Halliday says that language is a 'social semiotic') and Krashen's focus on acquisition rather than learning. Willis and

Willis agree with Krashen that a focus on meaning leads to acquisition whereas a focus on form leads to learning and argue that this is a logical consequence of the Hallidayan view of language as a meaning system.

A second strength to the argument in this chapter is the link that is made between the practical experience of teaching and learning a language and linguistic theories. The writers refer to the experience of many language teachers:

> Even though elementary learners know that to make questions in English you invert the subject and the verb or modal – *Where are you going?*, not *Where you are going?* – they go through a stage where they get this right when doing an exercise or a test, but when speaking spontaneously they often fail to produce it.

They link this phenomenon explicitly to Krashen's theories. Then at each point in the task sequence they relate what is happening in the classroom with the propositions at the beginning of the chapter.

A language tip   In this chapter we find examples of language that are relatively informal as well as examples that are more formal and academic.

The normally accepted mode of writing in an academic article is formal, as in 'The individual's presentation of self will vary according to the circumstances of communication (private or public).' This is not a long sentence, but it packs several ideas into a short space (using 'nominalization' as explained in chapter 3). These ideas include: 'We give an image of ourselves when we speak or write', 'Changing the way we speak or write changes the image we present', and 'We will change the image we present depending on the situation, and in particular whether we are in a private or a public situation.'

But occasionally this chapter addresses the reader more informally as in: 'The basis of TBT is the task itself. But what activities count as tasks?' This is informal because the sentences are very short, the second sentence begins with *but* (some people would object to this in formal language), and the second sentence interacts directly with the reader by asking a question. A more formal way of writing this example might be: 'The basis of TBT is the task itself, although it is not easy to specify which activities count as tasks.'

Why do you think the writers have chosen the more informal mode of presentation? Perhaps they want to involve the reader more actively in the construction of their message, and so they choose to address the reader directly. Perhaps, because, as they go on to admit, they are not entirely sure of the answer. So they temporarily abandon their formal role as experts and instead appeal to readers to apply their own expertise.

To think about   1   Have you used tasks yourself, as a teacher or as a learner? If so, do you feel that they are an effective form of language teaching? Do you agree with Willis and Willis that the task cycle they describe can be used to expose learners to new language as well as to practise known language?

2   Willis and Willis suggest that the task cycle is followed by a 'focus on form'. Some people would argue that there is too little emphasis on grammar and vocabulary in

tasks; others would argue that focus on form means there is too much emphasis on grammar and vocabulary. Do you agree with either view?

3   Can you explain in your own words how the ideas of Halliday and of Krashen are linked to task-based teaching?

CHAPTER 6

Six propositions in search of a methodology:
applying linguistics to task-based language teaching

Dave Willis and Jane Willis

Halliday (1975) gives an account describing the process whereby his son, Nigel, acquired his first language. Significantly, this book was called not *Learning how to talk*, not *Learning how to speak*, but *Learning how to **mean***. What children are doing in learning their first language is developing a *system for meaning*. It is true that this system is realized by wordings, but the children's aim is not simply to produce words, but to influence those around them. They want to get things done, to make social contact, to be part of the world of others. Language does not develop in a vacuum. It develops in response to the need to mean. Our first proposition therefore is:

> 1 *Language is a meaning system. And acquiring a second language entails acquiring a new system for realizing meanings.*

Our next two propositions are to do with acquisition and learning. One of the puzzles surrounding second language acquisition since the work of Selinker (1972), Corder (1967) and other interlanguage theorists some years ago is that there is often a gap between the language learners **know** and the language they **use**. Even though elementary learners know that to make questions in English you invert the subject and the verb or modal: *Where are you going?* – not **Where you are going?* they go through a stage where they get this right when doing an exercise or a test, but when speaking spontaneously they often fail to produce it.

The terms *learning* and *acquisition* are most closely associated with the work of Krashen (1985). He explained the fact that learners seem to know and at the same time not to know, by hypothesizing that learners operate two systems – the learned and the acquired systems. Learners may have learned about subject-auxiliary inversion and, given time to think, can produce language which incorporates this inversion. But they have not acquired these forms – they are not part of their spontaneous language behaviour. Krashen also argued that these two systems are quite separate, describing them as impermeable. He holds that the learned system has no influence on the acquired system – there is no leakage, no permeability between the two. The processes by which these systems are built up are also quite distinct: learning is a conscious process which we can to some extent control. Acquisition is an unconscious process. It is not controlled, and can only occur naturally, as a result of exposure to the language used in a meaningful context. Later research (see for example Long 1988; Skehan 1996) suggests that Krashen is mistaken in this, and that conscious processes and a focus on language form can contribute to acquisition. But this does not deny the paradox of knowing but at the same time not knowing. Our second proposition then is:

2 There is a distinction between learning and acquisition, but it is indistinct, and neither system is impermeable.

This links to our first proposition because we account for the difference between the two systems by pointing out they have a quite different focus – one on form and one on meaning. Learning focuses on particular forms of the language. Each pattern is separated out and practised in isolation, for possible future use, in the hope that it will be recalled/retrieved from memory when the need occurs, whereas acquisition occurs sub-consciously in meaning-focused situations.

So our third proposition is:

3 Acquisition is prompted by the need and desire to engage in meaning, and takes place through the process of meaning.

We have talked a good deal about meaning, but what do we mean by meaning? The most familiar idea of meaning encompasses telling people things, expressing ideas – what Halliday and Mathiessen (2004) call *ideational*. But Halliday's notion of meaning goes further than this – it is also about presenting ourselves to other people. We show what kind of person we are through the language we use. This is a different kind of meaning, which Halliday calls *interpersonal*. This brings us to our fourth proposition:

4 Language serves a wide range of functions, including the presentation of self.

This becomes clearer when we look at language varieties and at variety in individual language use. Labov (1970) showed us that we vary our language according to the circumstances we are in. Compare, for example, talking about your work in a bar over a couple of drinks with being interviewed for a job, speaking to a panel of interviewers. When we use language in a relaxed setting among friends, for a predominantly social purpose, we use those forms which come readily and easily. We feel little need to conform to a prestigious standard form of the language. But when we are in a more formal setting, we do feel the need to conform to an externally imposed standard. If you look at transcripts of spontaneous spoken English you will see this very clearly (Willis, D. 2003: 186–211). Our fifth proposition, then, is this:

5 Language is variable. We vary our language to meet different circumstances and different expectations.

We have argued so far that language is a meaning system; that, though conscious processes may contribute to learning, acquisition is prompted by the desire to engage in meaning; that language and language use are intensely personal; and that we vary our language to meet circumstances and demands. It seems to follow from this that we cannot and should not seek to impose language forms on others. And those others include learners. We cannot teach learners what forms of language to use. The best we can do is to provide them with *opportunities to engage in meaning*. We can supplement this acquisitional process by providing a *focus on language form* in the belief that this contributes to acquisition (Long and Crookes 1993: 37–39; Skehan 1996: 17–30). But we cannot impose a meaning system on learners. Ultimately they must work out their own ways of meaning. They must, and will, vary their language to meet differing demands. This, then, is our sixth and last proposition:

> 6 *Teaching for conformity to a standardized language norm is neither possible nor desirable.*

What, then, is the role of the language teacher? What classroom procedures, what kind of methodology will provide learners with the opportunity and incentive to develop their own meaning systems?

In broad terms, given the above propositions, what we need is:

1 a methodology which is rooted in meanings
2 a methodology which exploits natural language behaviour
3 additional activities which encourage a focus on form.

Foreign language courses often work on the premise that students will learn (and use) the forms they are taught if they repeat them accurately and often enough. But such students often leave school unable to interact effectively in the foreign language they have spent five years learning. Classrooms such as these provide insufficient opportunities for natural acquisition. Our six propositions find no home there. So let us look at the opportunities offered by a task-based approach to language teaching (task-based teaching or TBT).

Tasks and task sequences

The basis of TBT is the task itself. But what activities count as tasks? It is difficult to provide a watertight definition of what constitutes a task, and many people have tried. Willis and Willis (2007) attempt to characterize tasks along the lines suggested by Skehan (1998: 95–96). They write:

The more confidently we can answer *yes* to each of these questions the more task-like the activity:

a) Does the activity engage learners' interest?
b) Is there a primary focus on meaning?
c) Is there an outcome?
d) Is success judged in terms of outcome?
e) Is completion a priority?
f) Does the activity relate to real world activities?

If we evaluate activities in this way, we can see more precisely how to adapt them to make them more task-like. The important thing is that tasks engage learners in real language use; learners are free to use whatever language they can to achieve the task outcome, rather than using language that has been scripted or forms that have been prescribed in advance.

There are many different types of tasks such as comparing two pictures to find a set number of differences, listening to or reading instructions to trace a route on a map, solving a problem or creating a story from clues – these all have outcomes that can be shared with others. Willis and Willis (2007) offer ways to generate a varied sequence of tasks arising from a chosen topic.

We will now go on to look at a sample task sequence – a listing task, leading on to a classifying task, followed by a ranking task – and examine how it might accommodate some of the propositions above.

Even beginners can do simple tasks. Children often start by doing 'Listen and do' activities led by the teacher. Older learners can begin by listing and classifying familiar international words and phrases. We asked one group of beginners what words of English they knew already. They came up with *football, hotel, sandwich, internet, no problem* and many others. As teacher, you can take up their ideas and build on them: *Football – yes – who plays football? You do – five of you! Who watches football on TV? I don't. I don't like football. Who doesn't like football? You two. OK. What about tennis? I like tennis . . . What other sports do you like?* Learners need only give minimal responses at this point. The teacher-talk provides accessible input which will help learners begin to build up their own meaning systems.

Learners (possibly in pairs) can then classify their words into categories such as sport, food, media, adding more words to each category. So here we have the beginning of a task sequence – listing, then classifying. These could be followed by a ranking task – for example, rank the sports in order of cost, or in order of popularity in your country. Ideally after each task, learners would listen to a recording of fluent speakers doing the same task and compare results, reflecting on how they did it and exploring the language they used. We will look at the transcript of the recording made for this 'International Words' task in the section 'Integrating a focus on form'.

Tasks, then, allow learners to experience language used as a meaning system. Tasks are also motivating in themselves – it is satisfying to complete a task and achieve the goal. Tasks engage learners in real meanings and this prompts natural acquisition. Thus propositions 1 and 3 above find a home here.

A TBT framework

Task-based teaching, however, involves more than getting learners to do a series of tasks. A diet of nothing but tasks might well, as Skehan (1996) points out, result in learners developing fluency at the expense of accuracy and their language becoming fossilized. More linguistic challenge is needed to drive the learner's interlanguage development forward. Using tasks within a systematic methodological framework can help do this in line with the other propositions listed above.

A possible TBT framework, building on those described in Willis and Willis (1987, 1996) and Willis J. (1996), typically consists of three main phases:

Pre-task phase

Priming and Preparation activities, introducing topic and task

Task cycle

Task, Planning a report and Reporting back

Form Focus

Analysis and Practice

The *Pre-task priming* phase is where the teacher introduces the topic of the task, high-lighting useful words and phrases, and then sets up the task, giving instructions and the expected outcome. This again is consistent with propositions 1 and 3, since it provides meaningful teacher-talk in the target language which students must process in order to know how to attempt the task. Some silent preparation time will allow each individual to think of how to do the task and what to talk about, which enhances their engagement with the task and generally results in richer interaction (Foster 1996, Djapoura 2005, Ellis 2005: 3–36).

In the *Task cycle*, the Task gives opportunities for exploratory use of language, where learners work in the security of their pairs, in private, using whatever language they can recall. They then move to public, planned and more formal use of language at the Report stage where they report the results of their task to the class.

Doing the Task and Report involves learners in exchanging real meanings, in line with propositions 1 and 3. But now proposition 5 (language is variable) comes into play. To help learners bridge the linguistic gap between their private, exploratory *Task* language, where mistakes didn't matter, and the public *Report* stage, where accuracy will matter and where they will feel a natural desire to avoid error and to use more pres-tigious language, there needs to be an interim *Planning* stage.

As learners (usually in pairs) plan how to describe their task results clearly and appropriately to a wider audience, they will organize the content of what they want to say or write, experiment with wordings, check words and pronunciations or spellings, using the support of peers, dictionaries and their teacher. They will be moving from the highly interactive exploratory talk of the *Task* to the planned language of the *Report* – either oral monologue or in written form. We see then how learners get a chance to use and develop different varieties of the target language as they progress through the task cycle, and, in doing so, extend their own language use. This feature of language behaviour is illustrated in detail in Essig (2005) and Johnston (2005).

This aspect of methodology not only meets the demands of proposition 5, above, that language is variable, but also those of proposition 4. The individual's presentation of self will vary according to the circumstances of communication (private or public). Their changing roles at each stage open up opportunities for experiencing the multi functionality of language: at the *Task* stage, using language to explore meanings and suggest ideas or narrate experiences, at the *Planning* stage, using language to talk about language, and at the *Report* stage, using language to present polished ideas and to assert a group or pair identity.

The *Planning* and *Report* stages also support proposition 6. The aim here is not to present the learners with new language forms in a vacuum. It is to help them explore and expand their own language systems in response to a new communicative demand. At the *Planning* stage, the teacher responds to the learners' desire to express what they mean and to present themselves favourably. The teacher can do this by suggesting wordings that express learners' own meanings more clearly, thus extending the language they already have. Note that both teachers and learners are using language to respond to a communicative need. They are not simply engaged in the production of language forms for their own sake.

Variations on this TBT framework can be found in Edwards and Willis (2005) and Willis and Willis (2007). Repeating the task and reporting to different audiences also result in linguistic improvements (Bygate et al. 2001, Lynch and Maclean 2001, Pinter 2005).

The TBT framework described so far is, then, likely to provide an acquisition-rich environment. But what about proposition 2? How do we supplement acquisition with learning? This is achieved by the final phase of the framework: *Form Focus*.

Integrating a focus on form

This phase is based on explicit study of a written or spoken text used during previous task cycle(s). Let's go back to the task 'International Words' described in the section 'A TBT framework'. Once learners have finished listing the words they know, they could listen to a recording of fluent speakers doing a similar task, identify any words on their own lists, and try to add some more. They might then go on to classify their words, and report back to the class on their categories.

Later, in the *Form Focus* phase, learners could be given the transcript of the recording and asked to listen again and do some analysis exercises, practising useful phrases.

Here is part of a transcript of four people in the middle of this task, followed by some exercises.

E: Hamburger.
H: Mhm Mhm.
C: What about taxi?
E: Oh yes, that's a good one
W: Erm . . .
H: Picnic? What about that?
E: Oh yes, that's a good one. [. . .]
C: Yes. Hamburger?
All: Ah – we've done that one. Got that!
C: Oh, we've got that, sorry.
W: Hotel?
H: Yes, hotel, that's a good one.
E: Stop!
W: Stop. Mhm mhm. What about football?
H: Oh yes, that's a good one, yes.
E: Oh yes, definitely . . . [Pause] Oh dear . . .
W: And rugby. . .

H: Yeah.
C: Olympics.
H: Ah no, I'm not sure of that. [I don't think that's . . .
E: [That's Greek!

Exercises

a) Questions
Read the transcript as you listen to the CD. Underline the words and phrases that are questions. Can you find four? Practise saying them.

b) Ways of saying *Yes* and *No*
What do the speakers say when expressing *Yes* and *No* in English? Circle them in the transcript first, then listen to the CD and check. Practise any useful expressions.

c) Phrases with *that / That*
Read out to your partner all the phrases with the word *that.*
Think how you might classify them. Write them in two (or more) lists.
Compare your lists with other pairs' lists. Your teacher will help.
Choose two or three phrases you like and practise saying them to your partner.

d) *Erm* and *Oh dear*
How do you express these in your own language?

Commentary

All four exercises start from the language used in the task. Having done the task themselves, learners will already have expressed similar meanings, though not necessarily using the same wordings. These exercises give learners a chance to notice new things about the target language and to consciously learn and practise useful words and expressions, building on what they knew already. We are not telling them they must now use this language, nor are we seeking to impose a meaning system on learners. We are in line with proposition 6: teaching for conformity to a standardized language norm is neither possible nor desirable. We are saying 'Notice these language features, choose some to practise, note down useful expressions and – at some point in the future – they might be useful.'

Thus the *Form Focus* phase supplements the acquisitional processes begun in the *Pre-task* and *Task cycle* by providing an opportunity for conscious learning. This is directly in line with proposition 2: we are making a distinction between acquisition and learning, but accepting that it is indistinct and that neither system is impermeable. SLA research shows clearly that acquisition is rooted in meaning, but that a focus on form does make acquisition more efficient.

Concluding summary

Through its focus on meaning and its recognition of language as functional, Hallidayan linguistics provides a sound theoretical basis for language teaching. In terms of applications, it suggests a methodology which sees meaning as central and which is rooted in natural language behaviour, and which is supplemented, but certainly not dominated, by instruction and learning.

References

Bygate, M., Skehan, P. and Swain M. (eds) 2001. *Researching Pedagogic Tasks: Second language learning, teaching and testing*. Harlow: Longman.

Corder, S.P. 1967. 'The significance of learner errors'. *International Review of Applied Linguistics* 5: 160–70.

Djapoura, A. 2005. 'The effects of pre-task planning time on Task-based performance'. In Edwards, C. and Willis, J. (eds).

Edwards, C. and Willis, J. (eds) 2005. *Teachers Exploring Tasks in ELT*. Oxford: Palgrave Macmillan.

Ellis, R. 2005. 'Planning and Task-based performance: theory and research'. In Ellis, R. (ed) *Planning and Task Performance in a Second Language*. Amsterdam and Philadelphia: John Benjamins, pp. 3–36.

Essig, W. 2005. 'Story-telling: effects of planning, repetition and context'. In Edwards, C. and Willis, J. (eds).

Foster, P. 1996. 'Doing the task better: how planning time influences students' performance'. In Willis, J. and Willis, D. (eds), pp. 17–30.

Halliday, M. 1975. *Learning How To Mean*. London: Edward Arnold.

Halliday, M.A.K. and Mathiessen, C.M.I.M. 2004. *An Introduction to Functional Grammar*, 3rd edn. London: Edward Arnold.

Johnston, C. 2005. 'Fighting fossilisation: language at the Task versus Report stages'. In Edwards, C. and Willis, J. (eds).

Krashen, S. D. 1985. *Principles and Practice in Second Language Acquisition*. Oxford: Pergamon.

Labov, W. 1970. 'The study of language in its social context'. in P. Giglioli (ed) *Language and Social Context*. London: Penguin.

Long, M. 1988. 'Instructed interlanguage development'. In L. Beebe (ed) *Issues in Second Language Acquisition: Multiple Perspectives*. Rowley, Mass.: Newbury House.

Long, M. and Crookes, G. 1993. 'Units of analysis in syllabus design'. In Crookes, G. and Gass S. (eds) *Tasks in a Pedagogical Context: Integrating Theory and Practice*. Clevedon: Multilingual Matters Ltd, pp. 37–39.

Lynch, T. and Maclean, J. 2001. 'A case of exercising: effects of immediate task repetition on learners' performance'. In Bygate, M., Skehan, P. and Swain, M. (eds).

Pinter, A. 2005. 'Task repetition with 10-year old children'. In Edwards, C. and Willis, J. (eds) *Teachers Exploring Tasks in ELT*. Oxford: Palgrave Macmillan.

Selinker, L. 1972. 'Interlanguage'. *International Review of Applied Linguistics* 10: 209–31.

Skehan, P. 1996. 'Second language acquisition research and task-based instruction'. In Willis, J. and Willis, D. (eds), pp. 17–30.

Skehan, P. 1998. *A Cognitive Approach to Language Learning*. Oxford: Oxford University Press.

Willis, D. 2003. *Rules, Patterns and Words: Grammar and Lexis in English Language Teaching*. Cambridge: Cambridge University Press, pp. 186–211.

Willis, D. and Willis, J. 1987. 'Varied activities for variable language'. *ELT Journal* 41 (1): 12–18.

Willis, D. and Willis, J. 2007. *Doing Task-based Teaching*. Oxford: Oxford University Press.

Willis, J. and Willis, D. (eds) 1996. *Challenge and Change in Language Teaching*. Oxford: Heinemann Macmillan. (Chapters on aspects of TBL available on www.willis-elt.co.uk)

Willis, J. 1996. *A Framework for Task-based Learning*. Harlow: Longman Pearson Ed.

Introduction to chapter 7

This chapter deals with a topic that is important to the area of psycholinguistics: the topic of motivation. This might be seen as the 'other side of the coin' to the chapters on language teaching methodology, in that learners could be said to need two things in order to learn well: good teaching and the motivation to take advantage of it. The chapter presents the results of research that involves asking people questions about themselves, what they think and what they do. The results are presented not just numerically but also in terms of a theoretical model that will account for them.

The background to this chapter

Many teachers would say that motivation is the most important part of language learning. Indeed, you may have met people who have learnt a language under conditions that would seem to be impossible (without a teacher, and without interaction with any other speakers of the language, for example) just because their motivation was so strong. Conversely, even the best teacher might struggle to achieve success with a group of unmotivated students.

As Dörnyei points out in this chapter, for many years a view of motivation has been accepted which distinguishes between 'integrative' and 'instrumental' motivation. If you learn a language for integrative reasons, it is because you like the speakers of that language and want to integrate with them. If you learn a language for instrumental reasons, it is because it can help you pass an exam or get a better job. To reverse this, if you have no integrative motivation, you may prefer not to be associated with the people whose language you are learning; and if you have no instrumental motivation, you may expect to gain nothing material from learning the language.

In Dörnyei's view, the 'integrative'/'instrumental' distinction is only of limited use when accounting for typical language learning situations in the world today. In many parts of the world, people learn English, for example, to become part of a global society rather than a purely 'English' one. This suggests that integrative motivation will not be important. When Dörnyei did research in Hungary, however, he found that answers associated with integrative motivation were coming out very strongly. He accounts for this by taking another idea – the concept of 'possible selves' – and using it to explain his data. Instead of the original idea of integrative motivation, he proposes motivation to learn a language that stems from a possible self-image – I have a picture in my mind of myself as a competent speaker of language x, and that inspires me to work hard at learning that language.

Focusing on the argument

This chapter brings together different types of evidence, including statistics, intuition and available theories. The statistics themselves involve some complexity, as quantities need to be compared with one another to find which sets of results support or contradict each other. Notice, too, that the statistics themselves could be used to support the concept of integrative motivation, but that Dörnyei goes beyond this to develop a new theory. Further survey work is then used to test the new theory. It is interesting that Dörnyei uses intuition – the researcher's sense that something is not quite right, or does not quite fit – to move beyond old ways of thinking into new ones. It is this interpretation of results in new ways that changes the research map or paradigm.

A language tip   Dörnyei uses a number of technical terms in this chapter.

He uses the term *paradigm* to refer to a set of theories which is accepted by the research community, and the term *paradigm shift* to describe a major change from one set of theories to another.

He uses the word *correlation* to describe the relationship between two things which are connected statistically, in the sense that when one thing increases the other does too. A correlation can be interpreted to indicate a cause, but it does not prove the existence of a cause. For example, if an increase in smoking correlates with an increase in lung cancer it might be hypothesized that smoking causes cancer, but the correlation by itself is not a proof of this.

Notice, too, the term *construct*, used as in 'the schematic representation of the final construct'. The word *construct* here is a noun (with the stress on the first syllable) and means something like 'model' or 'theory', but with a sense that the theory has a number of different parts that fit together. Dörnyei uses the term quite a few times in this chapter, and he avoids confusion by not using the verb *construct* (with the stress on the second syllable), as in 'a theory was constructed'.

To think about

1 Can you explain the terms 'integrative motivation', 'instrumental motivation' and 'motivational self'? Can you apply them to yourself as a language learner, or to your students?

2 Scientists and social scientists almost never talk about having 'proved' something. In this chapter, find the ways in which Dörnyei expresses the idea that experiment results have shown a theory to be correct.

3 How relevant is the research on motivation to the teacher? Can you see ways in which a teacher might use the research reported in this chapter?

CHAPTER 7

Researching motivation: from integrativeness to the ideal L2 self

Zoltán Dörnyei

Language teachers frequently use the term 'motivation' when they describe successful or unsuccessful learners. This reflects our intuitive belief that during the lengthy and often tedious process of mastering a foreign/second language (L2), the learner's enthusiasm, commitment and persistence are key determinants of success or failure. Indeed, in the vast majority of cases, learners with sufficient motivation *can* achieve a working knowledge of an L2, *regardless of* their language aptitude, whereas without sufficient motivation even the brightest learners are unlikely to persist long enough to attain any really useful language ('you can lead a horse to water, but you can't make it drink').

Because of the central importance attached to it by practitioners and researchers alike, L2 motivation has been the target of a great deal of research in Applied Linguistics during the past decades. In this chapter I describe a major theoretical shift that has recently been transforming the landscape of motivation research: the move from the traditional conceptualization of motivation in terms of an *integrative/instrumental dichotomy* to the recent conceptualization of motivation as being part of the learner's self system, with the motivation to learn an L2 being closely associated with the learner's *'ideal L2 self'*. For space limitations I cannot provide a detailed review of the relevant literature (for recent summaries, see Dörnyei 2005; Dörnyei and Ushioda 2009); instead, my focus will be on illustrating how such a major paradigm shift has emerged through a combination of theoretical considerations and empirical research findings.

The starting point: 'Integrativeness' as a motivational factor

There has been a long-lived (and inaccurate) understanding in the L2 profession that language learning motivation can be divided into two main dimensions: *integrative motivation* and *instrumental motivation*. The former refers to the desire to learn an L2 of a valued community so that one can communicate with members of the community and sometimes even to become like them. Instrumental motivation, on the other hand, is related to the concrete benefits that language proficiency might bring about (e.g. career opportunities, increased salary). Thus, broadly speaking, it was thought that we learn a language either because we like it and its speakers or because we think it will be useful for us.

The integrative/instrumental distinction has been attributed (again somewhat inaccurately) to the influential work of Canadian social psychologist Robert Gardner (1985, 2001), who did indeed introduce these terms but whose theoretical motivation construct was much more elaborate than this simplistic duality. Furthermore, Gardner hardly ever discussed the nature and impact of instrumental motivation, because he was almost exclusively interested in the interpersonal/emotional aspect of motivation that he termed 'integrativeness'. He characterized this motivational dimension as follows:

> Integrativeness reflects a genuine interest in learning the second language in order to come closer to the other language community. At one level, this implies an openness to, and respect for other cultural groups and ways of life. In the extreme, this might involve complete iden-tification with the community (and possibly even withdrawal from one's original group), but more commonly it might well involve integration within both communities.
>
> (Gardner 2001: 5)

The concept of integrativeness/integrative motivation has become a popular and much researched concept in L2 research, but starting in the 1990s an increasing number of scholars began to raise issues about how generalizable the term was. In a multicultural setting such as Montreal, where Gardner first developed his theory, it made sense to talk about potential 'integration', but in learning situations where a foreign language is taught only as a school subject without any direct contact with its speakers (e.g. teaching English or French in Hungary, China, Japan or other typical 'foreign language learning' contexts), the 'integrative' metaphor simply did not make sense. In such environments what exactly would be – to quote Gardner (2001) – 'the other language community' that the learner would want to 'get closer to'? In many language learning situations, and especially with the learning of world languages such as English or French, it is not at all clear who 'owns' the L2, and this lack of a specific L2 community undermines Gardner's theoretical concept of integrativeness. This view has been shared by several scholars worldwide (e.g. Coetzee-Van Rooy 2006; Lamb 2004; Yashima 2000; for a review, see Dörnyei 2005), and, as a result, over the past decade I have been trying to find a broader interpretation of the notion that goes beyond the literal meaning of the verb 'integrate' but which also builds on the relevant knowledge and considerable body of research that we have accumulated in the past.

Towards the 'L2 Motivational Self System'

In 2005, I proposed a new motivation construct (Dörnyei 2005) – the 'L2 Motivational Self System' – that builds upon the foundations laid by Gardner (1985) but which at the same time broadens the scope of the theory to make it applicable in diverse language learning environments in our globalized world. The proposed model, which attempts to synthesize a number of influential new approaches in the field (e.g. Ushioda 2001; Noels 2003), has grown out of a combination of empirical research findings and the-oretical considerations (for a detailed description, see Dörnyei, 2009). Let us look at these more closely, starting with the former.

Empirical findings pointing to the need to reinterpret Integrativeness

Over the past 15 years I have been heading a research team in Hungary with the objective of carrying out a longitudinal survey amongst teenage language learners by administering an attitude/motivation questionnaire at regular intervals so that we can gauge the changes in the population's international orientation. So far three successive waves of data collections have been completed (in 1993, 1999 and 2004) involving over 13,000 learners (for a detailed summary, see Dörnyei et al. 2006). The survey questionnaire targeted attitudes towards five target languages: English, German, French, Italian and Russian. It was originally developed in collaboration with one of Robert Gardner's closest associates, Richard Clément, and therefore integrativeness and instrumentality had a prominent place in it, but we also measured several other attitudinal/motivational dimensions, such as *Direct contact with L2 speakers* (i.e. attitudes towards actually meeting L2 speakers and travelling to their country), *Cultural interest* (i.e. the appreciation of cultural products associated with the particular L2 and conveyed by the media; e.g. films, TV programmes, magazines and pop music), *Vitality of L2 community* (i.e. the perceived importance and wealth of the L2 communities in question), *Milieu* (i.e. the general perception of the importance of foreign languages in the learners' school context and in friends' and parents' views) and finally *Linguistic self-confidence* (i.e. a confident, anxiety-free belief that the mastery of an L2 is well within the learner's means).

In an analysis of the first two waves of the survey (Dörnyei and Csizér 2002), we computed correlations of the various motivation components with a criterion measure, *Language choice*, which referred to the degree of the learners' desire to learn a particular L2 in the next school year. Correlation is a conceptually straightforward statistical procedure: it allows us to look at two variables and evaluate the strength and direction of their relationship or association with each other. To do so, we compute a 'correlation coefficient' between the two variables, which can range from −1 to +1, with a high correlation indicating a positive relationship, zero correlation no relationship, and a

	English/UK		English/US		German		French		Italian		Russian	
	1993	1999	1993	1999	1993	1999	1993	1999	1993	1999	1993	1999
Integrativeness	.43*	.33*	.43*	.33*	.47*	.43*	.42*	.44*	.43*	.43*	.25*	.32*
Instrumentality	.28*	.25*	.28*	.25*	.30*	.30*	.27*	.30*	.29*	.31*	.20*	.21*
Attitudes towards L2 speakers/community	.23*	.16*	.17*	.16*	.33*	.30*	.31*	.33*	.32*	.31*	.12*	.21*
Vitality of the community	.12*	.09*	.12*	.09*	.11*	.12*	.13*	.16*	.16*	.18*	.07*	.10*
Cultural interest	.14*	.09*	.12*	.10*	.20*	.17*	.20*	.21*	.26*	.23*	.12*	.17*
Milieu	.12*	.12*	.12*	.12*	.01	−.00	.03	.04	.01	−.00	−.05*	−.10*
Linguistic self-confidence	.07*	.06*	.07*	.06*	−.00	.01	.03	−.02	−.01	−.02	−.02	−.04
Multiple correlations	**.44***	**.34***	**.44***	**.34***	**.49***	**.45***	**.44***	**.46***	**.45***	**.45***	**.27***	**.34***

* p < .001

Table 7.1 Correlations between the attitudinal/motivational scales and *Language choice* in the Dörnyei and Csizér (2002) study

negative correlation an inverse relationship (Dörnyei 2007). Thus, for example, learners' IQ is expected to have a high positive correlation with their mathematics grades and zero correlation with, say, the love of chocolate. Table 7.1 presents the results.

As can be seen in Table 7.1, three variables stand out consistently across the languages and the data points: *Integrativeness, Instrumentality* and *Attitudes towards L2 speakers/community*. This was, actually, to be expected given our previous understanding of L2 attitudes and motivation, but what surprised us was that when we computed multiple correlations (i.e. correlations between language choice and all the motivational variables together), the joint correlation was hardly higher than the correlation associated only with *Integrativeness*. For example, the correlation of the choice of English (UK) in 1993 was .43 with *Integrativeness* and .44 with all the altitudinal variables together. This suggested that *Integrativeness* played a principal role in determining the extent of a learner's overall motivational disposition.

To test the prominent position of *Integrativeness*, Dörnyei et al. (2006) submitted the data from all the three waves of the survey to a more complex statistical procedure, *structural equation modelling* (SEM). SEM is very useful to interpret the relationship among several variables within a single framework. Its strength is that we can specify directional paths (i.e. cause–effect relationships) amongst the variables and SEM then produces various goodness-of-fit indices to evaluate the feasibility of the whole model. In conducting the analysis, we took each language and each year separately (so we computed separate models for, say, German in 1993 and French in 2004), but the various models converged and with minor variations produced the same overall result. Figure 7.1 presents the schematic representation of the final construct.

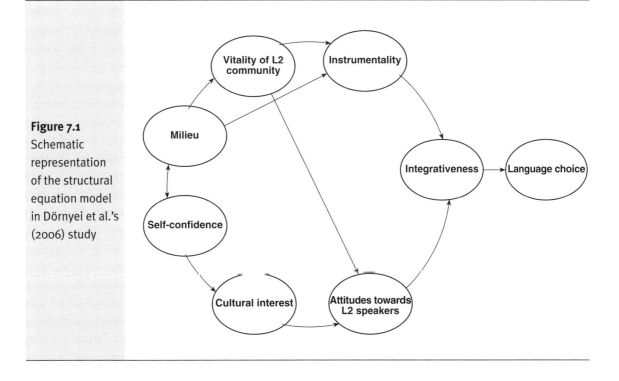

Figure 7.1
Schematic representation of the structural equation model in Dörnyei et al.'s (2006) study

The final model that emerged from our study, presented in Figure 7.1, confirms our earlier observation based on correlation analysis that *Integrativeness* plays a key role in L2 motivation, mediating the effects of all the other attitudinal/motivational variables on the criterion measure *Language choice* (and we obtained exactly the same results with another criterion measure, *Intended effort to study the L2*). Curiously, the immediate antecedents of this latent variable were *Attitudes towards L2 speakers/community* and *Instrumentality*; thus, the three variables that the correlations in Table 7.1 highlighted emerged as the central motivational components in the SEM model as well, and the model also gave us an indication about how these variables related to each other and to the criterion measure. What is more, this was a very consistent finding because it applied to all the different target languages and all the three waves of our survey. The only problem was that what we found did not make much theoretical sense: 'Integrativeness' turned out to be the principal motivation factor in an environment where 'integrating' was not very meaningful (since there was nothing really to integrate into) and, furthermore, integrativeness was closely associated with two very different variables: faceless pragmatic incentives and personal attitudes towards members of the L2 community. It was clear that we needed a new theory to accommodate these findings.

Theoretical considerations

Parallel to conducting the empirical research outlined above, I became familiar with an intriguing new theoretical approach in psychology that looked particularly promising with regard to applying it to L2 motivation: the conceptualization of *possible selves*. First introduced by Markus and Nurius (1986), the concept of the possible self represents an individual's ideas of what they *might* become, what they *would like* to become and what they are *afraid of* becoming. That is, possible selves are specific representations of one's self in future states, involving thoughts, images and senses, and are in many ways the manifestations of one's goals and aspiration. From a motivational point of view, two types of possible selves – the ideal self and the ought self – seemed particularly relevant (Higgins 1987). The former refers to the representation of the attributes that someone would ideally like to possess (i.e. representation of hopes, aspirations or wishes), whereas the latter refers to the attributes that one believes one ought to possess (i.e. a representation of someone's sense of duty, obligations or responsibilities) and which therefore may bear little resemblance to desires or wishes. The motivational aspect of these self-guides was explained by Higgins's (1987, 1998) *self-discrepancy theory*, postulating that motivation involves the desire for people to reduce the discrepancy between their actual and ideal/ought selves.

This self framework not only made intuitive sense to me but it also seemed to offer a good explanation of our Hungarian findings. Looking at 'integrativeness' from the self perspective, the concept can be conceived of as the L2-specific facet of one's ideal self. If our ideal self is associated with the mastery of an L2, that is, if the person that we would like to become is proficient in the L2, we can be described in Gardner's (1985) terminology as having an integrative disposition. Thus, the central theme of the emerging new theory was the equation of the motivational dimension that has traditionally been interpreted as 'integrativeness/integrative motivation' with the *Ideal L2 Self*.

Looking back at Figure 7.1, please recall that our Hungarian data showed that the immediate antecedents of the Ideal L2 Self in the model were *Attitudes towards the L2 speakers/community* and *Instrumentality*. Does this make sense? Yes it does: with regard to *Attitudes towards the L2 speakers/community*, we must realize that the actual L2 speakers are the closest parallels to a person's idealized L2-speaking self, which suggests that the more positive our disposition towards these L2 speakers, the more attractive our idealized L2 self. Or, to turn this equation around, it is difficult to imagine that we can have a vivid Ideal L2 Self if the L2 is spoken by a community that we despise. With regard to *Instrumentality*, because the ideal language self is a cognitive representation of all the incentives associated with L2 mastery, it is naturally also linked to professional competence that often requires the knowledge of the L2. Thus, to put it broadly, in our idealized image of ourselves we may want to be not only personally agreeable but also professionally successful.

We should note here, however, that from a self perspective the term 'instrumentality' can be divided into two distinct types. In conceptualizing the ideal/ought self distinction, Higgins (1987, 1998) highlighted a crucial difference between the two dimensions, a contrasting *approach/avoid* tendency: ideal self-guides have a *promotion* focus, concerned with hopes, aspirations, advancements, growth and accomplishments (i.e. approaching a desired end-state); whereas ought-to self-guides have a *prevention* focus, regulating the absence or presence of negative outcomes, concerned with safety, responsibilities and obligations (i.e. avoidance of a feared end-state). With this distinction in mind, we can see that traditionally conceived 'instrumentality/instrumental motivation' mixes up these two aspects. When our idealized image is associated with being professionally successful, 'instrumental' motives with a promotion focus – for example, to learn English for the sake of professional/career advancement – are related to the Ideal L2 Self. In contrast, instrumental motives with a prevention focus – for example, to study in order not to fail an exam or not to disappoint one's parents – are part of the Ought-to L2 Self.

The 'L2 Motivational Self System'

As we have seen above, both the empirical findings and the theoretical considerations seemed to support a reconceptualization of L2 motivation as part of the learner's self system. I have come to believe that the two elements discussed before, the ideal and the ought selves, are central components of this system, but I also felt that we needed to add a third major component, which concerns the direct impact of the learning environment (and which will not be discussed in this chapter in detail; for reviews, see Dörnyei 2001; Manolopoulou-Sergi 2004). Accordingly, I proposed (Dörnyei 2005) that the 'L2 Motivational Self System' was made up of the following three components (for more details on the self approach, see Dörnyei 2009; Dörnyei and Ushioda 2009):

- *Ideal L2 Self*, which is the L2-specific facet of one's 'ideal self'. If the person we would like to become speaks an L2, the *'ideal L2 self'* is a powerful motivator to learn the L2.

- *Ought-to L2 Self,* which concerns the attributes that one believes one *ought to* possess to meet expectations and to *avoid* possible negative outcomes.
- *L2 Learning Experience,* which concerns situated motives related to the immediate learning environment and experience (e.g. the impact of the teacher, the curriculum, the peer group, the experience of success).

Validating the L2 Motivational Self System

Over the last two years my research students – Stephen Ryan, Tatsuya Taguchi and Michael Magid – and I have been conducting large-scale survey research in Japan and China to validate the L2 Motivational Self System (for details of the surveys, see Ryan 2009; Taguchi et al. 2009). We believed that if we can support the main tenets of the theory by data coming from foreign language contexts that are very different from the Hungarian learning environment that the L2 self approach originated from, this would be a powerful validity argument of the construct. The studies did indeed confirm that our assumptions were correct; in the following I present some of the key findings: (a) correlations between traditional *Integrativeness* and the *Ideal L2 Self* to check whether the two constructs can indeed be equated; (b) correlations of *Integrativeness* and the *Ideal L2 Self* with criterion measures to see which variable does a better job at explaining motivated behaviour; (c) correlations between aspects of *Instrumentality* and the *Ought-to L2 Self* to check whether traditional instrumentality can indeed be divided into two distinct types.

The relationship between the Ideal L2 Self *and* Integrativeness

Table 7.2 presents correlations between *Integrativeness* and the *Ideal L2 Self,* in three different East Asian surveys involving over 5,300 participants, each consisting of different subsamples. As can be seen, there are substantial positive correlations in every subsample, suggesting that the two variables do indeed tap into the same underlying construct domain. The average correlation across the subsamples is .54, which is very high in L2 motivation research. These consistent results leave no doubt that the two concepts are very closely related.

Table 7.2
Correlations between *Integrativeness* and the *Ideal L2 Self*

	Total sample	University students (non-English majors)	University students (English majors)	Secondary school pupils	Adult learners
2,397 Japanese learners (Ryan forthcoming)	.59	.54	.53	.61	
1,586 Japanese learners (Taguchi et al. forthcoming)	.63	.63	.48		
1,328 Chinese learners (Taguchi et al. forthcoming)	.51	.46	.46	.66	.53

Note: All figures are significant at the p < .001 level.

The correlation of the Ideal L2 Self and Integrativeness with Intended effort

Table 7.3 presents the correlations of *Integrativeness* and the *Ideal L2 Self* with *Intended effort* in the same samples as in Table 7.2. These figures allow us to compare which variable does a better job at explaining the criterion measure, effort. Although *Integrativeness* does a consistently good job at accounting for the variance in the criterion measure, the *Ideal L2 Self* exceeds it in all but one subsample. The average variance (which is the average of the squared correlation coefficients) explained by *Integrativeness* across the different samples is 32 per cent, which can be considered high, but the same figure for the *Ideal L2 Self* is 42 per cent, which is almost 30 per cent higher!

		Total sample	University students (non-English majors)	University students (English majors)	Secondary school pupils	Adult learners
2,397 Japanese learners (Ryan forthcoming)	Ideal L2 Self	.77	.74	.71	.75	
	Integrativeness	.65	.61	.54	.71	
1,586 Japanese learners (Taguchi et al. forthcoming)	Ideal L2 Self	.71	.71	.61		
	Integrativeness	.63	.64	.49		
1,328 Chinese learners (Taguchi et al. forthcoming)	Ideal L2 Self	.55	.52	.51	.69	.51
	Integrativeness	.52	.47	.53	.63	.44

Note: All figures are significant at the p < .001 level.

Table 7.3 Correlations of *Integrativeness* and the *Ideal L2 Self* with *Intended effort*

The case of Instrumentality

Table 7.4 presents correlations that allow us to examine whether *Instrumentality* can indeed be divided into two types as outlined above. The data are drawn from Taguchi et al.'s (2009) Japanese and Chinese samples where the promotion and the prevention aspects of *Instrumentality* were measured separately. If Higgins's (1987, 1998) promotion/prevention distinction applies to our data, then we would expect to find higher correlations of the *Ideal L2 Self* with *Instrumentality-promotion* than with *Instrumentality-prevention*, and the *Ought-to L2 Self* should display the opposite pattern. This is exactly the case in Table 7.4. Furthermore, if the promotion and the prevention aspects are separate from each other then we would not expect a high correlation between them, and indeed both correlations are modest (with even the higher one explaining less than 12 per cent of the variance). Thus, these figures provide unambiguous confirmation that the traditionally conceived 'instrumental motivation' can indeed be divided into two distinct types: one relating to the Ideal L2 Self, the other to the Ought-to L2 Self. These two types are only moderately related to each other and show a distinct correlation pattern with the two self dimensions.

Table 7.4
Correlations between the *Ideal L2 Self, Instrumentality* and the *Ought-To L2 Self* in Taguchi et al. (forthcoming) Japanese and Chinese samples

	Ideal L2 Self		Ought-to L2 Self		Instrumentality – promotion	
	Japan	China	Japan	China	Japan	China
Instrumentality – promotion	.63*	.46*	.28*	.45*	–	–
Instrumentality – prevention	– .01	– .13*	.53*	.63*	.34*	.26*

* p < .001

Conclusion

This chapter discussed a major theoretical shift that has been taking place within the field of L2 motivation research. I described how a new paradigm has emerged from both theoretical considerations and research results, and then presented the main components of the newly proposed 'L2 Motivational Self System'. In the second part of the chapter I provided empirical data from three different surveys involving over 5,300 participants to validate the new construct. The correlational results clearly indicated that: (a) *Integrativeness* and the *Ideal L2 Self* tap into the same construct, but the *Ideal L2 Self* does a better job at explaining variance in the criterion measures; (b) the traditionally conceived concept of *Instrumentality* mixes up two types of pragmatic motives (with a promotion vs. a prevention focus) that show a rather different relationship pattern with the *Ideal* and the *Ought-to L2 Selves*. These results are all in accordance with the proposed theory and thus provide a strong validity argument for it. We should reiterate here that in the current study the third main component of the 'L2 Motivational Self System', the *L2 Learning Experience*, was not measured.

References

Coetzee-Van Rooy, S. (2006) 'Integrativeness: Untenable for world Englishes learners?' *World Englishes*, 25: 437–50.

Dörnyei, Z. (2001) *Teaching and researching motivation*, Harlow: Longman.

Dörnyei, Z. (2005) *The psychology of the language learner: Individual differences in second language acquisition*, Mahwah, NJ: Lawrence Erlbaum.

Dörnyei, Z. (2007) *Research methods in applied linguistics: Quantitative, qualitative and mixed methodologies*, Oxford: Oxford University Press.

Dörnyei, Z. (2009) 'The L2 Motivational Self System', in Z. Dörnyei and E. Ushioda (eds), *Motivation, language identity and the L2 self*, Clevedon: Multilingual Matters.

Dörnyei, Z. and Csizér, K. (2002) 'Some dynamics of language attitudes and motivation: Results of a longitudinal nationwide survey', *Applied Linguistics*, 23: 421–62.

Dörnyei, Z. and Ushioda, E. (eds) (2009) *Motivation, language identity and the L2 self*, Clevedon: Multilingual Matters.

Dörnyei, Z., Csizér, K. and Németh, N. (2006) *Motivation, language attitudes and globalisation: A Hungarian perspective*, Clevedon: Multilingual Matters.

Gardner, R.C. (1985) *Social psychology and second language learning: The role of attitudes and motivation*, London: Edward Arnold.

Gardner, R.C. (2001) 'Integrative motivation and second language acquisition', in Z. Dörnyei and R. Schmidt (eds), *Motivation and second language acquisition*, Honolulu, HI: University of Hawai'i Press.

Higgins, E.T. (1987) 'Self-discrepancy: A theory relating self and affect', *Psychological Review*, 94: 319–40.

Higgins, E.T. (1998) 'Promotion and prevention: Regulatory focus as a motivational principle', *Advances in Experimental Social Psychology*, 30: 1–46.

Lamb, M. (2004) 'Integrative motivation in a globalizing world', *System*, 32: 3–19.

Manolopoulou-Sergi, E. (2004) 'Motivation within the information processing model of foreign language learning', *System*, 32: 427–41.

Markus, H. and Nurius, P. (1986) 'Possible selves' *American Psychologist*, 41: 954–69.

Noels, K.A. (2003) 'Learning Spanish as a second language: Learners' orientations and perceptions of their teachers' communication style', in Z. Dörnyei (ed.), *Attitudes, orientations and motivations in language learning*, Oxford: Blackwell.

Ryan, S. (2009) 'Self and identity in L2 motivation in Japan: The ideal L2 self and Japanese learners of English', in Z. Dörnyei and E. Ushioda (eds), *Motivation, language identity and the L2 self*, Clevedon: Multilingual Matters.

Taguchi, T., Magid, M. and Papi, M. (2009) 'The L2 motivational self system amongst Chinese, Japanese and Iranian learners of English: A comparative study', in Z. Dörnyei and E. Ushioda (eds), *Motivation, language identity and the L2 self*, Clevedon: Multilingual Matters.

Ushioda, E. (2001) 'Language learning at university: Exploring the role of motivational thinking', in Z. Dörnyei and R. Schmidt (eds), *Motivation and second language acquisition*, Honolulu, HI: University of Hawaii Press.

Yashima, T. (2000) 'Orientations and motivations in foreign language learning: A study of Japanese college students', *JACET Bulletin*, 31: 121–33.

Introduction to chapter 8

This chapter focuses on an issue that is touched on also in other chapters (e.g. chapters 5, 7 and 12): the global spread of English and the consequences of this for learners and teachers of English. The topic belongs to sociolinguistics – the area of language study that prioritizes the interaction between language and society. A number of key concepts are introduced in this chapter, including globalization, new varieties of English, English as a lingua franca, and the contrast between 'centre' and 'periphery'.

The background to this chapter

There are many factors influencing language learners and teachers: teaching methods, the learners' motivation, the community of the institution in which the learning takes place, and the role of the language being learnt in the community of which teachers and learners are a part. Increasingly, for English particularly, that community is a global one.

As Kennedy explains, although English has been used worldwide for many years, its position in the world has changed subtly and in a number of ways. Traditionally, English is used in countries where a majority of the inhabitants are native speakers of English (e.g. US or Britain) or where it is used in government and education, often as a result of colonization (e.g. India, the Philippines). Earlier work by Kennedy and others focused on the role of governments and agencies such as Education Ministries in discussing which languages to encourage, and how to do so, in various political contexts.

Nowadays, however, English is sometimes used with symbolic rather than informational meaning. For example, English words are used in Japan in some product names and advertising, although their meaning may be puzzling to a speaker of English from elsewhere. (As Kennedy has pointed out elsewhere, this symbolic use of a language is not restricted to English. In Britain, for example, German phrases often appear in advertisements for cars and French ones in advertisements for cosmetics and perfume. It does not matter whether British consumers understand the German or French – they are likely simply to associate German with engineering quality and French with looking one's best. The difference, of course, is that English is not considered to be under threat from German, though standards of German are sometimes thought to be threatened by English.)

Most importantly, perhaps, English is now used as a common language (lingua franca) between people who either do not share another language or who do understand each other's language but who prefer to communicate in a third language – English – which does not give either of them an advantage over the other. English may even be used among native speakers of another language if there is someone present in the conversation who does not understand the other shared language.

Along with new situations for English come new kinds of English, and this is where questions of acceptability arise for teachers. Not only are there varieties of English associated with, for example, the US and Britain, there are also 'new' varieties spoken in countries such as India or the Philippines, and lingua franca varieties spoken around the world. Kennedy quotes researchers who document the growth and the characteristics of these varieties. The question for the language teacher is whether to accept these characteristics as 'correct' in English. For example, it is documented that speakers of lingua franca varieties regularly use the base form of a verb for all present-tense occurrences, not distinguishing, for example, between *I say* and *she says* but instead using *I say* and *she say*. Such usage is not illogical. If English can manage with *I say, we say, you say* and *they say*, why not also *she say*? For the English teacher, however, it may feel very uncomfortable not to correct *she say* in an essay. As time goes on, however, it may be that *she says* starts to sound rather old-fashioned, a marker of a local variety of English set against modern, global varieties.

Kennedy places the discussion about English in the context of other issues of globalization. The spread of English happens alongside political changes (the expansion of the European Union, for example) and commercial ones (the growth of multinational companies). The acceptance of or resistance to language issues may well be influenced by attitudes to political and commercial ones.

Focusing on the argument

Kennedy deals with contentious issues in this chapter, but his argument maintains a strict neutrality. For example, in discussing whether the use of English in Greek shops is a positive or negative influence on Greek, Kennedy sets out the terms of the debate: *This raises the question of the extent to which English is a negative force (reducing the status of local languages and cultures) or is part of a local community's identity.* He then quotes supporters of each side – shopkeepers who use English as part of a local marketing strategy, and those who believe that their identity as Greeks is being threatened by this use of English – without placing himself on one side or the other.

He uses a similar strategy in discussing English as a lingua franca. The argument is attributed to others, using phrases such as:

There are certainly those who believe . . .
[Seidlhofer] believes that . . .
Jenkins takes a similar view to Seidlhofer arguing that . . .

Rather than openly stating a view, Kennedy summarizes the area of disagreement:

Her ideas have met with a mixed reception . . .
. . . we are only just entering the period of discussion over these issues
Lingua franca research is raising a number of other interesting research questions . . .

You may wish to compare this chapter with others in this book, such as chapter 12, where the writer more clearly takes sides in an argument. You may also wish to consider how you react to Kennedy's neutral style: is he to be criticized for avoiding expressing an opinion, or to be congratulated for summarizing the issues without imposing his own view on the reader?

A language tip

This chapter, appropriately, illustrates how language might change to meet new demands. For example, although *English* is usually considered to be a non-count noun (I speak *English*, not *an English*), Kennedy quotes Graddol in using the plural form *Englishes* to emphasize that English in the future may be considered to be a number of different languages rather than only one. There may come a time when choosing to speak of *English* rather than *Englishes* represents a political decision, a rejection of multiple varieties of English, though it does not yet carry that meaning.

Another unfamiliar word in this chapter is *glocalization*, a merging of the words *global* and *local* to indicate the concept of merging the global and the local. The first time Kennedy uses the word he introduces it as an invented term with the phrase *which has been termed* . . . He then places *'glocal'* (and later *'glocalization'*) inside inverted commas. These devices signal that users of English cannot (yet) use the term without comment – it must still be marked as new.

To think about

1 What do you think is 'correct English'? How do you react when you encounter something from an unfamiliar variety of English?

2 Kachru talked about English in the world in terms of 'circles': inner, outer and expanding. Do you think this metaphor is still valid today?

3 Do you think that English as a lingua franca is a threat to other languages that you are familiar with?

CHAPTER 8

Learning English in a global context

Chris Kennedy

All human activities are socially based and a number are highly influenced by political and economic events. Learning English is certainly social but it is an activity that might not seem to be unduly influenced by political and economic forces. In fact, it is. Why people learn English, where and when they learn it, how it is learned, who learns it and what they learn can be traced back to political and economic forces and in many cases deliberate decisions on the part of governments, institutions and groups. Such decisions may benefit communities but there are as many cases where differential access to English can divide societies (Canagarajah 2006).

These politico-economic influences apply to the learning of any language, but it is the English language which is the focus of this chapter. English is a world language (Graddol 2006). There are more people using English (or Englishes as we shall see) around the world than any other language. Although this may change if centres of economic power shift, English is embedded as the major world language for the foreseeable future. The benefits and disadvantages of such a situation are hotly debated, particularly with reference to the influence of English on other cultures and languages. I shall be referring to some of these stresses and strains later in this chapter.

The development of English as a world language has inevitably led to attempts to manage its spread. These attempts at deliberate language policy (Spolsky 2007) either try to channel its uses in ways regarded as beneficial to affected communities, or, in those situations where its spread is regarded as harmful, to hinder its development. The learning of English, a part of language policy implementation, becomes a value-laden activity in these circumstances.

Globalization

We need to place the learning of English in its context since it is the forces of globalization that are driving the spread of English. One characteristic of globalization is the compression of time and space enabled by technological advance. Traditional political borders become less important to business organizations, and indeed to governments seeking inward investment to boost their economies. Businesses set up manufacturing operations and service industries wherever there is a skilled educated workforce and/or where labour costs are comparatively low, regardless of national borders. In customer-contact services, the availability of an English-speaking workforce will be a criterion in the decision where to locate, especially where global communication is an organizational requirement. Call centres are a case in point. Many UK/US businesses have outsourced their customer operations to those countries offering a supply of local educated English speakers, such as India, Kenya, the Philippines, Malaysia and South Africa, countries with relatively cheaper labour costs.

Although globalization is characterized by movements from 'centre' to 'periphery'

(I discuss these terms below) with global concerns influencing local contexts, globalization paradoxically has the effect of increasing localization. We can see this in the case of nationalist movements. International business may not operate according to traditional national boundaries, but local communities are increasingly developing their own identities and demanding greater political autonomy.

However, 'centre' and 'periphery' are not secure terms and their meaning may shift according to the political standpoint of whoever is using them. A 'periphery' may develop its own power and influence to become a 'centre' and a force for global activity, and 'peripheries' may have their own 'centres' and 'peripheries'. This fluidity can be seen in takeovers of 'centre'-based companies by a 'periphery' member (e.g. the takeover of Corus (formerly British Steel), and of Jaguar and Land Rover manufacturers by Tata Industries, an Indian global conglomerate). The same process is occurring in teaching English as a second or foreign language (ELT) with centres of expertise developing on the 'periphery' and 'periphery' countries attracting English-speaking students from other 'peripheries'.

As well as globalization causing a local reaction, there will often be a hybrid effect, which has been termed glocalization. The global and the local merge and in so doing produce a new 'glocal' form or event, some examples of which we shall see in relation to English later.

The activities arising from globalization processes involve spoken and written communication between participants. Since such communication takes place between communities that may not have access to each other's language (German-speaking and Chinese-speaking business communities for example) mediation is required. This may entail translating or interpreting the respective languages (German and Chinese in my example), but this can be an expensive and inefficient process. Alternatively, participants may decide to use a common third language. English often performs this function either institutionally where an English-language policy has been formally adopted, or informally with individuals' agreement.

English is a carrier of the globalization process and of the values and culture attached to it. The contestation of these values causes arguments around the power and influence of English and its benefits or disadvantages. As well as English performing particular functions in the world, its spread and the different roles it plays have led to local changes to grammar and discourse and more obviously vocabulary, to which I shall refer later.

The circles of English

Let us look at the roles of English in different areas of the world. Kachru (1985) suggested three concentric 'circles' of English language users: an inner circle, an outer circle, and an expanding circle. The inner circle consists of speakers of English as a first language, e.g. from the UK, North America, New Zealand and Australia. Outer circle speakers use English as a major additional language primarily for use within their nation. Many of the former British colonies in Africa and Asia (e.g. Kenya, Nigeria, India) fall into this category with English playing a major role since independence. The third, expanding circle increases year on year as more nations and the people within them realize the need for English for international communication (e.g. Brazil, Spain, Thailand).

The valid point Kachru was making at the time was that the direction of sociolinguistic influence (reflecting economic and political power) was from inner circle to outer and expanding circles, not the reverse, that is, from a powerful economic centre to a comparatively weaker periphery, and, in linguistic terms, from native speakers of English (NS) to non-native speakers (NNS). Linguistic standards and norms of use were derived from inner-circle countries (particularly Britain and the USA) as were ELT materials, methodologies and teacher supply.

Much has changed since the 1980s when the model was introduced. (At the time the Berlin Wall and the USSR still existed, and CDs and the Macintosh computer had only just been introduced.) The model was never intended to reflect a static state and it is not surprising if global socio-political changes (and a poststructuralist move from macro to more micro concerns on the part of applied linguists) have led to modifications. Some have suggested a different model reflecting a greater linguistic fluidity and hybridity (Kirkpatrick 2007), focusing on language proficiency rather than NS/NNS distinctions. It is true that users of English in Kachru's three circles cannot be as compartmentalized as they might have been (Pennycook 2007). Because of the spread of English, cross-borders migration arising from civil war and economic disparities, and the development of new economic centres, some communities within the inner circle might identify themselves as speakers of English as an additional or international language. Conversely, speakers in the outer and expanding circles may be as proficient in English as speakers in inner-circle countries and may indeed regard themselves as native English-speakers. Such groups exist for example in India, Singapore and Dubai. As economic conditions have changed in outer- and expanding-circle nations, and as political centres have developed, there is more interaction between outer- and expanding-circle countries and a new ownership of English and Englishes, not necessarily dependent on inner-circle norms.

Ownership of English

Communities have always absorbed elements of a contact language and made it part of their own culture and language. This is most obvious in the area of linguistic borrowings which are one result of English language spread. Japanese examples include *kiro* from *kilo* and *tero* from *terrorism* (Daulton 2004). Such borrowings, if regarded as carriers of foreign cultural values rather than local identity markers, can be politically unacceptable. National language academies may try to discourage borrowing, promoting locally created neologisms instead. The Icelandic Language Institute, for example, has a wordbank of alternatives to English loanwords. Rather than *computer*, it suggests *tolva,* created from two Icelandic words meaning *numbers* and *prophetess.* The degree of success of such deliberate attempts to manipulate individual linguistic behaviour is not high, especially in those situations where little linguistic capital is gained by adopting the neologism.

In the case of borrowings we could argue that English influence on a host language is externally driven but that the borrowings may eventually become a part of the host language and of a local identity, a form of 'glocalization' I referred to earlier. Other developments are more internally driven. One domain is that of media. English (and other languages) are frequently used in advertisements aimed at consumers who speak a first language which is not English and who may in some instances not understand

English. In an advertisement in a Japanese magazine for a Japanese car, the phrase 'FOR DRIVERS' appears amongst the Japanese text. The use of English in these domains is symbolic. English is perceived as appealing to innovation and high-status Western values. At the same time, mixing English and Japanese appears a response to a local Japanese identity. English is owned internally rather than imposed externally.

Further evidence of a local ownership of English can be gathered by examining aspects of the local linguistic landscape (Gorter 2006). Sakaguchi (2002) investigated the language of drinks cans sold from street kiosks and machines in Japan. 'FOR' and 'I LOVE KISS' (soda drinks) and 'LOVE BODY' (tea) are brands of Japanese drinks. The drinks consumer market is Japanese and English is a part of the brand. It is a variety of English which, to use Kachru's terms, inner-circle users would find inaccessible. English has spread to Japan as a consequence of globalization, but has been re-interpreted in creative, playful ways that make English in these consumer contexts a specific local variety owned by the Japanese drinks industry and its consumers. English has become part of a Japanese marketing style and design.

This raises the question of the extent to which English is a negative force (reducing the status of local languages and cultures) or is part of a local community's identity. In many cases there will be a local division of opinion. Katsaridi (2003) looked at shop signs in streets in Athens and found that English was used to create a perception in potential Greek customers that the shop sold high-quality goods and that they, the customers, belonged to the social group that would buy such high-quality products. English was being used as part of a clear marketing strategy. Opposition to the idea of English signage existed, however, as the following (translated) statement from a Greek shop owner illustrates (Katsaridi 2003: 51):

the Greek identity is completely lost. You can hardly survive in Greece . . . without English. [The Greeks] are trying their best to cast their identity away and buy a new one like some piece of clothing. I will have no part in this. This is . . . why I have kept my shop sign in Greek.

New varieties

Ownership of English and its effect on identity is closely connected with the emergence of new varieties of English associated with communities of English-users. New varieties are an example of the localization processes that take place in opposition to the centralizing effects of globalization.

In those contexts where the English language is being used as a medium of communication and where it is closely linked to the identity and culture of the users, local varieties, such as Nigerian English and Indian English, develop with their own lexis, grammar, phonology and discourse, and there will be sub-varieties or 'lects' ranging from formal to informal registers within the variety. Standard Singapore English (SSE) and its more informal variety, Singlish, is a good example. The Singapore government has conducted a long-standing campaign to try to persuade people to Speak Good English (in their terms SSE) with not unexpected opposition from groups wanting to preserve Singlish as an identity marker.

In some cases these varieties will not be second but first languages, raising once more the issue of who 'native-speakers' are and whether they should be solely assigned to 'inner circle' nations. Even where English is used for international rather than intranational purposes there are those who would argue that local varieties such as Korean English or Japanese English are emerging with their own characteristics, and that such varieties cannot be dismissed as deviations from an inner-circle standard, but are varieties in their own right. It is an open question whether over the longer term the various 'Englishes' will gradually diverge from one another particularly in the spoken mode or whether the influence of formal written English will be sufficient to maintain mutual intelligibility across varieties.

English as a lingua franca

There are certainly those who believe that the time has come to re-evaluate the power and influence of inner-circle standardized varieties such as British or American English and their hold over the targets we set learners of English as a second or foreign language.

Seidlhofer has collected a corpus of spoken English (the VOICE corpus) which is beginning to provide data for the existence of a European lingua franca. She believes that once certain linguistic features are established in the repertoire of a community of users, such features may no longer be legitimately regarded as non-standard by comparing them for example with a British or American standard (English as a native language – ENL) but must be accepted as an acceptable feature of an emerging variety of European English. Seidlhofer (2004) lists some of the characteristics she and her team have found:

- Dropping the third person present tense –s
- Confusing the relative pronouns who and which
- Omitting definite and indefinite articles where they are obligatory in ENL, and inserting them where they do not occur in ENL
- Failing to use correct forms in tag questions (e.g. isn't it? or no? instead of shouldn't they?)
- Inserting redundant prepositions, as in We have to study about . . .
- Overusing certain verbs of high semantic generality, such as do, have, make, put, take
- Replacing infinitive-constructions with that-clauses, as in I want that . . .
- Overdoing explicitness (e.g. black colour rather than just black).

Jenkins (2007) takes a similar view to Seidlhofer arguing that setting phonological ENL norms as targets for learners of English is unnecessary and impractical. She has tried to define a phonological 'common core' based on her research with NNSs that might provide syllabus targets for English as a lingua franca programmes. Her ideas have met with a mixed reception, not least from teachers themselves. As is the case with any innovation, the attitudes and beliefs of users are crucial for successful implementation, and we are only just entering the period of discussion over these issues.

Researchers are also looking at the pragmatics of lingua franca communication, showing that in those contexts where an outcome needs to be achieved with a minimum loss of face (e.g. a business negotiation), participants tend to ignore lexico-grammatical 'errors' (as measured by NS norms), and engage in considerable repair and support strategies so that the communication can reach a successful end. Such data suggests that existing models of second language learning where the performance of learners and users is judged against acquisition of NS norms will need to be revised to include lingua franca use (Firth and Wagner 2007).

Lingua franca research is raising a number of other interesting research questions which are likely to be of concern in the future. Implementation issues (e.g. whether teachers will introduce new norms and/or targets for learning English) relate to innovation theory including the importance of identity and of teacher and student attitudes towards the innovation. There is also the question of efficiency and just how much 'work' is required by the participants in lingua franca communication in order to reach understanding, and the related issue of intelligibility. There must be some minimum linguistic competence required for successful communication but what this is, and whether we can identify it, is an area that needs investigation. There is the further more general question of whether the present research agenda on lingua franca communication remains an imposition of Western values on non-Western professionals (Holliday 2005).

Conclusion

Globalization has produced a complex situation regarding English and the learning of English. English is one of the facilitators of globalization and as the language spreads some welcome it and others attempt to control its spread. As a paradoxical consequence of globalization, English becomes embedded in local conditions and contexts, and its ownership is no longer held by the traditionally defined native speaker, but is part of the culture and identity of all English-users worldwide. With localization come developments in the vocabulary, grammar and discourse of the various Englishes, and the emergence of one or several 'lingua francas'. Such new varieties raise questions regarding changing norms and targets for ELT and a new research agenda which includes issues of identity, attitudes and intelligibility.

References

Canagarajah, A.S. (2006) 'Negotiating the local in English as a lingua franca', *Annual Review of Applied Linguistics*, 26: 197–218.

Daulton, F. (2004) 'The creation and comprehension of English loanwords in the Japanese media', *Journal of Multilingual and Multicultural Development*, 25, 5: 285–296.

Firth, A. and Wagner, J. (2007) 'On discourse, communication, and (some) fundamental concepts in SLA research', *Modern Language Journal*, 91, 5: 800–815.

Gorter, D. (ed) (2006) *Linguistic landscape*, Clevedon: Multilingual Matters.

Graddol, D. (2006) *English next*, London: British Council

Holliday, A.R. (2005) *The struggle to teach English as an international language*, Oxford: Oxford University Press.

Jenkins, J. (2007) *English as a lingua franca: attitude and identity*, Oxford: Oxford University Press.

Kachru, B. (1985) 'Standards, codification, and sociolinguistic realism', in R. Quirk and H.G. Widdowson (eds) *English in the world: teaching and learning the language and literatures*, Cambridge: Cambridge University Press (pp. 11–30).

Katsaridi, A. (2003) 'The language of shop signs in Greece', unpublished Masters dissertation, Centre for English Language Studies, University of Birmingham.

Kirkpatrick. A. (2007) *World Englishes: implications for international communication and ELT*, Cambridge: Cambridge University Press.

Pennycook, A. (2007) *Global Englishes and transcultural flows*, London: Routledge.

Sakaguchi, T. (2002) 'Importing language', unpublished Masters dissertation, Centre for English Language Studies, University of Birmingham.

Seidlhofer, B. (2004) 'Research perspectives on teaching English as a Lingua Franca', *Annual Review of Applied Linguistics*, 24: 209–239.

Spolsky, B. (2007) *Language policy*, Cambridge: Cambridge University Press.

III Applied Linguistics in a wider context

Introduction to chapter 9

Ideology, particularly ideologies of language teaching, plays a part in several of the chapters in this book, but this chapter focuses on language and ideology and belongs to a tradition called Critical Discourse Analysis (CDA). CDA involves looking at texts from the point of view of how they influence, and are influenced by, the beliefs and value systems of the communities that read, hear and produce them. Critical Discourse Analysts work with texts of all kinds (including, for example, advertisements, politicians' speeches, textbooks and magazines) but often they investigate newspapers and other kinds of news discourse. They show how popular ideas about events and people come from the way those events and people are written about. The key concepts in this chapter are: Critical Discourse Analysis, metaphor, register and semantic prosody.

The background to this chapter

In this chapter O'Halloran refers to the ground-breaking and very influential work by Lakoff and Johnson on metaphor. We are all familiar with metaphors used in poems or other literary works, such as 'to suffer the slings and arrows of outrageous fortune' (from Shakespeare's play *Hamlet*), but Lakoff and Johnson argue that metaphor is also very common in ordinary conversation or writing. They also argue that metaphors group together to suggest a consistent interpretation of the world, and that because the metaphors are consistent with one another that interpretation seems 'natural', that is, it seems to be the only one that is possible. O'Halloran quotes the example ARGUMENT IS WAR, which comes from Lakoff and Johnson's book. Lakoff and Johnson point out that many phrases commonly used in English to describe an argument are metaphors taken from the field of warfare. Because of this, they suggest, people who speak English (and use or hear or read such phrases) come to associate argument with aggression and competition.

Arguments such as these are used by critical discourse analysts to suggest that common ways of saying something can have the effect of presenting an issue from a particular point of view. Lee's argument, quoted by O'Halloran, is that a newspaper article written about multi-racial South Africa presents a 'white' point of view because it uses words such as *simmer* and *erupted* to describe the actions of the (black) inhabitants of Soweto. These words, Lee argues, represent the Sowetans not as human beings but as a destructive natural force, such as a volcano.

Another term used in this chapter is 'semantic prosody'. This term was first used by Louw (1993), following suggestions by John Sinclair, to refer to the pragmatic or emotional effect of a phrase that might not be obvious from the individual words in the phrase. For example, it has been shown by Channell (2000) that the phrase *roam/roamed the streets* is nearly always used to talk about groups of people who are behaving in a violent or uncontrolled manner. The phrase therefore tends to suggest behaviour that the speaker or writer finds threatening, even though this cannot be guessed from the individual words *roam* and *street*. The term 'semantic prosody' is often used to indicate that a given word or phrase is often associated with positive (desirable) things or with negative (undesirable) ones. (In practice, for reasons that are not entirely understood, it seems that more semantic prosodies are negative than are positive.) O'Halloran's argument is that a semantic prosody may be specific to a particular register or kind of text. Sports writing, for example, may use words with a different sense of 'positive' or 'negative' than other kinds of journalism do. O'Halloran uses the new term 'register prosody' to refer to this phenomenon.

Focusing on the argument

In this chapter O'Halloran explicitly disagrees with another writer – Lee. However, he uses Lee as an example of a more extensive phenomenon, which he (O'Halloran) calls 'over-interpretation'. According to O'Halloran, Lee is mistaken in his interpretation of *The Guardian* news article. O'Halloran brings a kind of evidence that Lee does not use – evidence from a large collection of newspaper texts – in support of his contention that Lee's interpretation is incorrect. It is important to recognize that O'Halloran is not arguing against CDA itself, or with other things that Lee has said, but only with this specific instance.

As readers we have at least two choices – we can agree with Lee and disagree with O'Halloran, or vice versa. (Alternatively, we might choose to develop an entirely different argument that partially agrees or disagrees with both.) It is worth considering what we would need to accept in order to agree with O'Halloran.

- The word *erupted* can be said to lose its association with volcanoes, and with non-human destructive force, if it is more often used, in a particular register, with words indicating a human activity. So a phrase such as *the township erupted* does not dehumanize the people involved although it does imply the use of violence. In the context of hard news, *erupted* is <u>not</u> a metaphor linking human activity with volcanic activity.
- More generally, a word can be a metaphor in one register but not in another. If a word that begins as a metaphor (as *erupted* presumably did) is used very frequently in a given register, it loses its character as a metaphor.
- We can replicate the experience of, for example, readers of hard news by collecting a large number of hard news texts (a corpus of hard news texts). Conclusions drawn about the frequent use of a word or phrase in a corpus can be extended to conclusions about individual readers.
- The evidence from a corpus of texts can be used to counter (to argue against) one reader's interpretation of a text. This evidence will carry more weight than if a second reader simply disagreed with the first.
- Even more generally, one interpretation of a text can be said to be 'more correct' than other one.

A language tip

When O'Halloran reports what a writer has said, he uses language that either distances him from the writer's words or associates him with them. Here are some examples:

Distancing:
Chilton and Schäffner (1997: 222) <u>point to</u> the use of the *argument is war* metaphor in politics . . .
They <u>argue</u> that . . .
Now Lee's (1992: 93) <u>comments</u> . . .
Biber et al. (1999: passim) <u>comment</u> that . . .
This is why Biber et al. (1999: 477) <u>argue</u> . . .

Distancing may imply disagreement but it does not necessarily do so. Although O'Halloran disagrees with Lee, he agrees with Chilton and Shäffner's use of Lakoff and Johnson's work. He also does not disagree with Biber et al.

Associating:
<u>As</u> Stubbs (2001: 20) says . . .
Recent advances in corpus investigation have thrown up many <u>insights</u> about the nature of phraseological language

Associating always implies agreement. It would look very odd if O'Halloran went on to disagree with Stubbs or with corpus investigations of phraseology.

To think about

1 What is your reaction when you read the news story extract? Do you think of volcanoes when you see the word *erupted*?
2 Can you think of (other) examples of words or phrases that have one meaning in one register and another meaning in another register?
3 Can you think of (other) metaphors which are commonly used and which may make us interpret events in one way rather than another?

Reference

Channell, J. 2000, 'Corpus based analysis of evaluation texts', in Hunston, S. and Thompson, G. (eds) *Evaluation in Texts: Authorial stance and the construction of discourse.* Oxford: Oxford University Press, pp. 38–55.

CHAPTER 9

Investigating metaphor and ideology in hard news stories

Kieran O'Halloran

Critical Discourse Analysis (CDA) is a branch of linguistics which is concerned with discovering how values and ideologies are represented in text (see, for example, Caldas-Coulthard and Coulthard 1996; Fairclough 2001). In CDA, hard news stories are often analysed, because they are so important in contemporary culture. This chapter is embedded within the tradition of CDA and will also analyse hard news material. The following from Bell (1991: 14) provides a definition of hard news. I follow this definition in this chapter:

reports of accidents, conflicts, crimes, announcements, discoveries and other events which have occurred or come to light since the previous issue of their paper or programme . . . Hard news is also the place where a distinctive news style will be found if anywhere.

In the next section of this chapter we will look at a hard news story.

One focus of CDA is highlighting how metaphors can be ideologically significant – how metaphors can influence how people think about situations. For example, Chilton and Schäffner (1997: 222) point out examples such as *the opposition's claims were shot down in flames*, in articles about politics. Examples such as this draw on the metaphor that ARGUMENT = WAR. Chilton and Shäffner argue that when a metaphor such as this is used it makes readers think that it is natural to see an opponent's opinion as something to be destroyed. It would be possible to see an opponent's opinion in a different way; for example, perhaps when we hear two different views we can see them both as contributing to an attempt to solve a problem, rather than being opposed to each other. But a metaphor such as *the opposition's claims were shot down in flames* makes it difficult to think of these alternatives. In other words, the metaphor makes us see a particular approach to disagreement as the only possible approach. This view is very similar to that of Lakoff and Johnson (1980). Lakoff and Johnson also argue that using sets of metaphors makes us accept one way of seeing the world as the only way. CDA practitioners usually accept Lakoff and Johnson's view of metaphor. They often argue that when writers use a metaphor they are making readers see the world in a particular way.

This view of metaphor has much to offer, but sometimes it ignores the differences between kinds of writing. It is possible that a metaphor that 'means' one thing in one kind of writing can mean something else in another kind. This is what I shall argue in the case study below.

My argument is that in order to investigate how metaphor works we have to look at large collections of texts of a particular kind. This will allow us to see the language that readers of those texts are exposed to. We can then see how a word or phrase is usually used and what it means for those readers. This view is different from that of Lakoff and Johnson (and Chilton and Schäffner). They would seem to assume that a metaphor has the same meaning wherever it occurs. I argue that the meaning can be different in different contexts.

I will demonstrate this position via a case study, an analysis by Lee (1992) of metaphor in a hard news text. I shall examine Lee's analysis which is prototypical of the way CDA draws on Lakoff and Johnson (1980) to analyse metaphor. Using a large corpus of 260 million words which includes hard news text, I shall show how regular readers of hard news would be exposed to particular collocates and phraseologies around one metaphor that Lee (1992) identifies. On this evidence, I show where Lee produces an over-interpretation of his linguistic data as metaphorical when it is unlikely to be so for habitual readers of the hard news register.

Case study: Lee (1992)

Lee (1992) has proved to be a popular textbook, continuing to be recommended reading for courses on CDA. Lee's (1992) analysis of metaphor in a hard news text is then reasonably well known. Indeed, it is a salient example of Lakoff and Johnson (1980) inspired metaphor analysis in CDA since Lee (1992) devotes an entire chapter to Lakoff and Johnson's (1980) view of metaphor. Lee comments upon a hard news report from the British newspaper, *The Guardian*, on 4 August 1976, concerning events in Soweto in South Africa. Here is the headline and first paragraph of the article which Lee (1992: 91–2) reproduces:

Police open fire as Soweto erupts again[1]

From STANLEY UYS, Cape Town, August 4

The black township of Soweto, which has been simmering with unrest since the riots on June 16 and the shooting of 174 Africans, erupted again today.

Now Lee's (1992: 93) comments:

[A] feature of the first paragraph that could be said to derive from a white perspective is the metaphorical process that treats the people of Soweto as some kind of natural force, specifically here as a volcano which has been 'simmering' with unrest and then 'erupted' . . .

The effect of these processes of metaphor . . . is arguably to distance the reader from the subjects of the report . . . The situation is seen as resulting from some kind of inevitable set of natural laws rather than from human feelings and decisions.

In other words, Lee points out that the words *simmering* and *erupted* are often used in English to refer to the action of volcanoes. Volcanoes are, of course, not human, and they cannot be controlled. They are a natural force, something that is not controlled.

Lee argues that by using the same words to talk about a situation involving human beings the newspaper story makes the events seem to be a natural force, not the result of human decisions. The people of Soweto, according to Lee, are made to seem like a volcano.

But how far can one assume that a routine reader of the hard news register would see the words *simmering* and *erupted* and understand Sowetans in terms of a natural force/volcano? In this chapter I will address this question by focusing on the word *erupted* only.

Theory and method

Register and meaning

Halliday and Hasan (1985) use the term 'register' to refer to different kinds of spoken and written language that are found in different contexts. For example, recipes make up a register, school activities such as class quizzes make up a register, and hard news makes up a register. Registers are identified by their context (for example, who is speaking in what situation) and also by the words and grammar (the lexicogrammar) that are found in them. Sometimes we can identify a register from only a small sample of language. For example, a regular reader of recipes in English will immediately identify *Heat half a pint of milk* as belonging to a recipe. It has an imperative, *heat*, a quantity, *half a pint*, and the name of a food, *milk*.

Investigation of large corpora bears out the fact that there is a greater likelihood of some lexicogrammatical patterns in certain registers than others. So corpus investigation can show clearly the *distinctive style* of hard news (see earlier quotation from Bell, 1991). Exploring large corpora of news texts can provide a sense of what regular readers of news text are usually exposed to. As Stubbs (2001: 20) says with regard to this issue of convention:

our (unconscious) knowledge of what is probable . . . involves expectations of language patterns. Our knowledge of a language involves not only knowing individual words, but knowing very large numbers of phrases . . . and also knowing what words are likely to co-occur in a cohesive text.

My plan, then, is to examine the word *erupted* in a large corpus of hard news texts. If it can be shown through corpus investigation that:

1 *erupted* tends to have conventional meanings in hard news texts,
2 these meanings are different to the meanings Lee makes in his interpretation, then this will raise doubts about Lee's analysis of metaphor as inspired by Lakoff and Johnson (1980).

The corpus used in this investigation

To perform this investigation, I will draw upon the Bank of English, a corpus of 450 million words made up of separate subcorpora. It is particularly skewed towards newspapers, which suits my purposes. I shall use 260 million words from six newspaper subcorpora: 60 million, UK *The Times*; 30 million, UK regional newspapers; 45 million, UK *The Sun* and *The News of the World*; 51 million, UK national news; 38 million, US News; 36 million, Australian newspapers, from the period 1999–2003.[2] They are not 'pure' register corpora since they consist of many different newspaper texts, not just hard news. However, since the Bank of English allows the investigator to expand concordance lines to five lines of co-text, it is possible to establish whether the texts come from hard news or not by inspecting whether the text is in line with Bell's (1991) definition given in the introductory section of this chapter.

Collocation and phraseology

To get an initial sense of how *erupted* might regularly function in the hard news register, my first step is to look at its collocates using the 260 million word newspaper corpus. This is because we know what a word means only when we look at the words it co-occurs with. Or rather, meaning is actually spread across a number of words rather than belonging to a single word. Evidence of regular collocational patterning in hard news would tell us whether words such as *erupted* are associated with volcanoes in this register.

I look for collocates within a span of four places to the left and four places to the right of *erupted* (the maximum span possible in the Bank of English) and produce the raw frequencies for collocates. Comparing raw frequencies is useful in seeing which collocates are recurrent.

Recent advances in corpus investigation have thrown up many insights about the nature of phraseological language (Wray, 2002; Butler, 2005). Inspecting phraseologies of *erupted* forms the second part of my investigation.

Results and analysis

Collocates for erupted

Let me begin with a collocate search in the 260 million word newspaper corpus. *Erupted* is in the past tense in the Soweto text. But since the collocate search can only look for the form *erupted*, results will include collocates for the past participle *erupted* as well. The collocates that were found are shown in Figure 9.1 with their frequency.

There are 41 instances of *volcano*. Still, the number of instances of *volcano* and names of volcanoes (*Vesuvius* and *Nyiragongo*) as collocates actually amounts to only around 4 per cent of the total. The collocate with the largest frequency is *violence* at 214 instances. These instances of *violence* refer to human phenomena. So, overwhelmingly,

Figure 9.1 Collocates for *erupted* and their frequency

violence (214), row (190), fighting (87), fury (82), scandal (79), war (78), crisis (53), controversy (53), trouble (50), **volcano** (41), rioting (34), gunfire (32), battle (30), riots (28), dispute (28), clashes (21), furore (20), protests (19), conflict, (18), feud (14), protest (13), revolt (12), tensions (12), chaos (10), killing (8), struggle (8), **vesuvius** (8), **nyiragongo** (5).

erupted usually occurs when the newspapers are talking about human beings and their actions. In other words, this newspaper corpus suggests that we should not interpret the word *erupted* in the Soweto text as being associated with volcanoes.

Erupted in the past tense

There are 2509 instances of *erupted* in the 260 million newspaper corpus. Around 90 per cent of the instances of *erupted* are in the past tense. A random sample of 20 lines of *erupted* in the past tense from the 260 million word newspaper corpus is given in Figure 9.2.

Figure 9.2
A random
sample of 20
lines for *erupted*
in the past tense

```
          issue since the scandal in America erupted. "Behavior which might give
              in the West Bank and gun battles erupted in the Gaza Strip yesterday, a day
    called by passers-by after a dispute erupted between the driver of a Mercedes
          tourists. <p> Last week's fighting erupted around the old Spanish colonial
             at Kabul airport. Fresh fighting erupted yesterday in northern Afghanistan
    nto the city since renewed fighting erupted between Palestinians and Israelis
             one said. On Friday, when firing erupted in this corner of southern Kosovo,
       Officers slam 'cosy deal' <p> FURY erupted last night after a police chief
            <dt> 18 May 2002 </dt> <p> FURY erupted yesterday as an arsonist aged 15
               Terminal when the gunfire erupted. "It echoed all over the airport,"
         <p> The tension of the occasion erupted at odd moments. Speaking too long,
    Then seven years later the problem erupted again when the couple tried to
   <p> Rumbles of controversy recently erupted over the world of famed US jock
   the two clubs continues. <p> The row erupted last week when Andrew accused
          their silence. But the scandal erupted this year with new allegations of
   of the council that horrible scenes erupted. They held out no olive branch,
   the Marines. When a political storm erupted in April over an American spy
      but talks broke down and violence erupted in September. The Palestinians say
      village of Montrado when violence erupted after the murder of a Dayak boy.
   were sent to Bosnia when civil war erupted there in 1992. They quickly
```

Around 75 per cent of the instances are from the hard news register, and again are mostly about human beings and actions (e.g. *fighting erupted*; *row erupted*). The subject of *erupted* is usually an abstract noun referring to human actions (*scandal, dispute, fighting, tension, problem, controversy, political storm, violence* and so on). The usual phraseology of *erupted* in hard news, then, can be represented as 'abstract noun for human phenomenon + erupted in the past tense'. Because of this, a reader finding *erupted* in the past tense in hard news is most likely to think of violence, conflict etc. rather than volcanoes.

Register prosody versus semantic prosody

Since the meanings for *erupted* are overwhemingly negative, one might say there is a negative **semantic prosody** for *erupted* in the past tense. The concept of semantic prosody is widely used in corpus-based linguistics (e.g. Sinclair, 1991; Louw, 1993). Here is a definition from Sinclair (2003: 178):

A corpus enables us to see words grouping together to make special meanings that relate not so much to their dictionary meanings as to the reasons why they were chosen together. This kind of meaning is called a semantic prosody.

Sinclair (2004: 30–35) gives the example of the seemingly neutral phrase, *the naked eye*. Corpus investigation reveals a common phraseology, *visibility + preposition + the + naked + eye*, which in turn reveals a negative semantic prosody such as in *too faint to be seen with the naked eye* or *it is not really visible to the naked eye*.

However, there is a problem in saying *erupted* in the past tense has a negative semantic prosody. This is because *erupted* in the past tense is not always negative. Consider *the pub erupted*. This is an example, from the 260 million word corpus, of *erupted* in the past tense which has positive associations. It is not from the hard news register, but from the sports report register. Here is the expanded co-text:

Just as another undeserved German victory loomed, up popped Robbie Keane to score a dramatic last-minute equaliser. **The pub erupted.** Another heroic draw for the Irish to celebrate. I suspect Roy Keane would have been furious that they had failed to win.

Here, *the pub erupted* means that the people in the pub became very excited and happy (because their football team had just scored a goal). It does not mean they became violent.

What is interesting about this football report example is that there is no modification of *erupted* with a postmodifier such as *with joy*. However, we would understand *erupted* here in a positive sense since football supporters are celebrating a goal. Other collocates, in the sports report register, such as *crowd, ground, press box, room* and *stadium* all relate explicitly to eruptions of applause, joy, etc. while watching a sports game. Therefore, in hard news, *erupted* tends to have a negative prosody (it is associated with 'bad things' such as violence) whereas in sport reporting it has largely a positive prosody (it is associated with celebration). I would like to suggest the term 'register prosody', as opposed to 'semantic prosody' to describe this. I should stress that the concept of register prosody is a probabilistic one. While the meanings around *erupted* in the past tense in hard news are overwhelmingly negative, there are a small number of instances of *erupted* in the past tense in hard news which carry positive meanings (e.g. *fireworks erupted and champagne corks were popping* in a story about the first day of the new millennium).

Register prosody and information compression

Biber et al. (1999: passim) comment that the need for economy affects the choices of grammar and vocabulary in news given the need to save space in hard news and maximize what is new. Biber et al. (1999: 477) argue that this is why the short passive is common in news (e.g. Doherty was arrested in New York in June). Applying this to the use of *erupted* in the Soweto text, one might say that because *erupted* in the past tense carries a negative register prosody in hard news, its use allows the writer to imply in a very few words that violence is present without 'violence' actually having to be mentioned. Similar things could be said with regard to *erupted* in the sports report register. Here *erupted* would seem to have a positive register prosody and so communicate 'joy' without it having to be inscribed in the text.

Endpoints

Widdowson (2004) uses the term **pretextual** to describe how certain scholars, particularly some critical discourse analysts, interpret texts in ways which corroborate their values while implicitly assuming that target readers will understand the text in the same way. First, I have shown how corpus evidence is useful in avoiding pretextual metaphorical lexicalization of textual data from the perspective of readers who have been routinely exposed to the text's register. Second, I have shown how difficulties can arise in applying Lakoff and Johnson's (1980) position on metaphor to texts in a specific register. This suggests that applying Lakoff and Johnson to other register-based critical analyses of metaphors is potentially problematic.

Notes

1 Lee (1992) does not provide the headline of this extract.
2 Clearly in using contemporary corpora, I am not attempting to reconstruct how a reader in August 1976 would have come to the Soweto text. This would be difficult to achieve since to the best of my knowledge there is no corpus of newspaper texts of comparable size (260 million words) from the early to mid-1970s, let alone a sizeable corpus of *Guardian* hard news texts up to August 1976. Since my purpose is ultimately to show how CDA metaphor analysis, which imports an approach from the discourse level to a register level, can be problematic, I treat the text non-historically (like Lee).

References

Bell, A. 1991. *The Language of News Media*. Oxford: Blackwell.

Biber, D., S. Johansson, G. Leech, S. Conrad and E. Finegan. 1999. *Longman Grammar of Spoken and Written English*. Harlow: Longman.

Butler, C. 2005. 'Formulaic language: an overview with particular reference to the cross-linguistic perspective' in Butler, C., Gómez-González, M. and Doval-Suárez, S. (eds.). *The Dynamics of Language Use*. Amsterdam: John Benjamins.

Caldas-Coulthard, C.R. and M. Coulthard. (eds.) 1996. *Texts and Practices: Readings in Critical Discourse Analysis*. London: Routledge.

Chilton, P. and C. Schäffner. 1997. 'Discourse and politics' in T. van Dijk (ed.), *Discourse as Social Interaction*. London: Sage.

Fairclough, N. 2001. *Language and Power*, 2nd edn. London: Longman.

Halliday, M.A.K. and R. Hasan. 1985. *Language, Context and Text: Aspects of Language in a Social-Semiotic Perspective*. Oxford: Oxford University Press.

Lakoff, G. and M. Johnson. 1980. *Metaphors We Live By*. Chicago: University of Chicago Press.

Lee, D. 1992. *Competing Discourses: Perspective and Ideology in Language*. London: Longman.

Louw, W. E. 1993. 'Irony in the text or insincerity in the writer?' in Baker, M., G. Francis and E. Tognini-Bonelli (eds.), *Text and Technology. In Honour of John M. Sinclair*. Philadelphia and Amsterdam: John Benjamins.

Sinclair, J.McH. 1991. *Corpus, Concordance, Collocation.* Oxford: Oxford University Press.

Sinclair, J.McH. 2003. *Reading Concordances.* Harlow: Longman.

Sinclair, J.McH. 2004. *Trust the Text: Language, Corpus and Discourse.* London: Routledge.

Stubbs, M. 2001. *Words and Phrases: Corpus Studies of Lexical Semantics.* Oxford: Blackwell.

Widdowson, H.G. 2004. *Text, Context, Pretext: Critical Issues in Discourse Analysis.* Oxford: Blackwell.

Wray, A. 2002. *Formulaic Language and the Lexicon.* Cambridge: Cambridge University Press.

Introduction to chapter 10

This chapter is one of four that looks at Applied Linguistics outside the context of the language classroom. It describes some of the activities of forensic linguists, that is, people who use linguistic expertise to advise police investigators, disciplinary boards, authors who believe their work has been copied, and similar cases. This sometimes ends in the forensic linguist giving evidence in court, although much of the case work provides sufficient information to prevent things going that far. In this chapter, some of the techniques, and the difficulties, of establishing authorship of a text are described. The chapter is also one of a number that describes how a large corpus of texts might be used to investigate language. In this chapter a corpus is used to show when an aspect of language use is unusual and so unlikely to happen by chance. The key concepts introduced in this chapter are: Forensic Linguistics, evidence, plagiarism and collusion.

The background to this chapter

The field of Forensic Linguistics is an intriguing one and is capturing the imagination of a growing number of Applied Linguistics students. The range of topics covered is quite large. A forensic linguist might advise on whether a suspect has understood the police caution when arrested, on the meaning of the wording of a statute (law), on whether a confession is written in the suspect's own words, or on what the 'rational interpretation' of a given text might be. As Johnson and Woolls say in this chapter, a forensic linguist is only able to give an opinion, and only on matters of language. He or she cannot say whether someone is innocent or guilty of a particular crime or breach of regulations.

Forensic linguistic techniques may be used in circumstances that lie well outside the courtroom. Of the examples given in this chapter, only the first one is taken from a court case. This is also the only example that compares one text (in this case an SMS text message reportedly sent by a teenaged girl) with a body of other texts known to have been written by that person. The aim is to establish whether the writer of the one text and the writer of all the other texts is the same person. This example is different, too, in that it relies on spelling and punctuation to make its case, rather than grammar or phraseology.

The other examples in the chapter relate to plagiarism: the use (by students) of other people's words or ideas. The examples are: applicants to universities who work together in writing their 'personal statements', and students who copy into their essays ideas and phrases from books they have been reading. Essay markers often find it easy to guess when work has been plagiarized. They may find that two essays are remarkably similar in their ideas, or that the style of one sentence or paragraph is very unlike the others in an essay. Features such as this make the marker aware that plagiarism may be present.

Proving plagiarism is rather more difficult. First, the source text has to be identified. Then, a measurement of similarity has to be established. As Johnson and Woolls point out, students who plagiarize often do not copy whole phrases or sentences exactly. Rather, they change some words, phrases and even sentences from the original, either because they believe that if they do so they are not plagiarizing, or because they hope to escape detection in that way.

Students are often very anxious about plagiarism. They know that it is severely punished when found, but they are afraid that they might accidentally plagiarize something they have been reading. Plagiarism can be avoided by (a) being careful to give a reference when ideas have been taken from a source and by (b) avoiding using the words and phrases in the original source unless a direct quotation is being used.

Focusing on the argument

Johnson and Woolls begin their chapter with three assumptions. These are important and worth exploring a little further here. The first assumption is that most sentences in English (for example) are unique, so two identical sentences are likely to have been produced by copying. Johnson and Woolls point out that there is some tension between this observation and a contrary one: that much of the phraseology of English is repeated many times. Phrases such as *on the other hand* or *communicative language teaching,* for example, are very far from unique, and it would be surprising if two essays on the same topic did not contain some identical sequences of this kind. Separating 'innocent' repetition from plagiarism is one of the tasks of the forensic linguist.

The second assumption partly answers the question raised by the first – long sequences are less likely to occur frequently than short ones. It is known that whereas there are very many bi-grams (recurring two-word phrases) in English, there are far fewer consistently repeated six-word phrases. Johnson and Woolls go further and argue that a sequence of five adjectives in a row is unusual, irrespective of what those adjectives are. They also argue that the researcher needs to look at the amount of repetition in a passage as a whole. Although re-use of one two-word phrase may not amount to plagiarism, repeating several words and phrases in a short passage may well do so.

Finally, Johnson and Woolls state the assumption that language will tend to be different in different contexts, so language taken from one context to another (for example, from a textbook to a student essay) will look out of place and suggest to the reader that some form of plagiarism has taken place.

A language tip

In this chapter we might look at the ways that the writers use to link each section, apart from the first, to the one(s) before. The sections begin:

- *Elements other than words can also form part of an idiolect . . .*
  This forms a contrast with what has gone before, signalled by *also.*

- *One of the greatest problems which confronts a forensic linguist . . .*
  The previous section has established that doing forensic linguistics is far from straightforward. This section moves on to the main problem for such researchers.

- *In some cases the challenge is quite different.*
  Here the connection with the previous section is one of contrast.

- *As pointed out above, we are surprised as readers . . .*
  The section begins with 'old' information, signalled by *as pointed out above.* The old

information is then linked to a 'new' question: *the question of the point at which similar moves to dissimilar.*

* *We have attempted to show . . .*
  The concluding section begins conventionally with a summary of the argument in the chapter as a whole.

**To think
about**

1 Is the idea of plagiarism familiar to you? If not, make sure you ask about it when you start your course.

2 Look at the example of the passage from Coates and the student text. Do you agree that the student has behaved wrongly in writing as he/she did?

3 According to these writers, can a corpus study prove guilt or innocence?

CHAPTER 10

Who wrote this? The linguist as detective

Alison Johnson and David Woolls

Our chapter title was provided by the editors. The question it asks takes us straight to the heart of the problem we shall address. To ask such a question implies that it is reasonable to expect a particular 'this', a piece of writing which has a particular 'who' as an author. What we explore is why this is a reasonable assumption and why, despite this fact, the task of the linguist as a detective is by no means straightforward.

This form of linguistic analysis is usually described as Forensic Linguistics, because it requires the linguist to provide data of evidential value to a court or disciplinary hearing. We will first examine the sort of questions of the 'Who wrote this?' type that are asked and how they may be answered. We also examine the effect of the amount of data which is available to assist the linguist as detective in coming to a decision, which is generally, but not always, quite small. And finally we discuss what we mean by two texts being linguistically similar.

Here are some examples of areas where the question 'Who wrote this?' is asked of linguists:

1 A set of emails with different sender names are suspected to be from one author. Can a common linguistic link be found?
2 A series of anonymous extortion or threatening letters are received by a company. Are there linguistic grounds which point to one person as the sender or are more people involved?
3 Two students admit to having colluded but each is blaming the other. As the disciplinary consequences are different for the copyist and the supplier of the original, are there linguistic indications of the direction of the copying?
4 An organization has a large set of data which should all be independently produced. Is it possible to identify automatically all individual sentences which are shared in exact or modified form in the whole set?

What all these questions have in common is that a linguist is asked to give an opinion. It is important to realize that an opinion is all that can normally be given. Even with the very large collections of material available electronically, and the amount of text of different sorts available to any internet user, there is no equivalent of a linguistic fingerprint unique to an individual (see Coulthard 2004; Coulthard and Johnson 2007). However, there is considerable evidence of what is called 'idiolect' (Coulthard 2004), a particular way of selecting and putting words together, and it is this that allows an opinion to be formed on which one of two or three potential authors or speakers was likely to be responsible for a particular text or series of utterances.

Three fundamental assumptions

The first assumption is that most sequences of words are unlikely to be selected and arranged in the same order by two individuals, whether writing on the same topic or not. Pinker (1994: 87) presents it thus:

> Go into the Library of Congress and pick a sentence at random from any volume, and chances are you would fail to find an exact repetition no matter how long you continue to search. Estimates of the number of sentences that an ordinary person is capable of producing are breathtaking. If a speaker is interrupted at a random point in a sentence, there are on average about ten different words that could be inserted at that point to continue the sentence in a grammatical and meaningful way.

While Pinker's statements are assertions, since it is impossible to empirically demonstrate either proposition, they are the assumptions which lie behind suspicion of plagiarism that arises when a reader even partially recognizes a sentence. And his second assertion (If a speaker is interrupted) is relatively simple to demonstrate.

If one were to interrupt a speaker after 'The . . .', the number of potential words which might follow covers the full range of nouns, adjectives and adverbs in English. If one were to interrupt after 'On the other . . .' the possibilities might appear to be more limited. The word 'hand' might have occurred to you, but in fact any noun that might fill the slot would be acceptable, for example 'side' (of a street, a postcard), 'bank' (of a river), 'page' (of a letter), unless the speaker was making a contrast with a previous statement, in which case 'hand' would be by far the most probable.

The second assumption is that extended common sequences are even more indicative of a common source. Consider these two lists of adjectives:

idle, poor, profligate, cowardly, gentle
productive, wealthy, thrifty, brave, violent.

These can be found in successive sentences in *SparkNotes* (Ward and Said, 11 November 2007):

> Unoka was idle, poor, profligate, cowardly, gentle, and interested in music and conversation. Okonkwo consciously adopts opposite ideals and becomes productive, wealthy, thrifty, brave, violent, and adamantly opposed to music and anything else that he perceives to be 'soft,' such as conversation and emotion.

They are also found in successive sentences in three student essays, with the feature of parallelism between the pairs of antonyms retained almost exactly. Both the extent of the adjective list and the parallelism are certain to catch the attention of the marker of the set of essays. We explore this in more detail later.

The third assumption is that the nature of the content should be appropriate to the situation. This is because all writing is part of a text and has a functional and generic context. Writers are restricted by who they are writing for, so SparkNotes has a different audience than a student essay and the reader recognizes this, both in the stylistic choices of the writer (a didactic, highly descriptive one) and in the imagined audience (less knowledgeable students). The section of SparkNotes in which this entry appears is Analysis of Characters, which accounts naturally for the compactness and parallelism we have noted. The question that the three students were answering was 'How do post-colonial literatures represent the diverse roles of men and women?' By placing these two SparkNotes sentences, contrasting two males with sets of behaviours that are not notably feminine or masculine, into their essays almost without change and failing to employ such contrast as is there to address the essay question, the students drew attention to them as contextually unusual and textually inappropriate.

Non-lexical differences

Elements other than words can also form part of an idiolect, in particular in email and phone text message correspondence, where punctuation conventions and styles of abbreviation are sometimes adopted and are so consistent and different from the other material under review that it is possible to arrive at an opinion on the likely origin.

In terms of text messages, abbreviations are often particular to an individual or a peer group, and these can be difficult to simulate accurately and consistently. Text messages formed part of the evidence in the trial for murder of Stuart Campbell, the uncle of the victim Danielle Jones, in 2002. Two text messages were sent to his phone after she disappeared, both of which were suspected to have been sent by him rather by Danielle. The first message was written as:

> HIYA STU WOT U UP 2.IM IN SO MUCH TRUBLE AT HOME AT MOMENT EVONE HATES ME EVEN U! WOT THE HELL AV I DONE NOW? Y WONT U JUST TELL ME TEXT BCK PLEASE LUV DAN XXX

The message displays linguistic choices which were absent or rare in the murdered girl's messages:

> the use of capitals rather than sentence case, the spelling of 'what' as 'wot', the spelling in full of the morpheme 'one' in 'EVONE', rather than its substitution by the numeral '1', the omission of the definite article in the abbreviation of the prepositional phrase 'AT MOMENT' and the use of the full form of the word 'text' rather than an abbreviation in the phrase TEXT BCK.

> (Coulthard and Johnson 2007: 202)

Close examination of any texts under review is required to observe, quantify and express an opinion on the significance of such features in the context of the question being asked. In most such cases, the small number of possible authors allows any distinctive pattern to appear. Text messages and company emails are frequently stored and monitored, or retained by the individuals to whom they are sent. In such circumstances there is less need for supporting evidence from wider corpora, because this would only add a measure of the general probability of such features occurring. However, it is also the case that if eight out of twenty emails possessed a particular feature – for example, the use of ellipsis instead of full stops – and even one of the eight could be shown to be from a known different author from one of the other seven, the ellipsis feature would have no evidential value on its own.

Scale –
smallness of
sample

One of the greatest problems which confronts a forensic linguist is the lack of material and in particular the lack of appropriate comparative material. Even a series of threatening letters is likely to comprise a relatively short set, and finding comparable material from the suspected potential writers is not always a simple matter. Even when some material is available, the nature and purpose of that material may well be distinctly different and constrained by its communicative intent, which is unlikely to be of a threatening nature.

In recent years it has become possible to compare the features which can be extracted from any text, in relation to its syntax or use of vocabulary, with the large collections of electronic material collected in corpora such as the British National Corpus (BNC) and the Bank of English (BoE). By comparing observed patterns in the questioned material with their observable occurrence in such corpora, it is possible to form an opinion on the distinctiveness or otherwise of the pattern. We return to our SparkNotes example, starting with the two lists of adjectives:

> idle, poor, profligate, cowardly, gentle
> productive, wealthy, thrifty, brave, violent.

Apart from discovering whether the actual words have appeared together in a corpus that has been collected, tagged corpora allow a search for adjectives to find out how often, if at all, five successive adjectives are chosen together. Results in the 50 million word Bank of English revealed the following occurrences:

> *was* + 1 adjective`   45456
> *was* + 2 adjectives   1104
> *was* + 3 adjectives   103
> *was* + 4 adjectives   16
> *was* + 5 adjectives   2
> *was* + 6 adjectives   zero

This demonstrates that the use of five adjectives is extremely rare and, in the Bank of English at least, found only in novels, rather than essays. Where five adjectives are found together, each example uses different adjectives from the other:

1 talented, wonderful, beautiful, funny, musical
2 patient, thorough, steady, witty, capable.

Therefore, the probability of two individuals choosing the same five adjectives within a parallel structure is extremely unlikely. What led the researcher to the source that the students S1, S2 and S3 had used was that, even though the three students independently found the same source and used it in slightly different ways, they all had the multiple adjective pattern and the parallelism. In the extracts below, words that replace those in the source are in italics, words that have been added are underlined, and omitted words shown with Ø. Other words are exactly the same as in the source text.

EssayA

lazy, <u>effeminate</u>, poor Ø cowardly and gentle
productive, wealthy, thrifty, brave, violent,
EssayB
idle, poor, Ø, cowardly gentle
productive, <u>rich</u>, Ø, brave, violent
EssayC
idle, poor, <u>wasteful</u>, cowardly, gentle
productive, wealthy, <u>economical</u>, brave, violent

Note that EssayA breaks the parallelism by replacing 'wasteful' with 'effeminate' and then placing 'effeminate' before 'poor'. This is a helpful indicator that EssayA was (mis)using the source. Note also that the change of one word in all but the second set of EssayA makes searching for the set as a whole very difficult in a web search engine, because in such searches words are either treated as individual elements which all have to be present, or as phrases which have to be there in their entirety.

Size of collection

In some cases the challenge is quite different. In the example given next the linguist was asked to find a way of checking a very large number of texts very quickly, that is, within 10 minutes of the arrival of each text in the database concerned. The British Universities and Colleges Admissions Service (UCAS) handles nearly 500,000 applications to United Kingdom universities per year. Each application has to include a personal statement and each statement has about 30 sentences in it. UCAS required a linguistically based system for examining these statements for signs of plagiarism and collusion. The problem here is being able to find a single sentence matching another in a collection of several million. This can only be attempted and achieved with a computer program and a powerful computer. The task involved accurate identification of both identity and similarity at sentence level from a set starting at 30 million sentences (over two years) and growing. The system, *Copycatch Investigator* (Woolls 2007), was implemented in September 2007, and at the end of the major application cycle in January 2008 was taking a maximum of six minutes to check an incoming batch of 125 statements against the 500,000 statements in the index. The processing included finding the matches, identifying the most matched pairings, marking up the similar sentences and storing the output in the main database.

A pilot study for the project had shown that there was both minor and major adaptation of some sentences, to make them applicable to the particular student or course, for example. So the system has to be able to identify such changes accurately, even if they are quite extensive. This raises the issue of exactly what we mean by linguistic similarity.

Similarity

As pointed out above, we are surprised as readers when we see two, let alone three examples of what probably strike us as identical sentences. Then we are surprised again to discover that what seemed to be identical sentences actually are all slightly different from each other. Borrowed material is frequently adapted in some way, making it similar rather than identical, which then raises the question of the point at which similar moves to dissimilar. This is not generally a simple matter of counting word changes. Change can happen at both the lexical and the semantic levels. For example, if one word is changed to a thesaural equivalent, the similarity is near identity. But if the wrong substitute choice is made, the sentence can take on a different meaning while remaining lexically and structurally much the same. Or if a structural change is made, the meaning might again be disrupted. Such disruptions can be of assistance when faced with the third type of question exemplified at the start of the chapter.

Figure 10.1 shows an example taken from a student essay. The student text is on the right and the source text on the left is from Coates (1993).

| **Figure 10.1** Adapting a source | Lower-middle-class **women** style-shift very sharply: in the least **formal** style, they use quite a high proportion of the **stigmatised** variant, **but in the** three **more formal styles, they** correct **their speech to** correspond to **that of the class above them (the middle middle-class)**. **Labov** argues (1972a:243) that extreme style-shifting of **this** kind, often resulting in **hypercorrection**, is particularly marked in LMC **women**. Coates (1993: 70) | Lower middle class **women** used the **stigmatised** form frequently in their less **formal** tasks **but in the more formal styles they** then corrected **their speech to** match **that of the class above them** which is **the middle middle-class**. Such style shifting like **this** is referred to as **hypercorrection** and **Labov** (1972) states that lower middle class **women** often endorse this type of shift. Student text |

There are 62 words in the original, counting hyphenation as forming a single word, and 63 in the student work. Of these, the 26 words marked in bold are exact in form but not necessarily in use. There are a further six underlined words or word groups, where there are changes of hyphenation ('style-shifting' versus 'style shifting'), expansion ('LMC' becomes 'lower middle class') or tense ('use' becomes 'used').

The omission of hyphenation loses the classification element signalled in the original for both 'lower-middle-class', encapsulated as 'LMC' in the second sentence and for 'style-shifting'. In the original, Coates is describing the phenomenon of sharp style-shift, contrasting 'the least formal' with the 'three more formal'. The student has interpreted this in the first instance as relating to use in particular situations, while carrying out 'less formal tasks'. This implies that 'tasks' is synonymous with 'styles' which is neither what Coates wrote nor makes a great deal of sense.

The changes of tense in 'used' and 'corrected' (in the student text) implies that this is a report on research. Coates is reporting an observation of usage. The replacement of 'quite a high proportion' with 'frequently' potentially overstates the level of occurrence of the stigmatized variant. Replacing 'correspond' with 'match' is a much closer thesaural equivalent.

In the second sentence the changes made amount to a complete misrepresentation both of Labov and what Coates was reporting. The student equates style shifting with hypercorrection, as opposed to the style-shifting often resulting in hypercorrection, and turns Labov's 'argument' into a 'state[ment]' and the observation of style-shift occurrence as 'marked' into an 'endorse[ment]' <u>by</u> the women of their action.

This example has been used to illustrate that although the lexical identity or similarity in both sentences is sufficient for a computer program to identify that the sentences are related to each other, it requires human analysis to decide whether they are two ways of saying the same thing. Where it is decided they are not, it also requires a human to determine the direction of the dependence. We argue in this case that, whether we knew the origin or not, it is easier to explain the misinterpretation as explicated above than the re-interpretation which would have been required to generate the Coates text from that of the student.

Conclusion

We have attempted to show that speakers and original authors leave evidence of both their idiolect and their purpose in the transcribed or written texts a forensic linguist is given to examine. And we have also attempted to show how those seeking to misuse, imitate or conceal leave their own traces and fail to remove all evidence of the original author. It is important to understand that such identification and explanation is all a linguist is being asked to do. This is true of all detective work. The task of assembling the evidence for a prosecution or defence case is undertaken by those for whom the evidence is requested. The task of deciding on innocence or guilt is that of a judge, a jury or a disciplinary board. In assessing the texts available, the linguist must attempt the maximum objectivity. This is not always easy to achieve, because we will normally have been approached by the prosecution or defence who will have outlined what their position is and who are clearly hoping for linguistic evidence to support their case. And, as we have pointed out, knowledge of the context in which the texts were produced is an essential part of the linguist's evaluation of what is found. But objectivity allows us to view the texts as texts, in their particular setting and purpose, and provide an opinion on whether the texts show evidence of interference, attempted concealment of copying, attempted imitation of style or any other feature, and to provide a measure of certainty about the significance of such features in respect of the texts, but not directly in respect of the case of which the texts form a part.

References

Coates, J. (1993) *Women, Men, and Language: a sociolinguistic account of gender differences in language*. London: Longman.

Coulthard, M. (2004) 'Author identification, idiolect and linguistic uniqueness', *Applied Linguistics*, 25, 4, 431–447.

Coulthard, M. and Johnson, A. (2007) *An Introduction to Forensic Linguistics: Language in Evidence*. London: Routledge.

Pinker, Steven (1994) *The Language Instinct: How the Mind Creates Language*. New York: William Morrow and Company.

Ward, Selena and Said, Zahr. *SparkNote on Things Fall Apart.* Online. Available HTTP: http://www.sparknotes.com/lit/things/ (accessed 11 November 2007).

Woolls, D. (2007) *Copycatch Investigator* an automated, large-scale computerized plagiarism detection program. Online. Available HTTP: http://www.copycatchgold.com (accessed 21 November 2007).

Introduction to chapter 11

The background to this chapter

This chapter is one of four chapters dealing with topics in Applied Linguistics that do not relate directly to language teaching. The chapter gives us a demonstration of how a translator tackles the various decisions that translating a text throws up, at the same time relating these decisions to issues in translation theory. The key concepts in the chapter are: semantic similarity (or commonality, or resemblance), domestication and foreignization, cultural and contextual variance (or difference).

Translation is a paradox. One aim of the translator is to produce a text that 'means the same' as the original text. Yet it is clearly impossible for words or sentences in one language and culture to 'mean the same' as those in another. If two apparent synonyms in one language (e.g. *lady, woman* or *flat, apartment*) are not in fact the same at all, how much less can two utterances in different languages be anything like the same? In theory, translation should be impossible. Yet, in the real world, translation happens all the time – indeed, it is one of the main tasks of linguists to make translations happen. The world is full of translations, and if it were not so, people from different countries would find communication almost impossible.

In this chapter Malmkjær makes it clear that a translator is always working to find a way of making the translated text 'the same' as the original. The sameness might be semantic, finding at least a semblance of similarity of meaning between the two. It might be idiomatic – finding an expression that is as colloquial, or as strange, or as funny, as one used in the original text. It might carry the same kind of resemblance to other texts or customs or cultural artefacts in the target language as the original text does in its own language. It might have a similarity in terms of sounds or rhythm. It is unlikely that a translated text can be the same as the original in all these ways at once, and the translator is constantly finding a balance between them all.

At the same time, however, a translator might choose sometimes to avoid sameness and to emphasize the difference of the translated text, to remind the reader that they are reading something originally written in a foreign language. The reader might be expected to work harder at interpreting the translation, mimicking perhaps the experience of reading something in a foreign language and working out what it means.

The chapter demonstrates how the translator works through a text finding a series of balances between 'same' and 'different' and between different kinds of 'same'. The text used to demonstrate this is a famous story by the Danish writer Hans Christian Andersen, which has often been either translated or re-told in English. The best-known title in English is 'The Princess and the Pea'. The essence of the story is that a princess is invited to sleep on a mattress under which a pea has been placed. The princess is so sensitive that she cannot sleep, even when many mattresses are piled on top of each other. According to the story, her sensitivity proves that she is a genuine princess.

Focusing on the argument

Malmkjær sets out the essence of her argument in the introduction to the chapter and the remainder of the chapter demonstrates the process of working through a translation. We follow all the debates and decisions that the translator has to take in pro-gressing sentence by sentence through a text. Each decision relates to one or more of the principles set out at the end of the introduction, often balancing one against the other.

In terms of constructing an argument, this is an unusual chapter, because it proceeds sequentially through an activity rather than presenting, say, one side and then another of a debate. It works well, though, in bringing together all that a translator does in a genuine context, and impressing us with just how much a good translator knows about both the languages and the cultures she (in this case) is working with.

A language tip   Two of the tasks of the translator represented by Malmkjær are, in my opinion, quite difficult to process. An example of the first is:

a translator creates semantic resemblance out of linguistic variance

This uses nominalization (as described in chapter 3) in *resemblance* and *variance*. We might unpack the noun groups to say:

‘two texts resemble each other in semantic terms’ and
‘two languages are quite different from each other’

We need to add to this the structure ‘a translator creates x out of y’ to get a paraphrase such as:

‘A translator must write a text that resembles another one in meaning even though the languages they are written in are quite different from each other.’

The second difficult sentence is:

a translator selects target language norm conforming forms that are as close as possible to the source text formalities

This has a wonderfully long noun phrase: *target language norm conforming forms*. It might be paraphrased as ‘forms that are usual for the target language’. Another slightly shorter noun phrase is: *source text formalities* which might be paraphrase as ‘forms that are found in the original text’.

To think about

1   What do you understand by ‘Foreignization’ and ‘Domestication’? Can you find examples of both in Malmkjær’s translation?
2   What special problems do discourse particles present to the translator?
3   Malmkjær frequently discusses a single word but then chooses to reproduce the effect of the word by choosing a different phrase altogether. Can you find and explain one example of this?

CHAPTER 11

The translator's choice

Kirsten Malmkjær

A translated text is made on the basis of a translator's understanding of another text, which is usually immediately present while the translator is translating. Often, the purpose of translating is to convey at least some of what is conveyed by this immediately present text which will therefore both exercise a major influence on the translation and be evident in it (to people who have access to both texts). In other words, there is usually an expectation of strong semantic similarity between a text and its translation. The standard expectation with regard to the languages involved is, however, the opposite – that there will not be evidence of the language of the source text in the translation; such evidence is described using the pejorative terms, 'false friends'[1] and 'translationese'.[2] But insofar (and it is very far) as linguistic formalities contribute to meaning they must nevertheless be respectfully considered and dealt with in translating.

With regard to the treatment of cultural and contextual factors in translation, translators make strategic choices between either including cultural and contextual markers from the original, or adjusting to the norms of the culture where the translation is to function. This type of choice has been discussed throughout the history of translation theory, especially famously in terms of Schleiermacher's (1838) distinction between taking either the reader to the text or the text to the reader, and most recently in the guise of Venuti's (1995) distinction between Foreignization and Domestication. Whether all the manifestations of the distinction are actually manifestations of exactly the same distinction need not detain us here.[3]

Obviously, any (competent) reader will form an understanding of a text that they are reading; but whereas readers typically keep their understanding to themselves unless asked to reveal it, translators can hardly help displaying aspects of their understanding in their translation. This is most evident in cases of ambiguous source texts. For example, in the Viking Ship Museum in Oslo is a piece of wood with a runic inscription, given in Norwegian as *lite klokt menneske* ('little clever human'). The English translation provided is 'unwise person' and the German *kleiner kluger Mensch* ('small clever human').

A translator's understanding of the purpose of and the audience for the translation considerably affects the degree to which the translator decides to comply with the expectation of semantic commonality between the source text and the translation. For example, it is probably Mary Howitt's (1846) desire to produce a set of 'Wonderful Stories for Children' – and Victorian children at that – which causes her to play fast and loose with the semantic commonality expectation in examples such as the following:

From Andersen (1839), *Storkene* ('The storks' my translation)
      'Now we'll be revenged!' they said.
   'To be sure' said the mother stork. 'My plan is just right!

From Howitt (1846: 126–7) 'The storks':
            'Now let's have revenge,' said they.
         'Leave off talking of revenge,' said the mother. 'Listen to me, which is
   a great deal better.

So, in making a translation, a translator (i) creates semantic resemblance out of linguistic variance; (ii) selects target language norm conforming forms that are as close as possible to the source text formalities; (iii) decides how to deal with cultural and contextual variance; and (iv) considers the purpose of and audience for the translation – all against the background of (v) his or her understanding of the source text. This task presents translators with numerous types of choice and opportunities for creativity, as I shall seek to illustrate in the remainder of this article, which describes a process of translating a short, literary text.

Making a translation

The text to be translated was written in 1835 by the Danish writer Hans Christian Andersen. I will describe the process of translating it in the context of 20 existing translations – a small selection of the English translations of this text – occasionally referring to the choices made there. The original text is in italics; my translation is in bold.

The story's title, *Prindsessen paa Ærten*, means, straightforwardly,

'The princess on the pea'

Translators through the 173 years that separate us from the story have also chosen (earliest use only mentioned):

The princess and the peas (three in Boner's translation)
The princess and the parched pea (De Chatelain)
The real princess (Peachy, picking up a story theme)
The princess on the bean (Wehnert – unclear why a bean should be preferred)
The princess and the pea (Paull – 'and' is chosen regularly, despite the original and despite the princess clearly being on the pea).

The story begins

Der var engang en Prinds ('**There was once a prince**').

The text is of the genre known in English as the fairy tale, and *der var engang* is the standard opening for the corresponding Danish genre. In English, the standard opening is 'Once upon a time', so the translator may decide between domesticating the text, choosing 'Once upon a time' or foreignizing it, using the semantically much closer 'There was once'. The existing translations are evenly split among the two.

I opt for the foreignizing translation, because I want my translation to maintain its cultural identity and I do not think that my choice at this point will be so odd as to alienate any potential reader.

Next, we learn that

han vilde have sig en Prindsesse ('he [the prince] would have himself a princess')

Here, Andersen has chosen one of the colloquialisms for which his story style is famous: '*han vilde have* sig', using the reflexive *sig*, although *han vilde have en prinsesse* ('he would have a princess') would have been perfectly possible. In English, 'he wanted to have' is a similarly unnecessarily elaborate form compared to the minimalist 'he wanted', so I opt for

'he wanted to have a princess'.

We now read,

men det skulde være en rigtig Prindsesse ('but it should be a real princess').

Quite obviously and unproblematically, in compliance with English linguistic conventions, 'it' becomes 'she', 'should be' becomes 'would have to be', and I select 'a real princess' for the rest, making

'but she would have to be a real princess'.

I use that adjective for each occurrence in this text of *rigtig*. This reproduces a link established in the story between the princess and the story itself by the use of the adjective *rigtig* to modify nouns denoting the princess or princesses in general in four of 11 cases where such a noun occurs, and, in the final line of the story, to modify the noun that self-refers to the story, *en rigtig Historie* ('a real story') (see also Malmkjær 1995, 2003). I know this because I have read the story through before beginning to translate.

But adjectives typically provide numerous possibilities in translation, and as well as my choice, the following have been used in my corpus of translations: 'really and truly a princess'; 'genuine'; 'proper'; 'truly real'.

Saa reiste han hele Verden rundt, for at finde saadan en, ('then travelled he the whole world around for to find such one'),

we now read, and this can be adjusted to English linguistic conventions without difficulty: 'Then he travelled the whole world around to find one'. A Dane will feel some pain at the use of the starkly unmodified 'one' where the original has the softly rhythmic 'saadan en', an expression so common in spoken Danish that Danish novice English speakers are often heard transferring its cadence to English: 'to find such a one'. Of course, this loss will never strike an English reader, and it is for an English reader that the translation is being made. Nevertheless, I try to make some amends by infusing my translation with the rhythm of 'hele verden rundt' and writing

'Then he travelled all around the world to find one',

because 'all around the world' has its stressed and unstressed syllables arranged exactly like *hele verden rundt*.

The continuation of the sentence poses an interesting problem concerning the ordering of clauses and obviously, therefore, the ordering of the information they contain:

> *men allevegne var der noget i Veien, Prindsesser vare der nok af, men om det vare rigtige Prindsesser, kunde han ikke ganske komme efter, altid var der noget, som ikke var saa rigtigt* ('but everywhere was there something in the way, princesses were there enough of, but whether it were real princesses could he not quite come after, always was there something which not was so right').

I will pass over in silence most of the linguistic adjustments to be made here, to concentrate on how to deal with *men om det vare rigtige Prindsesser, kunde han ikke ganske komme efter, altid var der noget,* ('but whether it were real princesses could he not quite come after, always was there something'). It would be perfectly possible to write in English:

> 'but everywhere something was wrong, there were plenty of princesses, but whether they were real princesses, he could not really tell (or 'not quite decide'; or . . .), always something was not quite right'

but I think that the following sounds more natural:

> **'but everywhere something was wrong, there were plenty of princesses, but he could never be quite sure whether they were real princesses, there was always something that was not quite right about them'.**

But making this choice, I lose the foregrounding through fronting of the question of 'whether they were real princesses' and of 'always' relative to 'he could not tell' and 'there was something . . .' respectively, and this may be a problem in light of the focus in the story on how to identify a princess.

So far, I have pretended, by way of absence of comment, that glossing a text with the words of another language is unproblematic, and I have slyly used words rather than morphemes in my gloss. It looks cleaner and easier to gloss, for example, *Verden* as 'the world' than as 'world DEF'; but the next sentence introduces a complication that forces me to come clean:

> *Saa kom han da hjem igjen og var saa bedrøvet, for han vilde saa gjerne have en virkelig Prindsesse.*

It is the fourth word, *da*, which causes the problem:

> 'then came he *da* home again and was so sad, for he wanted so fain to have a genuine princess'.

Da is a discourse particle, and as Allen et al. remark (1995: 366), 'it is not always possible to provide a literal translation' into English for words of that class. They suggest that 'surely' provides a rough guide to the meaning of *da* generally, and that is so. Nevertheless, I choose

> **'So then he came home again and was very sad, because he wanted so much to have a genuine princess'.**

This is because the Danish discourse particles are unstressed and slip their contribution into stretches of text almost unnoticed, like the 'So' in front of 'then' does in my chosen English expression; besides, in the original, *da* conveys a sense that what the expression reports is a consequence of what has been reported before it, just as 'so' seems to me to do in my English choice.

In this sentence we also meet the second (and only other) adjective used to modify nouns that denote the princess in this story, *virkelig*. I translate it as 'genuine', because I think the story is partly about how to decide whether a princess is genuine or simply conforms to a princess stereotype, and that Andersen signals this by means of a contrast between being 'rigtig' (stereotypical, socially conformist) and being 'virkelig' (genuine) throughout his entire opus (see Malmkjær 1995, 2003). I know this because I have read a good deal of this opus and I have noticed the pattern because I am accustomed to stylistic analysis. All the translators in my corpus select 'real'.

In the first sentence of the second paragraph of the story we meet *da* once more, but here it arguably functions as an adverb of time:

> *En Aften blev det da et frygteligt Veir; det lynede og tordnede, Regnen skyllede ned, det var ganske forskrækkeligt! Saa bankede det paa Byens Port, og den gamle Konge gik hen at lukke op.* ('One evening became it then a terrible weather; it thundered and lightened, the rain poured down, it was quite frightful! Then knocked it on the town's gate, and the old king went along to open up.')

I make of this:

> **'Then one evening the weather turned truly awful; there was thunder and lightning and pouring rain, it was quite terrible! Then there was a knock on the town gate and the old king went along to open it.'**

I use 'truly', not to convey any sense of *da*, because I think its sense here is 'then', but to give emphasis to the nastiness of the weather by adding extra syllables to its modification. The translation may seem to over-emphasize sequentiality by fronting the temporal adverbials ('then') twice in close succession (where the original only fronts *Saa*), but this is not unusual in texts of this genre.

As we learn who the visitor is, we come across a feature which no translation that I have ever seen of this or any other story by Andersen has retained, namely the exclamation *Gud* ('God'):

> *Det var en Prindsesse, som stod udenfor. Men Gud hvor hun saae ud af Regnen og det onde Veir! Vandet løb ned af hendes Haar og hendes Klæder, og det løb ind af Næsen paa Skoen og ud af Hælen, og saa sagde hun, at hun var en virkelig Prindsesse.* ('It was a princess who stood outside. But God how she looked from the rain and the evil weather! The water ran down from her hair and her clothes, and it ran in through the nose of the shoe and out through the heel, and then said she that she was a genuine princess.')

I retain the exclamation, however, in the interest of the cultural identity mentioned earlier; again, this amounts to a foreignizing decision:

> **'It was a princess who was standing outside. But God what a sight she was with the rain and the evil weather! Water was running down her hair and her clothes, and in at the toes of her shoes and out at the heels, and yet she said that she was a genuine princess'.**

Next, we hear how the old queen intends to test this strong claim:

> *»Ja, det skal vi nok faae at vide!« tænkte den gamle Dronning, men hun sagde ikke noget, gik ind i Sovekammeret, tog alle Sengklæderne af og lagde en Ært paa Bunden af Sengen, derpaa tog hun tyve Matrasser, lagde dem ovenpaa ærten, og saa endnu tyve Edderduuns-Dyner oven paa Matrasserne.*
>
> *Der skulde nu Prindsessen ligge om Natten.*

> ('Yes, that shall we *nok* get to know!' thought the old queen, but she said not anything, went into the bedroom, took all the bedclothes off and laid a pea on the bottom of the bed, thereupon took she twenty mattresses, laid them on top of the pea, and then yet twenty eiderdown-quilts on top of the mattresses.
>
> There should now the princess lie at night.)

I find myself unable to gloss the discourse particle, *nok*, in the highly idiomatic phrase of speech which opens this passage. Nevertheless, it causes me no translation difficulty because there is a similarly idiomatic phrase in English, which I select:

> **'Well, we'll soon see about that!' thought the old queen, but she didn't say anything, went into the bedroom, took all the bedclothes off and put a pea on the bottom of the bed, then she put twenty mattresses on top of the pea, and then another twenty eiderdown-quilts on top of the mattresses.**
>
> **That was where the princess was to lie that night.**

It happens often in translating that the contribution to a text of an item without a formal equivalent is unproblematically rendered, neatly illustrating the fact that words do not make their contribution to text individually, but in unison, and that the meaning of a stretch of text is more or other than the meanings of its parts.

The princess goes to bed, we must assume, and then,

> *Om Morgenen spurgte de hende, hvorledes hun havde sovet.*
> *»O forskrækkeligt slet!« sagde Prindsessen, »Jeg har næsten ikke lukket mine Øine den hele Nat! Gud veed, hvad der har været i Sengen? Jeg har ligget paa noget haardt, saa jeg er ganske bruun og blaa over min hele Krop! Det er ganske forskrækkeligt!«*

('In the morning asked they her how she had slept. 'Oh terribly badly!' said the princess, 'I have almost not closed my eyes the whole night! God knows what there has been in the bed? I have lain on something hard, so I am quite brown and blue over my whole body! It is quite terrible!')

Again, the exclamation, *Gud* ('God') has not been used in any existing translations. With regard to the discolouration of the princess's body, the existing translations all agree that bruising is black and blue in English, and on this occasion I feel no need to maintain the Danish language habit:

In the morning they asked they her how she had slept. 'Oh terribly badly!' said the princess, 'I have hardly closed my eyes the entire night! God knows what was in that bed? I've been lying on something hard, so that I am black and blue all over! It is quite terrible!'

And everyone is happy that the test has worked:

> *Saa kunde de see, at det var en rigtig Prindsesse, da hun gjennem de tyve Matrasser og de tyve Edderduuns Dyner havde mærket Ærten. Saa ømskindet kunde der ingen være, uden en virkelig Prindsesse.* ('Then could they see that it was a real princess as she through the twenty mattresses and the twenty eiderdown quilts had felt the pea. So tenderskinned could there no one be except a genuine princess.')

Ømskindet ('tender skinned'), which is mainly used in Danish as a metaphor for mental hyper-sensitivity, is used in this passage to denote the princess's skin's susceptibility to injury, which, in turn, is believed to be a sign that the princess is real and/or genuine. It is difficult to encapsulate all this in an English expression: 'thin skinned' does not connote 'refined' and 'tender skinned' lacks the familiarity enjoyed by *ømskindet*. The existing translations give: 'tender'; 'delicate ((sense of) feeling)' 'so very fine a sense of feeling'; 'sensitive'; 'have such delicate skin'; 'tender skin'; and 'tender skinned'. I go with the two translators who have 'tender skinned', since none of the other expressions come any closer to conveying all that *ømskindet* conveys, and because it will at least show itself as a metaphor, given the number of quilts and mattresses that separate the princess from the pea. I credit my readership with the ability to working out the metaphorical implications productively:

'Then they could see that she was a real princess as she had been able to feel the pea
through the twenty mattresses and the twenty eiderdown quilts. No one but a
genuine princess could be that tender skinned'.

And the quest is at an end:

Prindsen tog hende da til Kone, for nu vidste han, at han havde en rigtig Prindsesse, ('The
prince took her then to wife, for now he knew that he had a real princess'),

with sweet irony insofar as it is the princess's skin – a surface feature – that has been
tested. Does that make her genuine? No, it makes her stereotypical, and again I use the
adjective 'real':

'So the prince took her as his wife, for now he knew that he had a real princess.'

But there is more:

og Ærten kom paa Kunstkammeret, hvor den endnu er at see, dersom ingen har taget den.
('and the pea came on the art chamber, where it still is to see if no one has taken it').

Only minimal adjustment is necessary here:

'and the pea was put in the royal collection where it is still to be seen if no-one has
taken it'.

But these clauses remind the initiated of the sad affair of two horns made of gold, dating
from around 450, which were unearthed in 1639 and 1734 respectively in a field in
southern Jutland and subsequently stolen from the royal collection in 1802 by a
goldsmith who melted them down. This piece of history is so far from being directly
written in as to be beyond even the pragmatics of the text (let alone the semantics) and
I do not include it within my translation. I would add it in a footnote to a scholarly
edition (in either language: not every Dane would make the connection).

 And now we are at the end of the story and Andersen addresses the reader directly,
using the imperative form to frame a declaration that the story matches the princess in
one respect:

See, det var en rigtig Historie! ('See, that was a real story')

And it was, if 'real' indicates stereotypicality: a story of a prince on a quest which is accom-
plished with the help of the old queen who has the wisdom to test the object of the quest;
but is it? but does she? the ambiguities remain to the end, but by retaining the adjective
patterning I allow the reader to decide for themselves where the irony, if any, resides.

'You see, that was a real story.'

Notes

1 Terms in two (or more) languages that resemble each other formally but not semantically can be false friends. Mary Howitt's (1846: 45) 'listened' is a false friend of the
Danish term *listede* ('tip-toed') in the following clause from *Tommelise* (Andersen 1835):

Andersen   *Næste Nat listede hun sig   igjen   ned   til den*
GLOSS   next night tip-toed she REFLEXIVE again down to it
Howitt   Next night she listened again

2 'Translationese' is a term used to characterize stretches of a translation in which the
structure of the language of the source text is clearly evident and unusual or inappropriate in light of the conventions and rules of the language of the translation, as in
the following clause from a tourist brochure translated into English from Italian:

English: The date of building of the fortress and of the Rivellino (which is the coun-
terfort) is presumably around the year 1000.

Italian: La data di construzione della Rocca e del Rivellino (che è il suo contrafforte) si
fa risalire intorno all'anno 1000.

3 A clear example of domestication/taking the text to the reader is Barbara Ker Wilson's
translation of (1975) *Alice in Wonderland* (Caroll 1865), in which, for example, the
White Rabbit with its fan and gloves becomes the Kangaroo with a dilly-bag and
digging-stick and in which the illustrations show, not a typically English Alice in a
typically English landscape, but an Aborigine girl whose name is Alitji, gracing an
Australian landscape.
   Examples of foreignizing translations include *The History of Danish Dreams*, Barbara
Haveland's (1995) translation into English of Peter Høeg's (1988) *Forestilling om det
Tyvende Århundrede*, which retains all characters' and place names in Danish, but which
compensates for this by including at the back a list of historical characters, with brief
biographies, to assist the English reader who would otherwise find it difficult to grasp
the import of, for example, a scene which deals with a party at which both Casper
Bartholin (1585–1629) and Ole Rømer (1644–1710) are present.

References

Allen, Robin, Holmes, Philip and Lundskær-Nielsen, Tom 1995 *Danish: A Comprehensive
   Grammar* London and New York: Routledge.
Howitt, Mary 1846 *Wonderful Stories for Children. By Hans Christian Anderson* [sic], *Author
   of 'The Improvisatore' etc.* London: Chapman and Hall.
Høeg, Peter 1988 *Forestilling om det Tyvende Århundrede.* Copenhagen: Munksgaard/
   Rosinante. Translated from the Danish by Barbara Haveland, *The History of Danish
   Dreams.* London: The Harvill Press, 1995.
Ker Wilson, Barbara (ed) 1975 *Alitjinya Ngura Tjukurtjarangka (Alitji in the Dreamtime)*,
   translated from the Pitjantjatjara adaptation and translation of Carroll's *Alice in
   Wonderland* by Nancy Sheppard. South Australia: University of Adelaide.
Malmkjær, Kirsten 1995 'What's in an adjective?: Using cross-textual patterns of collocation
   in translating' *Norwich Papers in Languages, Literatures and Cultures* 3: 44–54.

Malmkjær, Kirsten 2003 'On a pseudo-subversive use of corpora in translator training'. In Federico Zanettin, Silvia Bernardini and Dominic Stewart (eds) *Corpora in Translator Education*. Manchester: St. Jerome, pp. 119–134.

Schleiermacher, Friedrich Daniel Ernst 1838 'On the different methods of translating' ('Ueber die verschiedenen Methoden des Uebersezens'). Lecture 3 of *Abhandlungen gelesen in der Königlichen Akademie der Wissenschaften*, pp. 207–245 in Volume 2 (1838) of *Zur Philosophie* (9 volumes) Berlin: G. Reimer. English translation in Douglas Robinson 1997 *Western Translation Theory: From Herodotus to Nietzsche*. Manchester: St. Jerome, pp. 225–238.

Venuti, Lawrence 1995 *The Translator's Invisibility* London and New York: Routledge.

Source for Andersen's original texts

H.C. Andersens Eventyr: Kritisk udgivet efter de originale Eventyrhæfter med Varianter ved Erik Dal og Kommentar ved Erling Nielsen. 1963–1966. Copenhagen: Hans Reitzels Forlag.

Sources for the translations of the example text

In chronological order of date of publication.

A Danish Story-Book by Hans Christian Andersen. With numerous illustrations by Count Pocci. Charles Boner, London: Joseph Cundall, 1846.

Tales and Fairy Stories. Madame de Chatelain, London: Routledge & Co, 1852.

Danish Fairy Legends and Tales. Caroline Peachey, London: Henry G. Bohn, 1861.

Hans Christian Andersen's Stories for the Household. H.W. Dulcken, London: Routledge, 1866. Re-issued as *The Complete Illustrated Works of Hans Christian Andersen*. London: Chancellor Press, 1983; 1994.

Andersen's Tales for Children. Wehnert, Alfred, London: Bell & Daldy, 1869.

Hans Andersen's Tales for the Young. A New Translation by Mrs. H. B. Paull. London: Warne, 1872.

The Complete Andersen, I–VI. All of the 168 stories by Hans Christian Andersen (some never before translated into English, and a few never before published) now freshly translated [...] by JEAN HERSHOLT with an Appendix containing the unpublished tales, a Chronological Listing, an Index, and the Notes, and with hand-colored illustrations by FRITZ KREDEL. The Limited Editions Club, New York. 1949.

Hans Christian Andersen: Fairy Tales. Translator not named. London etc.: Hamlyn. 1959.

Hans Andersen's Fairy Tales: A Selection. Translated from the Danish by L.W. Kingsland. London: Oxford University Press, 1959.

Hans Christian Andersen. Fairy Tales and Stories. Translated, with an Introduction, by Reginald Spink. London, 1960. Republished in the series Everyman's Library Children's Classics, London, 1992.

Hans Christian Andersen: Fairy Tales. Translated by Marie-Louise Peulevé. Odense: Skandinavisk Bogforlag. No Date (but pre-1966).

Hans Andersen's Fairy Tales. Translated by Pat Shaw Iversen. New York: Signet, 1981 (1966).

The Complete Fairy Tales and Stories. Translated from the Danish by Erik Christian Haugaard. Foreword by Naomi Lewis. London: Gollanz, 1974. Also published, with a foreword by Virginia Haviland, New York: Doubleday & Co. New Edition, Gollancz Children's Paperbacks, 1994.

Hans Christian Andersen: Eighty Fairy Tales. Translated by R.P. Keigwin. Odense:

Skandinavisk Bogforlag, 1976. With an introduction by Elias Bredsdorff. New York: Pantheon Books, 1982.

Tales from Hans Andersen. Translated by Stephen Corrin, 1978. London: Guild Publishing, 1989.

Hans Andersen's Fairy Tales. Translated by Naomi Lewis. London: Puffin Books, 1981.

'The Princess on the Pea', Sara and Stephen Corrin. In *The Faber Book of Favourite Fairy Tales*, London and Boston: Faber and Faber 1988.

Hans Christian Andersen. Stories and Fairy Tales selected, translated and illustrated by Erik Blegvad. London, 1993.

Hans Christian Andersen Fairy Tales. Translated by Tiina Nunally, Edited and Introduced by Jackie Wullschlager. London and New York: Penguin Books, 2004.

The Stories of Hans Christian Andersen. Selected and Translated by Diana Crone Frank and Jeffrey Frank. London: Granta Books, 2004.

Introduction to chapter 12

This chapter addresses an issue in the general area of inter-cultural communication. Researchers in this area have sometimes distinguished between different types of society and have attempted to characterize various national or cultural groups. One of the topics they sometimes deal with is that of a 'stereotype'. If you have a stereotype of the people in another country you believe that all the people in that country have certain characteristics. For example, you may believe that British people are unfriendly – this would be a negative stereotype. Or you may believe that British people are polite – this would be a positive stereotype. Both positive and negative stereotypes are likely to be untrue. No doubt some British people are unfriendly, some are polite, and some are both, but many are only slightly unfriendly, or not polite at all, and so on. In fact, if you describe an opinion as a stereotype you mean that it is not true. In this chapter Adrian Holliday discusses two views of such stereotyping, asking whether it is harmful or beneficial, and suggests how someone visiting or working in another country might respond to stereotypes. The key issues introduced in this chapter are: the characterization of cultures; critical applied linguistics; and inter-cultural communication.

The background to this chapter

There is an established research tradition which investigates and measures attitudes in different countries and uses the results to characterize the cultures of those countries. Hofstede, who is mentioned in this chapter, is one of the earliest and best-known writers to use these measurements. He proposes a number of ways in which societies can vary from one another, including a distinction between societies oriented towards the 'individual' and those that prioritize the 'collective'. In general, by these measurements, societies in Western Europe and North America are considered to be 'individual' and those in the rest of the world are considered to be 'collective'.

Such cultural characterizations can be seen to be 'stereotypes'. As the quotation at the beginning of this chapter makes clear, if you call an idea a 'stereotype' you mean that it is ill-considered and over-simple – in short, it is harmful. Holliday quotes several people who suggest that cultural characterizations of the type made by Hofstede and others are always harmful, for several reasons. First, the characterizations make it seem that everyone in the country concerned is the same as everyone else. Second, they emphasize the differences between countries and cultures instead of acknowledging the similarities. Third, characterizations are often biased – for example, it may be considered better to be 'individual' than to be 'collective'. This may be because cultures have more often been characterized by researchers from Western countries than by those in Asia (for example), so the interpretations reflect Western ideas.

Holliday makes an interesting link between the notion of stereotypes and discussions about methods in English Language Teaching. He argues that stereotypes make people think of other cultures as 'different' and as 'inferior'. Many writers also argue that ideas about ELT such as 'communicative language teaching is the best method' or 'native speaker teachers are better than non-native speaker teachers' also encourage teachers from Western countries to regard other cultures, and the teachers who come from them, as 'different' and 'inferior'.

Focusing on the argument

In this chapter Holliday quotes two sides of an argument: stereotyping is always harmful and misguided; and stereotyping is often harmful but can on occasion be useful. Although both sides of the argument are presented, it is clear that Holliday is more in agreement with the first than with the second. Interestingly, though, he finds that the second argument (stereotyping can be useful) provides him with a challenge that leads him into new ideas. He responds to this by considering how an individual who is going to live and/or work in a foreign country should use stereotypes. Should that individual try to ignore stereotypes because they are wrong and harmful? Or should he/she listen to the stereotypes in order to get hints about how to behave in the new country? Holliday suggests a third alternative: the travelling individual should ask him/herself about the stereotypes he or she has in their mind so that he or she is not ruled by those ideas but is able to question them.

A language tip

At various points in this chapter Holliday uses the word *other* as a noun, and with a capital 'O'. Here is one example:

cultural stereotypes are in the main overgeneralizations which are based on the describer's imagination of an inferior Other rather than with objective information about what the people being described are actually like.

You may also find the word used as a verb, as in:

non-native speaker teachers are Othered as culturally deficient.

Put (over-)simply, if you Other someone, you talk or write or think about them as being totally different from you in an inferior way. We might say that you are looking at the world as though it was divided into two: the Self (which is superior) and the Other (which is inferior). Usually it is Western societies who are accused of 'Othering' in this way. Every time Holliday uses this word in this way he makes the association with the imagined inferiority explicit: he talks about *an imagined, deficient, non-Western Other* and he uses the verb 'correct': *a missionary quest to correct the cultures of a non-Western Other.*

To think about

1   Think about a country you have never visited. What stereotypes do you have in your mind about that country? Now think about a country you have visited or lived in. What stereotypes did you have before you went? When did you realize that your stereotypes were untrue, or only partly true?

2   Which opinion do you most agree with: that stereotypes are always harmful, or that stereotypes can sometimes be useful?

3   What do you understand by the phrase 'moral imperative', which Holliday uses in the last paragraph of the chapter?

CHAPTER 12

Interrogating the concept of stereotypes in intercultural communication

Adrian Holliday

The *Compact Oxford Dictionary* defines stereotype as 'a preconceived and over-simplified idea of the characteristics which typify a person or thing'. A simple example might be 'Iranian businessmen put family loyalty before business'. The issue of cultural stereotypes is central to the business of intercultural understanding and also connects with a broader cultural politics within international English language education. I shall begin by setting out two basic arguments and then present my own analysis of the way forward. The first argument derives from concerns that cultural descriptions may be chauvinistic and encourage racism. The second is the more popular belief that stereotyping is normal and useful. I shall leave this until second because, against expectations, it is the more complex view and leads to the greatest part of the debate.

The cultural chauvinism argument

This argument is that cultural stereotypes are in the main overgeneralizations which are based on the describer's imagination of an inferior Other rather than with objective information about what the people being described are actually like. In a browse through my own annotated bibliography almost every reference to stereotypes emphasizes this suspicion. For example, Homi Bhabha (1994: 94) asserts that the stereotype is 'the major discursive strategy' in establishing fixed notions of how people are, and that this can be used to justify the cultural improvement which was a stated aim of European colonization. Clark and Ivanič (1997: 168) associate stereotyping with the way in which writers impose 'a view of the world' on readers, and give the example of sexist or 'any language that presents powerless groups of people in a stereotyped and/or unfavourable light'. Kim M-S (2005: 105) tells us that 'empirical data have consistently shown the stereotypical model to be false' with 'massive variation' and 'overlap within and across cultures'. Even Hofstede (2001: 14, 17), who has been a major source of national cultural characterizations, warns us against the ethnocentrism of 'heterostereotypes' about others, such as 'all Dutch are tactless', and 'autostereotypes' about our own groups, such as 'we Dutch are honest'. Kumaravadivelu (2007: 65–9) maintains that cultural stereotypes which are believed to be egalitarian by their users are an influential underpinning of US notions of cultural assimilation which in turn impose ethnocentric cultural viewpoints.

The issue with cultural stereotypes has been linked with professional prejudices in English language teaching in which 'non-native speaker' teachers and students have been characterized as culturally deficient (e.g. Kubota 2002; Holliday 2008). Kumaravadivelu (2003: 715–5, 2007) locates chauvinistic stereotyping within what he considers to be an essentially racist Western society which generates binary 'us'–'them' categories. My own work (Holliday 2005, 2007b) relates this further to the way in which a modernist, technicalized 'native speaker' English language teaching methodology sets out on a missionary quest to correct the cultures of a non-Western Other through the imposition of prescribed learning behaviour. This cultural chauvinism argument is generally rooted in critical applied linguistics (e.g. Pennycook 1998; Canagarajah 1999), and Edward Said's (e.g. 1978, 1993) influential theory of Orientalism. Said argues that negative stereotypes of the non-Western Other (as dark, immoral, lascivious, despotic and so on) are constructed by Western art, literature and political institutions. Especially after September 11 we have seen a confirmation of Said's assertion in the form of Islamophobia, in which 'all Muslims' are characterized as 'terrorists'.

Stereotypical models of national and regional cultures have been used extensively in intercultural communication research and training. One such model, which was developed by Hofstede (op. cit.) in the 1960s and has sustained in popularity, distinguishes between two cultural types. On the one hand, individualist cultures, situated in North America, Western Europe and Australasia, are described as prioritizing self-determination. On the other hand, collectivist cultures in the rest of the world are described as prioritizing group conformity (Triandis 2004, 2006). Elsewhere (Holliday 2007a) I argue that this distinction, while pretending to be an objective measure based on empirical research, is in fact ideologically constructed along the lines described in the previous paragraph – so that individualism represents an idealized Western Self, and collectivism represents an imagined, deficient, non-Western Other. Kim (op. cit.: 108) also notes that Hofstede's model 'forced a single bipolar dimension of individualism and saw collectivism as an absence of individualism' that was derived from the need to negatively Other 'barbarians'.

The practicality argument

The cultural chauvinism argument thus suggests that stereotypes cannot be objective measures of what people are really like and are always going to be culturally chauvinistic. In contrast, the practicality argument suggests that cultural stereotypes are natural and useful mechanisms for aiding understanding of cultural difference, and that, although we know that they are over-generalizations, they are good as starting places. This view is the one that has been more established and supported by psychometric research such as that of Hofstede, and also fits better with popular belief. Waters (2007a, 2007b) sees stereotypes as almost always inevitable and ordinary starting points for perception, and feels that recognizing and accepting this will provide a firmer footing than attempting to outlaw them – thus working towards replacing negative stereotypes with more accurately positive ones. He describes such a process as follows:

Step 1: I am working in a culture which is unfamiliar to me. I feel it might help if I got some basic information about it, in order to begin to get to know it better.
Step 2: In the light of this knowledge, what can I do (i) to limit culturally inappropriate behaviour on my part, and (ii) improve my ability to understand/accept behaviour on the part of locals?
Step 3: In the longer-term, how can I use this information to give me a basis for building up a better general picture of how expatriates and locals can live and work together as well as possible, and to help me perceive the individual person behind the cultural 'mask'?

(2007a: 284)

He sees this as 'acquiring knowledge that will be used not as a static end in itself, but dynamically, as a means to gradually increasing understanding and contributing to the development of productive inter-cultural relations' (ibid.).

An extension of the practicality argument, which Waters (2007a, 2007b, 2007c) presents in some detail is that the cultural chauvinism argument amounts to an imposition of 'political correctness'. Citing the work of social theorist Browne (2006), he defines political correctness as a hegemonic force which has become dominant in English-speaking Western society and creates the impression that everyone is either an 'oppressor' or a 'victim' (Waters 2007b: 354). His response to the cultural chauvinism argument in English language teaching is that this imagined oppressor–victim relationship is portrayed indiscriminately as native speakers versus non-native speakers, teachers versus learners and '"global" versus local methodologies' (ibid.: 355).

Waters (2007a) cites a number of early theorists, such as Lippman (1922) and Allport (1954), to support the point that while there is an early acknowledgement that stereotypes are 'defensive, partial and rigid representations of the world, which obscure variety and particularity, and which the individual should resist', to deny the usefulness of stereotypes in 'economizing attention' would be to 'impoverish human life', and to deny the categorical nature of all human perceptions, and the possibility of working with their complexity and diversity to arrive at more valid truths. He therefore makes the following claim:

Suspension or suppression of stereotypes is an impossibility, a vain attempt at 'thought control', and all perception can be seen, to a greater or lesser extent, as inevitably stereotyped, for both better or worse. Thus, rather than stereotyping all stereotyping as innately unhealthy or aberrant, because *some* forms of stereotyping from *some* points of view are seen to have negative consequences, the starting point needs to be one based on accepting the immanency of stereotyping, instead of attempting to deny its rationality and central role in the development of perceptions. Such a stance recognises that some stereotypes will offend, but why this is so and what might be done about it can then be approached from a very different perspective.

(ibid.: 228, his emphasis)

Intercultural communication methodologies

Waters' warning against a knee-jerk demonizing of all stereotyping needs to be taken seriously. However, while it claims more realism than the cultural chauvinism position, his argument may also be naïve in its lack of belief about how easily the best intentioned people can be taken in, not by the hegemony of political correctness, but by the discoursal power of, in his words, the apparently innocent 'economized' explanations that stereotypes provide. Much can be learnt here from another branch of Applied Linguistics, that of Critical Discourse Analysis, which shows us how prejudices can easily be hidden in apparently neutral everyday talk, and in institutional, professional and political thinking (e.g. Fairclough 1995). Kumaravadivelu (2007: 52) puts this very well:

Even people with an egalitarian, non-prejudiced self-image can act prejudicially when interpretive norms guiding a situation are weak. In such a scenario, people easily justify their racially prejudiced acts and beliefs on the basis of some determinant other than race.

Kumaravadivelu's view of society, as an inherently racist system, is very different to that of Waters. Waters suggests that an initial, stereotyped understanding may subsequently be modified or abandoned in the light of experience. If we accept Kumaravadivelu's view, however, it is difficult to accept Waters' opinion. Once the easy repertoires of stereotypes are in place they provide basic structures of understanding that are very difficult to remove. In Western cultural history destructive narratives of an imagined uncultured East repeat themselves again and again. The cultural chauvinism and the practicality arguments each produce a methodology for intercultural communication which falls on either side of this tension.

Awareness through cultural descriptions

The practicality argument encourages the established, dominant approach where people are introduced to a description of the new culture they are about to be introduced to – very much following Waters' steps. Taking the example of Iranian society, with which I am familiar, this methodology would very probably introduce the prospective visitor to aspects of Iran as a collectivist and a Muslim society. These two macro characterizations may deal with such detail as 'Iranian businessmen put family loyalty before business' (the example from the beginning of this chapter) or 'it is not appropriate to deal directly with women'. On arriving in Iran the visitor would hopefully begin to discover that there are many 'exceptions' to such rules; and, indeed, much current intercultural communication theory does warn against the danger of over-generalization (e.g. Gudykunst 2005; Samovar and Porter 2006).

Awareness through interrogating issues of Self and Other

The cultural chauvinism argument is very cautious of the cultural description route. As argued above, macro characterizations such as collectivism are perceived to be ideologically motivated; and, especially in an era of Islamophobia, any form of characterization of Islam has to be treated extremely cautiously. The methodology emerging from the cultural chauvinism argument would therefore avoid imposing cultural descriptions. The focus would instead be on the structure of prejudice arising from the stereotyping process, and the development of disciplines for avoiding them. The prospective visitor to Iran would therefore be asked to interrogate her or his prejudices about Iran and to address inhibitions to understanding arising from them. Behaviour considered 'exceptions' to the stereotype in the cultural description methodology would be considered normal until found otherwise. The model of society would therefore be one of complexity rather than cultural unity, with an emphasis on looking for commonality rather than foreignness, given that many stereotypes are founded on a chauvinistic expectation of difference. Statements such as 'Iranian businessmen put family loyalty before business' or 'it is not appropriate to deal directly with women' would not therefore be taken as descriptions of how things are, but as 'easy answers' which need to be deconstructed in terms of a superior Western Self imagining a deficient non-Western Other. In other words, stereotypes are perceived as problems rather than solutions.

This sort of methodology can be found in Holliday et al. (2004: 48–49), and might involve disciplines for seeing such as: (a) excavate and put aside preconceptions and ready-made systems for understanding, (b) appreciate complexity, (c) avoid over-generalizing from individual instances, (d) submit to the unexpected and what emerges from experience, (e) seek a deeper understanding of how negative stereotypes are formed, and (f) accept that even innocent looking beliefs can have political and patronizing undertones. These disciplines have much in common with those of qualitative research, where the emphasis is on finding out the nature of culture without being influenced by preconceptions. Similarities may also be found in the work of Byram and colleagues (e.g. Byram and Feng 2006), who encourage foreign language students to carry out their own personal ethnographic research projects while visiting other people's countries – to find out for themselves the nature of other cultures. They are encouraged to begin by making sense of what is going on in its own terms, employing a 'willingness to seek out or take up opportunities to engage with otherness in a relationship' (Byram 1997: 57).

Loose ends

In conclusion it needs to be emphasized that I have presented an over-tidy picture of the issues surrounding stereotypes – learning something from Waters in appreciating how easy it is to stereotype arguments about stereotypes. The question of stereotypes needs to be looked at within the context of complexity. Either because the world is changing, within a process of globalization, or because we are more tuned to appreciate it, the nature of culture is far from straightforward. Culture is something that flows and shifts between us. It both binds us and separates us, but in different ways at different times and in different circumstances. There are many aspects of our behaviour which are culturally different. We must, however, be wary not to use these differences to feed chauvinistic imaginations of what certain national or ethnic groups can or cannot do – as exotic, 'simple', 'traditional' Others to our 'complex', 'modern' selves. The foreign is not always distant, but often participant within our own societies; and the boundaries between us are blurred. Culture is therefore cosmopolitan, and as such resists close description.

What is clear, however, is the moral imperative which underpins issues in intercultural communication and problematizes stereotypes – to counter what Kumaravadivelu (2007) projects as a major activity of the twentieth and twenty-first centuries, one half of the world chauvinistically defining the other as culturally deficient.

References

Allport, G. W. (1954). *The Nature of Prejudice*. Cambridge, Mass: Addison-Wesley.

Bhabha, H. (1994). *The Location of Culture*. London: Routledge.

Browne, A. (2006). *The Retreat of Reason*. London: Civitas.

Byram, M. (1997). *Teaching and Assessing Intercultural Communicative Competence*. London: Multilingual Matters.

Byram, M. and Feng, A. (2006). *Living and Studying Abroad: research and practice*. London: Multilingual Matters.

Canagarajah, S. (1999). *Resisting Linguistic Imperialism in English Teaching*. Oxford: Oxford University Press.

Clark, R. and Ivanič, R. (1997). *The Politics of Writing*. London: Routledge.

Fairclough, N. (1995). *Critical Discourse Analysis: The critical study of language*. London: Addison Wesley Longman.

Gudykunst, W. B. (eds) (2005). *Theorizing about Intercultural Communication*. Thousand Oaks, CA: Sage.

Hofstede, G. (2001). *Culture's Consequences: comparing values, behaviours, institutions and organizations across cultures*. London: Sage.

Holliday, A. R. (2005). *The Struggle to Teach English as an International Language*. Oxford: Oxford University Press.

Holliday, A. R. (2007a). 'The persistence of constructions of superiority and inferiority in cultural description'. Unpublished paper, Department of English and Language Studies, Canterbury Christ Church University.

Holliday, A. R. (2007b). 'Response to ELT and "the spirit of the times"'. *ELT Journal* 61/4: 360–6.

Holliday, A. R. (2008). 'Standards of English and politics of inclusion.' *Language Teaching* 41:1, 115–26.

Holliday, A. R., Hyde, M. and Kullman, J. (2004). *Intercultural Communication*. London: Routledge.

Kim, M.-S. (2005). 'Culture-based conversational constraints theory'. In W. B. Gudykunst (ed.), *Theorizing About Intercultural Communication*. Thousand Oaks, CA: Sage, 93–117.

Kubota, R. (2002). (Un)ravelling racism in a nice field like TESOL. *TESOL Quarterly* 36: 1, 84–92.

Kumaravadivelu, B. (2003). 'Problematizing cultural stereotypes in TESOL.' *TESOL Quarterly* 37/4: 709–19.

Kumaravadivelu, B. (2007). *Cultural Globalization and Language Education*. Yale, CT: Yale University Press.

Lippman, W. (1922). *Public Opinion*. New York: Macmillan.

Pennycook, A. (1998). *English and the Discourses of Colonialism*. London: Routledge.

Said, E. (1978). *Orientalism*. London: Routledge and Kegan Paul.

Said, E. (1993). *Culture and Imperialism*. London: Chatto and Windus.

Samovar, L. A. and Porter, R. E. (eds) (2006). *Intercultural Communication: a reader*. Belmont, CA: Wadsworth.

Triandis, H. C. (2004). 'Forward'. In Landis, D., Bennett, J. M. and Bennett, M. J. (eds), *Handbook of Intercultural Training*, Third Edition. Thousand Oaks, CA: Sage, ix–xii.

Triandis, H. C. (2006). 'Culture and conflict.' In Samovar, L. A. and Porter, R. E. (eds), *Intercultural Communication: a reader*. Belmont, CA: Wadsworth, 22–31.

Waters, A. (2007a). 'Native-speakerism in ELT: Plus ça change . . .?' *System* 35, 281–92.

Waters, A. (2007b). 'ELT and 'the spirit of the times'. *ELT Journal* 61/4: 353–9.

Waters, A. (2007c). 'Ideology, reality, and false consciousness in ELT'. *ELT Journal* 61/4: 367–8.

SECTION 2

STUDY SKILLS FOR APPLIED LINGUISTICS STUDENTS

IV Doing research in Applied Linguistics

Introduction to chapter 13

This is one of four chapters dealing with ways of carrying out research in Applied Linguistics. Aileen Bloomer's chapter covers some of the issues that a researcher has to think about when planning a questionnaire. The key concepts in this chapter are: questionnaire design, informants, pilot study and ethics.

The background to this chapter

Questionnaires are a very popular format for obtaining information for research. Often even research that is text-based rather than person-based involves some form of data-gathering through a questionnaire. If a researcher is collecting essays written by learners of English for analysis, he or she may ask the students to complete a short questionnaire, asking for their age, sex and how long they have been learning English, for example. This information means that the essays can then be compared: younger learners against older learners, boys against girls and so on.

For the most part, however, questionnaires are used as the main part of the research, to find out about an aspect of the behaviour of a particular group of people. For example, a researcher may use a questionnaire to find out what exposure a group of learners has to the language they are learning, outside the classroom. How often do the learners watch films, listen to songs or read books in the language they are learning? Do they communicate with people in other countries using the internet? Do the learners who do more of these activities get better marks in tests than the less active learners do? Information of this kind can be obtained with a questionnaire.

Other questionnaires test attitudes (see chapter 7 for an example of this kind of research using questionnaires). Attitudes – do you prefer this or that, how much do you like or dislike this or that, what are your fears and ambitions – are difficult to pin down with a questionnaire, and many of the problems around questionnaire design relate to this area. It is all too easy to write questions that hint to the informants that one answer would be considered 'better' than the other.

Questionnaires are often a mixture of open questions, where the informant is asked to write a few sentences giving an opinion, and closed questions, where the informant has to tick a box to indicate the answer. Both kinds of questions have advantages and disadvantages. Open questions give the informants scope to say exactly what they wish to, without being constrained by the researcher's assumptions. On the other hand, open questions can be time-consuming and difficult to answer, and they do not offer the researcher a ready way to quantify the results. Closed questions are ideal for quantification but only work if they are very well designed.

It is worth also thinking about alternatives to questionnaires. Often a researcher feels that more complete information will be obtained if the informant is interviewed rather than given a questionnaire (see chapter 14 for more information about interviews). An interview can follow up unexpected answers and explore attitudes in greater depth. If an interview is thought to put the informant under too much stress, a focus group (where several people are asked questions together) might be preferable. Focus groups have the additional advantage that people might agree with what one person says but possibly would not have thought of that answer themselves. But interviews and focus groups are time-consuming to run, and the data has to be recorded in some way, such as through transcription, before the results can be analysed. This is also hugely time-consuming, and limits the number of informants that can be used. If the aim is to survey large numbers of people, a questionnaire is really the only answer.

Focusing on the argument

In this chapter, Bloomer is offering advice and instruction rather than constructing an argument. The chapter is organized around a series of headings, each covering an area of possible difficulty for the researcher. Problems are posed and questions asked, either directly or indirectly. Although advice and instruction are the aim, note that in many cases Bloomer does not offer precise answers to questions but rather suggests a number of alternatives and asks the reader to consider the pros and cons of each. The chapter is thought-provoking even though it is not argument-based.

A language tip

Bloomer uses the word *nuanced* in two contexts:

[Closed questions] can often exclude more nuanced answers . . .
[Multiple choice questions] do not allow for a range of nuanced thoughts to be expressed . . .

A paraphrase of *nuanced answers* might be 'answers that do not express a simple yes or no but that give a quite detailed opinion'. An example of a nuanced answer is Bloomer's own answer to the question: Are you a good language learner? She might say: 'I'm not really sure. I have learnt some languages really quickly but others have been more difficult. And I often find that I start learning a language very successfully but I quickly get to a point where I seem to be making little progress.'

To think about

1 Why are questionnaires designed to find out about how speakers use language usually unsuccessful?
2 What are the problems in writing questions for questionnaires? How can these be avoided?
3 What are the problems in presenting the results from questionnaire? How can these be avoided?

CHAPTER 13

Designing a questionnaire

Aileen Bloomer

Questionnaires have long been seen as useful methods to research a wide range of topics and are often used in market research contexts to find out people's views on a given product or range of services or in political arenas to find out the range of opinions held by a chosen group of people. They are useful in applied linguistic research if the intention is to find out about people's attitudes to language change or to the target language being learnt; to the teaching and learning methods used in their second language learning classes; to discover different motivations for learning or for using a second language; to explore which languages are being used in a certain geographical area or in a particular business organization; to gather information about cultural beliefs or practices. Questionnaires are usually presumed to be in a written format (whether electronic- or paper-based) but many of the points made here will apply equally to oral interviews and to focus group discussions.

Questionnaires exploring an individual's language use tend to be less helpful. Human beings are not good at reporting verbatim what has just been said or what was the last sentence of the paragraph they have just read, though they are good, usually, at reporting the content of such language chunks. It is not always clear that human beings act in accordance with what they claim to be their views about language use (or about anything else, for that matter). They can only tell you what they think they believe or think that they do. I well remember an incident when I claimed vigorously that I did not like and never used the suffix -*wise* as found in some of the perhaps more modern examples such as *traffic-wise, weather-wise, clothes-wise* (though I did accept happily the term *streetwise*) and then continued to use exactly that suffix several times in the ensuing discussion in similar modern contexts: alert students pointed out the mismatch between my behaviour and my claim. Questionnaires tell us what the informant (or the subject) thinks they think and tells us how they think they behave but in the latter case, particularly, further research needs to marry up actual behaviour with perceived behaviour.

This chapter will provide advice on what a researcher needs to think about when designing a questionnaire. Several issues – the informants, the questions, pilot studies, presentation and ethical issues – will be discussed.

The informants need to match the area being researched. If second language learner (SLL) attitudes are to be sought, then the results of the questionnaire are invalid if any of the informants are not SLL learners. If the intention is to explore teacher attitudes to particular learning/teaching methodologies recently introduced, there is no point in asking the students for their opinion: their opinions belong to a different (probably linked) research project and different questions will be needed. It is only fair to give the informants (often giving up their time voluntarily to answer the research questions) a clear idea of what will be involved. Questionnaires are most often in written form and, in second language research projects particularly, it is important that the questions are written in language that the respondent will be able to understand and that the subjects have the language to formulate a sensible response: it is unfair to ask a target language (TL) beginner to speculate on the value of a particular methodology or to express their views on previous learning experiences in the target language if their current abilities in that target language will not allow them to give answers which will provide the content that they want to provide. In such a case, a structured interview might resolve some of the difficulties but there are other problems related to such interviews.

How many informants are needed is another vexed question and the answer here cannot be particularly helpful. It depends. The more informants there are, then the greater validity can be claimed for any statistical results of the survey and the wider the implications might seem. The fewer there are, the less widely applicable the results might seem but the more focused the results might be.

How are the informants to be chosen? The obvious answer to this question might seem to suggest that a random sample is always best – but is it? If the research project is to explore how overseas students at UK universities receive feedback from their UK tutors as opposed to how they receive feedback from their home country tutors, then the informants must all have been exposed to feedback in the two different contexts that form the basis of the comparison that is fundamental to the research project itself. The home countries might be different but the essential two experiences must be maintained, perhaps with care being taken to note where there are similarities between different home country feedback. In such a case, the researcher might have to use their own judgement to decide which students to ask to respond to the questionnaire. However, it is not only the research topic itself that will determine whether a random sample or a 'judgement' sample is indeed the better way to choose the informants: another point to consider is whether the informants will give honest answers or whether they come from a background where officialdom is never to be criticized (as a result of which the answers they give may well be constrained by that cultural belief).

How to formulate the questions

Many people will argue that the best way to get information from somebody is to ask them a direct question, but there are pitfalls to this approach. If presented with the direct, closed question 'Are you a successful language learner?', I would have responded confidently 'Yes' if asked the question before I had attempted to learn Chinese; I would have answered 'no' if the question had been asked in the period when the struggle to learn Chinese appeared completely overwhelming; and now I would answer 'I have no idea' based on all my experiences of learning different TLs as well as concern about how 'a successful language learner' might be defined. To explore success in language learning, more insightful and helpful answers might be gained from indirect questions such as 'Have you ever learnt vocabulary items by rote?' and 'In what ways was this helpful?', or 'List the problems (or list the three main problems) that you have experience when learning TLx'. To respond to the direct question 'Do you like the new seating arrangements in the classroom?' will involve not just issues about the seating arrangements but also issues of politeness: is it acceptable to suggest that the new arrangement (presumably an idea of the current teacher) might not be better than the old arrangement? While in the TL culture such critical comment might be easily accepted, the cultural background of the student might make the only answer possible one that supports the change because of power relationships perceived to pertain between tutor and student. Indirect questions about how easy it is to contribute to plenary discussion or to participate in group discussions might produce more honest answers. Some informants just might want to be nice to the researcher and therefore not give an honest answer but give the answer they think the researcher wants to hear.

Open questions will provide masses of data and the problem then emerges of how to analyse it. Classic open questions ask *Why . . .?*, *What do you think about . . .?*. Closed questions do limit the information that is recorded and make it easier to process the responses as it is often possible simply to count them. Closed questions provide useful detail (e.g. How long have you lived in the UK? What is your highest educational qualification?) but they can often exclude more nuanced answers (how would you answer the question 'Do you like answering questionnaires?') and can sometimes appear patronizing, which can lead to flippant and unhelpful answers.

Sometimes more helpful responses can be gained by the use of attitude scales or Likert Scales to allow more room for manoeuvre in an answer whilst still maintaining some control for the researcher over the possible responses (see Figure 13.1).

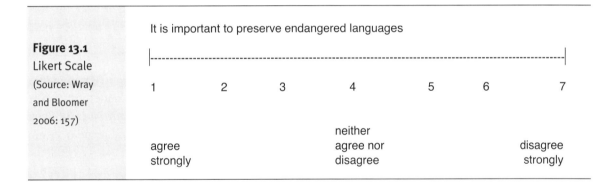

Figure 13.1
Likert Scale
(Source: Wray
and Bloomer
2006: 157)

Multiple choice techniques also limit the possible responses but multiple choice questions and their possible responses need to be written very carefully to ensure that only one answer is possible and acceptable. Whilst they might indicate an ability to use language (see Figure 13.2), such language is often decontextualized and therefore perhaps of only limited interest. Multiple choice questions are not particularly helpful in trying to ascertain attitudes, experiences or opinions as by their nature they do not allow for a range of nuanced thoughts to be expressed.

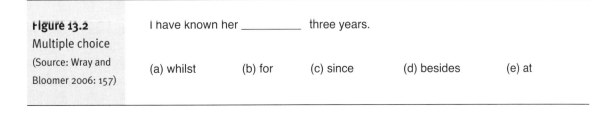

Figure 13.2
Multiple choice
(Source: Wray and
Bloomer 2006: 157)

Another way of eliciting information is to use ranking scales which might, for example, ask informants to rank from most to least helpful for them individually different approaches to organizing the seating in the classroom or of different ways of presenting a new syntactic structure. Simple ranking requires a response from top to bottom in list format but diamond ranking allows informants to choose the most helpful and the least helpful and allows them to place other responses in equal positions such that their final response may be diamond-shaped (or roughly that shape) rather than a single list:

Diamond response

In such cases, make sure that you offer your informants a wide range of possible responses, or better still ensure that you provide as complete a range of answers as possible to ensure that a respondent is not troubled by not finding the response that they really want to offer in the list available. You might choose to leave one response blank for the student to complete as in the example in Figure 13.3. A pilot study (see below) should help.

Whatever questioning techniques are employed (and there is a good argument for mixing open and closed questions with other elicitation techniques), questions in any questionnaire should be simple and unambiguous. Do not ask questions such as 'If you have learnt a second language what problems did you encounter, and if you have not learnt a foreign language, what problems might you anticipate?' Trying to cover all the bases in this way simply causes problems for the informant who may just give up at this point. Avoid loaded questions which make assumptions (e.g. 'Why do you think older people have more difficulty in learning a second language?') that the respondent might not share and avoid leading questions (e.g. 'If somebody has been brought up bilingually, wouldn't you expect them to find learning another language easier than somebody who has been brought up monolingually?') which indicate what might be perceived to be a right answer. Put easier questions before more difficult questions. Always try to include one or two pairs of cross-referencing questions (perhaps ask for the same information in different ways) to allow you to check the validity of the answers you are being given.

Always do **a pilot study** of the questionnaire before embarking on the questionnaire for the main research project. In this way, potential problems can be identified and removed before they cause too many difficulties. A pilot study should always include analysis of the results to ensure that any unforeseen difficulties in analysis (as well as in question design) can be resolved.

The responses to any questionnaire may be the data on which a project is based: the opinions provided by the respondents on, say, matters of language change may provide

What do you think is the most important reason for you in (*specify your country of interest*) to learn English? Rank these responses in diamond fashion. Number 16 is left blank for you to put in another reason, if you wish to.

1   to get a better job
2   to earn more money
3   to be able to travel outside the country
4   to be able to travel inside the country (*NB: I assume my enquiry is in a multilingual country*)
5   to be able to read English literature
6   to pass the end-of-compulsory-school state examination
7   to study at a university in this country
8   to study at a university in another country
9   to train the mind by the language learning process
10 to understand pop music lyrics
11 because I am good at it
12 because I enjoy it
13 because English is (*one of*) the official language(s) of this country
14 because employers require employees to be fluent in English
15 because my boy/girl-friend speaks English
16 (*If none of the reasons above are your real motivation, write your own motivation here and use this number 16*)

Possible response A	Possible response B	Possible response C
12	1	15
11 10 5	2 14 6	2 3 6
6 7 8 9 14	3 4 8	7 8 11 14 12
3 4 13	7 9	9 10 13
2 15	13	4 5
1	15 10 11 12	1
	5	

NB Student responses need not conform totally to a diamond shape (as in B).

Figure 13.3
Diamond ranking

qualitative information on which a theoretical argument can be based. Equally, quantitative data might be developed and presented, if the responses were processed to show, for example, the percentage of respondents giving each answer.

Presenting a questionnaire can create problems. Always provide some covering information which explains to your informants what you are researching and why. If this would detrimentally affect the project, then find some way to explain why the questions are necessary without giving away secrets that will invalidate the results. Make sure that the instructions are clear and, especially in second language research, in language that the respondents will be able to understand. Make the task look easy rather than difficult and leave plenty of space around the questions but avoid making the questionnaire look too long, a feature which can be very demotivating to informants.

Always indicate if there is another page to come and when the informant has reached the end of the questionnaire. Make sure that pages in paper-based questionnaires cannot get separated from each other as losing one page of answers from an informant can invalidate that individual's responses entirely. Always thank your informants for the time they have given in answering the questionnaire and for returning it to you.

Consider whether the questionnaire is to be distributed on paper or electronically – each of which can present different problems. Electronic presentation might allow for computerized analysis of the responses but presumes that all the respondents are computer literate at least to the level demanded by the questionnaire. It is harder to make electronic responses genuinely anonymous. It might be cheaper to distribute electronic questionnaires and it might also be easier to have informants from a wider geographical area if the electronic media are used. It is always possible to post paper copies of a questionnaire to informants, but how will you ensure that the responses are returned (include a stamped addressed envelope) and in time to be useful for you (provide a date by which you need the responses to be returned to you)? Is there any benefit in having all the respondents in the same room at the same time as they complete the forms with the researcher (or somebody else) being there to answer any queries that may arise? Might it be easier for the researcher not to be present as the questionnaires are completed?

Ethical issues are as relevant to questionnaire design as to other forms of research methodologies. Before asking for personal information, ask yourself whether you need this information and how it will help you in your own research project. Only ask questions which are relevant to your project. How (or why) is it relevant to ask an informant their age unless age is the differing variable that is the target of a project researching the possible effect of age in the process of learning another language? Ethnicity, gender and educational background may be relevant to your project in which case you must find an appropriate way to ask about them. If they are not relevant, do not ask the question. Make sure that you can keep any promises made to your informants. If you promise them that responses to the questionnaire will be anonymous, then you must keep this promise however difficult it might be to do so. With written responses, for example, distinctive handwriting styles might reveal who provided a given set of responses (and therefore there is no anonymity here) particularly if the researcher knows some or all of the informants. If you cannot keep the promise, do not make it in the first place.

Reference

Wray, A.M. and Bloomer, A.M. (2006) *Projects in Linguistics* 2nd edn, London: Hodder Arnold.

Introduction to chapter 14

This chapter is a 'research story': Macksoud recounts the way she designed and carried out her research. The research method it focuses on is that of the interview, used to find out what teachers' attitudes are to a particular issue. Macksoud discusses finding research subjects, conforming to ethical requirements, designing interview questions, transcribing, coding and interpreting the data.

The background to this chapter

It is very important to find out what teachers, and students, think and feel about issues that affect them, such as teaching methods or the things that help them work better. But it is also very difficult. In chapter 13, Bloomer suggests ways in which questionnaires can be designed to find out this kind of information; this chapter looks at an alternative technique – the interview. Interviews are more time-consuming than questionnaires, so they can get results from fewer people. On the other hand, it is possible to get more detailed information, because people are speaking relatively freely and are not constrained by the design of the questionnaire.

The decision to use interviews throws up a number of practical and academic problems for the researcher. On the practical side, people have to be found who are willing to be interviewed. The researcher may have relatively little control over who volunteers. For example, a researcher may wish to interview equal numbers of men and women, but if far more women than men volunteer, this may not be possible. Care has to be taken over the recording of information so that ethical considerations are respected. In most cases the interview is recorded, but this then raises a problem of how to transcribe the recording so that information can be taken from it. It can take many hours to write down everything an interviewee has said, and voice recognition software does not respond well to several different voices. Macksoud suggests an ingenious solution to this problem.

Turning to more academic matters, the researcher has to decide what questions to ask. This can be a difficult task and it is certainly important, as once the interviews are finished the researcher cannot easily go back and ask more questions if some important information is missing. So the research questions – what the researcher wants to know – have to be very clear, and the interview questions need to be designed so that they give the right information. It is also important that questions do not 'lead' the interviewees too much. If it is obvious what the interviewer thinks is the 'correct' answer to a question, then that is the answer the interviewee will be most likely to give.

The second task for the researcher is to analyse the data. This is more difficult than with questionnaire answers, as the interviewees will not necessarily use the kind of language the researcher is expecting. For example, if 20 teachers are asked about the training they have received, they may use 20 different ways to talk about it. However, the researcher cannot work with 20 separate replies. He or she will need to classify the responses into a small number of possibilities – the training was very general, or directly relevant to the speaker's current post; the training was practical or theoretical; the training was useful or not. The task then is to identify which categories each of the responses falls into.

What Macksoud demonstrates is that doing research is not simply a matter of following a set methodology – it is not like following a recipe to make a cake. Instead the researcher is faced with a series of decisions, each of which is important to the ultimate outcome of the research.

Focusing on the argument

This chapter is a narrative rather than an argument, and it proceeds in a chronological order, with each step of the research explained in turn. It is apparent, however, that each step is not only described ('this is what I did') but also justified ('this is why I did it'). There is, therefore, an implicit argument: that a piece of research has to be very carefully planned, with the end result in mind from the beginning.

A language tip

This chapter is written in a very personal style; it contains a large number of instances of the word *I*, for example. As a way of explaining what the researcher did, this is very effective. Most academic essays and dissertations, however, are written in a less personal style, though *I* is often used to emphasize where personal decisions or actions were taken. For example, here is a paragraph from the chapter:

When designing the interviews, I began by searching the literature to see if there were any published sets of interview questions that I could adopt or adapt for my study. However, the specific topic I was looking at had not been studied before so I was unable to find any existing instruments. Therefore, I had to develop an original set of interview questions.

This is how the paragraph might appear in an essay:

A literature search revealed that the specific topic that was the focus of this research had not been studied before and there were no existing instruments that could be used. I therefore developed an original set of interview questions. OR An original set of interview questions was therefore developed.

It is interesting to look at other paragraphs in the chapter to see how they might be re-written in this way.

To think about

1 Have you ever done research using questionnaires or interviews? What did you find to be the difficulties and how did you solve them?

2 Look at the questions that Macksoud quotes in the chapter. Would you find it easy to answer them? If not, can you suggest how they might be changed to make them easier?

3 Macksoud talks about her coding categories as 'relatively parallel' and 'discrete'. What do you understand by these terms? Can you see why having parallel and discrete categories is a good thing?

CHAPTER 14

Using interview data in case studies

Ruby Macksoud

This chapter is based on a project (a dissertation) that was designed to investigate teachers' feelings of preparedness to teach English for specific academic purposes (ESAP). The project was a qualitative and quantitative case study of university ESAP teachers in Canada and in the United Kingdom. The main research questions were as follows:

1   In what ways, if any, do teachers feel sufficiently prepared when teaching ESAP?
2   In what ways, if any, do teachers feel insufficiently prepared when teaching ESAP?
3   What general attitudes do English for academic purposes (EAP) teachers have about teaching ESAP?

I collected data over a three-month period from six university ESAP teachers as well as from six teachers of general university EAP. Each ESAP teacher participated in one 60-minute interview and completed an attitude questionnaire. For the general EAP teachers, data were collected using an e-mail questionnaire with a similar set of questions to the interviews and an attitude questionnaire. In addition, after each interview and electronic contact, reflective notes were recorded in a researcher journal. These notes were used to cross-examine the data collected using the other techniques as recommended by Nunan (1992).

Within this mixed-method research design, the primary source of data was the face-to-face interviews with the six university ESAP teachers. In this chapter I will focus on this part of the research design, describing how the interview participants were found, how the interviews were designed, how the data were gathered and transcribed, and how the data were interpreted in order to answer the research questions.

The participants

The technique I used to find participants for the interviews was convenience sampling as described by Bogdan and Biklen (1998). I needed to find participants who were currently teaching ESAP in a university context; this meant that I searched for participants who fit this basic criterion and who were available. Once I identified individuals, I sent e-mail letters to them and met with them briefly to invite them to participate in the study. In this way, I was able to find six ESAP teachers (four women and two men) to participate in the interviews.

One of my concerns when choosing participants was how many to aim for and how this might impact the balance in my study between detail and generalizability. I decided to include only a small number of participants because interviews are usually time-consuming and labour intensive (e.g. because of the need to transcribe the recordings and analyse the transcripts). Keeping the number of participants small allowed me to gather very detailed data, while cutting down on time spent transcribing. However, in using a small number of participants, I had to be careful to not over-generalize when drawing conclusions from these data.

Ethical issues   When searching for participants, I kept ethical issues in mind. I wanted to ensure that the individuals I invited did not feel pressured to participate in the study. To avoid this I stated clearly in my invitation that, while the study was important and their participation would be very helpful, participation was completely voluntary. I also wanted to ensure that the participants would not be put at any risk; for example, that they could not be identified. I explained to them that I would take steps to ensure their confidentiality. These included keeping data (i.e. interview recordings and original transcripts) in a safe location and not allowing anyone else access to them, removing names and other identifying features from the transcripts, and not using the names of individuals or institutions in reporting the findings.

Designing the interviews   When designing the interviews, I began by searching the literature to see if there were any published sets of interview questions that I could adopt or adapt for my study. However, the specific topic I was looking at had not been studied before so I was unable to find any existing instruments. Therefore, I had to develop an original set of interview questions.

I developed this set of interview questions in several steps. First, I considered whether I could use the study's research questions directly as interview questions. However, the research questions did not lend themselves neatly to an interview situation. The research questions were in some ways general and abstract, and I thought they may not be sufficiently clear for the participants. I decided instead to use the research questions as a foundation for generating interview questions that would be clear for participants. As long as I maintained a close relationship between the interview questions and the research questions, the interview questions would get the participants to provide information that would answer those research questions. For example, based on the first research question (which asked whether and how teachers felt prepared to teach ESAP), I created the following interview question:

What aspects of your professional history (i.e. education, professional training/ experience) do you usually draw on when you are teaching an ESAP course? Please describe with an example(s).

This question took the abstract notion of 'preparedness' from the research question and made it more concrete for the participants.

Second, when I had developed a draft set of questions, I asked for feedback on the overall design of the set of questions from two ESAP researchers working in Canada and the United Kingdom. According to Berg (1995), this is an important step to ensure the suitability of research instruments and to help check for researcher bias in the interview questions. I then used the feedback from these individuals to revise the questions.

Once the overall design of the set of questions was revised, I piloted the interview questions with seven university ESAP teachers. These teachers gave me feedback on how participants might respond to the interview questions and where I might need to ask follow-up questions for clarification.

The result of this process was a clear, concrete set of interview questions as follows:

1   Can you please describe briefly the ESAP course(s) you teach (or have taught)? (e.g. Who are the students? What are the goals?)

2   (a) What aspects of your professional history (i.e. education; professional training/experience) do you usually draw on when you are teaching this ESAP course(s)? Please describe with an example(s).

    (b) Why do you usually draw on these aspects of your professional history? Please explain with an example(s).

3   Has there ever been a particular time or incident in your ESAP teaching when you felt that your professional history was insufficient preparation for what you were doing? *If so*, please describe the particular situation and explain why you felt this way. *If not*, why do you think this hasn't happened?

4   Generally speaking, do you feel your professional history was sufficient preparation for teaching ESAP? Please explain.

The semi-structured nature of the interviews would allow for spontaneous expansion on responses from both the participants and the interviewer (Robson, 2002). In this study, the possibility of expanding on teacher responses was important to elicit personal stories about concrete teaching-related incidents and experiences. As Woods (1996) argued, this technique of eliciting data from teachers is based on the assumption that feelings and attitudes are not always consciously accessible for teachers and so need to be constructed through having teachers talk about concrete teaching events.

Gathering and transcribing the data

Once the set of interview questions was designed, I had to decide how I would gather data during the interviews. My main choices were either to take notes by hand or to use an audio recorder. I decided to record the interviews for several reasons. First, this would result in more accurate preservation of raw data. Second, as Bogdan and Biklen (1998) suggested, it would free me during the interviews to take notes on relevant issues without having to document everything the participants reported in real time. Third, it would allow me to maintain eye contact with the participants, which was important to help keep the interview climate comfortable and dynamic and the participants responsive to the questions. However, I was aware that there may also be drawbacks to audio recording interviews. According to Lamie (2001), for example, one criticism of recording interviews is the uneasiness a participant may feel in response to being recorded. I attempted to address this issue during the interviews by asking participants to refer to samples of their own instructional material to illustrate answers. I thought this might help distract participants from the fact that they were being recorded.

Once I had completed the interviews, I had to decide how I would transcribe the recordings. I made two key decisions in terms of transcribing. One decision was to use voice recognition software instead of a transcriber machine because time constraints meant that I had to transcribe the data in the quickest way. By training voice recognition software to recognize my voice, I was free to listen to the recordings, repeat the words into a microphone, and have the software generate the text on a computer screen for me. In this way, the voice recognition software would eliminate hours of manual work. However, I was aware that there may also be drawbacks to transcribing with voice recognition software. One example of a drawback is the accuracy of the software. Since I was using an original coding strategy to identify themes in the transcripts (see examples below), it was important that I generate accurate and careful transcriptions. As Bogdan and Biklen (1998) noted, the accuracy with which the transcribing of interviews is done influences how easy it is to work with the reported data from the interview participants. I attempted to address this issue by monitoring the text being produced on the screen and making any corrections manually. The second decision to transcribe only the main ideas as they related to my interview questions made my task easier. This meant that I did not need to transcribe filler words, overlapping speech or pauses, as I was not interested in the linguistic aspects of the interviews.

Interpreting the data

When the transcribing was complete, I used a coding strategy to identify themes in the interview transcripts that were directly related to the three research questions. I designed the coding strategy based on suggestions in the literature on qualitative data analysis (Lincoln & Guba, 1985; Miles & Huberman, 1994) and used the original research questions to create a general framework for the analysis. Within this framework, I used an interpretive approach to identify relevant themes in the interview data. Each unit of analysis, or 'segment of text . . . [which] contains one idea, episode, or piece of information' (Tesch, 1990, p. 116), related to the research questions was placed into one or more categories that reflected emerging themes. In total, I identified and categorized 105 units of analysis in the interview transcripts for the first research question and 62 units of analysis in the interview transcripts for the second research question. (I did not use the interview transcripts to answer the third research question.)

After I completed the initial coding, I performed the constant comparative method as described by Miles and Huberman (1994) and Bogdan and Biklen (1998) with my emergent codes. This meant that I reviewed all of my data to cross-examine the codes which had been applied. This process involved comparing units of analysis within and across transcripts to identify any overlap between coding categories that had emerged from the data. The result was a set of relatively parallel, discrete coding categories.

To illustrate, for the first research question, coding of the interview transcripts resulted in the emergence of eight different categories that represented sources of influence on these participants' feelings of preparedness to teach ESAP (see Table 14.1). Further, I divided some of these categories into narrower sub-categories in order to generate more detailed findings. For example, when participants said they drew on their teacher training when teaching ESAP, some participants referred to English language teaching (ELT) teacher training, and others referred to non-ELT teacher training.

Category	Sub-category
Education	Language-instruction Non-language-instruction
Teacher training	ELT Non-ELT
Teaching experience	EAP ELT Non-ELT
Professional training/ experience	Non-ELT training Non-ELT experience
Current EAP work environment	–
Intuition	–
Personal characteristics	–
Knowledge of broader current context	–

Table 14.1
Sources
teachers drew
on when
teaching ESAP

One example of this process of coding units of analysis involves the category *education* (see Table 14.1). I identified relevant units of analysis in the transcripts by looking for references the participants made to their educational backgrounds as influences on what they did in the ESAP classroom. Some of the teachers' educational backgrounds were in language-related areas such as literature, linguistics and foreign languages; other teachers' educational backgrounds were in non-language-related areas such as natural sciences, business and engineering. In order to take into account the range of educational backgrounds among the teachers, I divided this category into two sub-categories: *language-instruction-related education* and *non-language-instruction-related education*.

The following excerpt from an interview transcript is one of the units of analysis I coded as *education*. This teacher credited his language-instruction-related education with giving him the ability to analyse different texts confidently in his ESAP course:

Well, one of the things I would say that I draw on consistently is the fact that my *education* was really about close reading . . . I mean, when I was an undergraduate, those texts were romantic literature and Chaucer and those kinds of things. Now they are engineering texts . . . the ability to read closely, the ability to understand the material from the context, all that kind of stuff you get really at an undergraduate level in an *English language education*, which makes you very in touch with the text.

(Teacher E, italics added)

The following excerpt is another example from a different teacher. This teacher drew on his non-language-instruction-related education to help him deal with subject-specific content in his ESAP course:

Yes, well, I thought I can understand how things work because I have got *the economics background*.

(Teacher B, italics added)

To illustrate this coding process further, another category was *current EAP work environment* (see Table 14.1). I identified relevant units of analysis in the transcripts by looking for elements of the participant's current work environment, such as other colleagues or resource materials, that s/he reported drawing on when teaching ESAP. These elements would have been set up by the institution or the individual teacher. The following excerpt from an interview transcript is an example of one of the units of analysis I coded in this category. This teacher explained specifically how she drew on her colleagues to deal with materials development in her ESAP teaching:

You realize though that when you *share materials with other people*, you think, ah yes, and you immediately identify with it and you think that is a really good thing because *it fits the model or framework that you have about pedagogy*.

(Teacher F, italics added)

When I had completed the coding, I addressed the issue of reliability by asking another individual (who had experience with qualitative data analysis) to re-code 10 per cent of the data using the list of categories and sub-categories that I had generated. I compared the codes that individual assigned to the data with the codes I had assigned to the same data to see how closely we agreed. This resulted in an inter-rater reliability value of 91 per cent. Then, I re-coded 10 per cent of the data myself, and examined how closely my coding decisions overlapped with my original coding decisions with those data. This resulted in an intra-rater reliability value of 98 per cent.

Writing about the data

My challenge in writing about the interview data was to convey to readers the categories that I had generated through the coding process described above. I had spent a lot of time reading through the transcripts and reducing the highly contextualized data in those transcripts into categories that were represented by very short labels (e.g. education; teaching experience). However, since my readers would not have had the benefit of having read through all the interview transcripts, I had to make clear to the readers what the categories that I had generated meant. I decided that the best way to do this was to use a simple formula. In the findings section of my dissertation, when I listed the categories that had emerged from my analysis of the interview data, for each category, I gave a detailed definition of the category followed by an example of a unit of analysis that had been coded in that category; the coding details and transcript excerpts above are presented in a similar way.

Writing about the interview data contrasted with the way I wrote about the quantitative data that I had gathered through the attitude questionnaires. Compared to the qualitative data for which transcription and the coding process had been somewhat challenging, writing about the quantitative data was much more straightforward. I analysed the responses from the attitude questionnaires and then generated descriptive statistics. In the findings section of my dissertation, for each statement, the number of teachers who had selected each choice on the eight-statement Likert scale was counted. Once the data were organized, a graphic was generated and presented to the readers.

Conclusion   The interviews that I have described in this chapter formed only part of the research design of my study. Besides the interviews, the ESAP teachers completed an attitude questionnaire that provided quantitative data. The general EAP teachers, on the other hand, completed a written questionnaire that included similar questions to the interviews and an attitude questionnaire through e-mail. Using a mixed-method design like this was helpful, because it allowed me to try to answer my research questions with different types of data. In other words, mixing methods in the research design was a way to triangulate the findings in my study.

However, the interviews by themselves were the central part of this study. Using interviews to gather data allowed me to elicit responses about concrete ESAP teaching-related incidents and experiences from teachers in a very detailed and meaningful way. Given the open-ended nature of the research questions, and the fact that this was exploratory research on a topic that had received little if any attention, interviews were critical to the success of this project.

References   Berg, B. (1995). *Qualitative research methods for the social sciences*. Needham Heights, MA: Allyn & Bacon.

Bogdan, R., & Biklen, S.K. (1998). *Qualitative research in education: An introduction to theory and methods (3rd edition)*. Boston, MA: Allyn & Bacon.

Lamie, J.M. (2001). *Understanding Change: The impact of in-service training on teachers of English in Japan*. New York: Nova.

Lincoln, Y.S., & Guba, E.G. (1985). *Naturalistic inquiry*. Beverly Hills, CA: Sage Publications.

Miles, M.B., & Huberman, A.M. (1994). *Qualitative data analysis: An expanded sourcebook*. Thousand Oaks, CA: Sage Publications.

Nunan, D. (1992). *Research methods in language learning*. Cambridge, UK: Cambridge University Press.

Robson, C. (2002). *Real world research*. Oxford, UK: Blackwell Publishers Inc.

Tesch, R. (1990). *Qualitative research: Analysis types and software tools*. New York: Falmer Press.

Woods, D. (1996). *Teacher cognition in language teaching: Beliefs, decision-making, and classroom practice*. Cambridge, UK: Cambridge University Press.

Introduction to chapter 15

The background to this chapter

Doing research into spoken language usually involves making a written transcription of that language. This chapter discusses some of the issues involved in making such a transcription and is one of a number that focus on methods of carrying out research. Key concepts introduced in this chapter include: transcription conventions; layout; transcription as theory; multimodal transcription.

Writing down what people have said ('transcription') sounds like a fairly simple task, but as anyone who has tried it will confirm it is actually quite difficult. One of the difficulties is that the transcriber has a lot of choices to make, and each choice will affect the outcome of the research that the transcription is a part of. One choice is what to transcribe: just the words spoken, or gestures and facial expressions used by the speakers as well? Another is how to set out the transcription, and how to show when different speakers start and stop speaking. Finally, many choices have to be made about representing intonation, or different pronunciations, accents and languages. In most cases there will not be only one 'correct' way of doing transcription; as Joan Swann demonstrates in this chapter, the same section of talk can be represented in a number of different ways, each one appropriate to a different kind of research.

A transcription takes something (a piece of speech) that was interpreted by listeners in a particular way when it was spoken, and puts it on the page so that it is available for interpretation by readers. One aim for a transcriber is to make the likely reading interpretation similar to the likely listening interpretation (though note there may be slightly different interpretations by different listeners). Ochs, who is quoted in this chapter, was one of the first to point out how transcription layout affects interpretation. Consider a situation where two people are speaking more or less at the same time. This might 'sound like' one person being rude and constantly interrupting the other, or it might sound like two friends enthusiastically agreeing with and supporting each other. If a traditional transcription layout is used, so that the conversation resembles a play script, it may look as though neither speaker can finish an utterance before the next speaker interrupts. But if a different layout is used, such as that shown in Figure 15.10, where the different speakers are shown like the instruments in an orchestra, it looks as though two people are both contributing whole utterances, but sometimes at the same time.

However good and detailed a transcription is, the transcriber will often feel dissatisfied and worry that they have had to leave out a good deal of information that was present in the recording (audio or video) that they are working from. It is difficult for a written representation of intonation to convey exactly how something was said, or for a comment to describe a tone of voice. When we take part in a conversation, we interpret many different signals at the same time; pulling these apart to put them into a transcription does not put the same thing in a different medium, it actually tells us something different.

Focusing on the argument

In this chapter Swann argues against a point of view that might be expressed like this: a transcription is a neutral representation of an interaction; anyone can be trained to do transcription; the linguist comes along afterwards and does the analysis; so the transcription and the analysis are completely separate and the second does not depend on the first. Swann argues that this is not true, that the transcription is part of the analysis itself, because decisions made about how the transcription is done will affect what information is available for (further) analysis. These contrasting points – transcription is difficult and time-consuming, not quick and easy, and transcription is part of the subjective analysis, not an objective preparation of data – are expressed in the introduction of the chapter. Everything that follows is an elaboration of this opinion, and is designed to persuade us, the readers, of the validity of the writer's point of view. Swann uses various devices to help in that persuasion, such as a number of examples including contrasting transcriptions, and bringing in other writers to support her case. Note too that a lot of information is included in the chapter, such as the various transcription models available, and the research that different people have done.

The blending together of information (e.g. these are the transcription conventions used by conversation analysts), practical advice (e.g. do a quick transcription of a long interaction then pick out parts to be transcribed in more detail), and argument (e.g. you need to transcribe gestures and facial expressions to be able to interpret what people have said) make this a very effective chapter.

A language tip

This chapter is written in an accessible style – it is easy to read. However, it also packs a lot of information into a small space, so many of the sentences contain a lot of information. Here is an example that might be explored:

Use of punctuation represents a trade-off between legibility and accessibility of the transcript and what might be a premature and impressionistic analysis of the data.

The information in this sentence can be 'unpacked' and expressed in a series of sentences, as follows:

- Punctuation can be used in transcription to make the transcription easy to read (because it is like written language). [*legibility*]
- The transcription can then be read by anyone, not just someone who is practised in reading transcriptions. [*accessibility*]
- But, using punctuation in this way can lead to an analysis of the interaction that does not pay enough attention to the detail in the interaction and is superficial. [*premature and impressionistic*]
- A transcriber probably wants the transcription to be relatively easy to read but also wants it to be analysed properly.
- The transcriber therefore has to balance 'easy to read' and 'proper analysis' when deciding what punctuation to use. [*trade-off*]

Swann has herself used a 'trade-off' here, balancing something that is easy to read, but too long, with something that is more difficult to process but gives a lot of information in a short space.

**To think
about**

1   Before you read this chapter, try doing some transcription yourself. Record two people having a 5-minute conversation, in any language (remember to ask their permission first). Now write down exactly what they have said, and try to represent how they said it. How long does it take you to do this? What problems do you encounter? Try the same exercise after you have finished reading the chapter.

2   What issues are involved in using non-standard spelling in transcriptions?

3   Swann argues that transcription layout is never neutral. Take one example of transcription from the chapter and consider what attitudes or ideologies it conveys.

CHAPTER 15

Transcribing spoken interaction

Joan Swann

CONTENTS

In this chapter I discuss different ways of transcribing spoken interaction. Transcription is valuable not simply as a means of representing speech, but also as an analytical tool. It is often the slow, repetitive process of transcription and retranscription that begins to reveal to analysts aspects of an interaction that may be worth further investigation. At the same time, transcription is not a neutral exercise in which features of an interaction are objectively identified. Transcriptions necessarily correspond to a researcher's interests and what they see as the analytical potential of their data, as well as their wider beliefs and values. It is in this sense that transcription is said to constitute both a representation and the beginnings of an interpretation of data. As Elinor Ochs has argued, in a now classic account of 'Transcription as theory', it is 'a selective process reflecting theoretical goals and definitions' (1979: 44). This point is illustrated by the different forms of transcription considered below. I shall discuss, in turn, conventions for transcribing spoken interaction; the representation of languages, varieties and styles; ways of laying out a transcript; and multimodal transcription.

Transcription conventions

Researchers sometimes use conventional punctuation in transcribing spoken interaction, but it is unusual for linguists to do this. Punctuation represents written features of language such as sentence boundaries, but people do not usually speak in complete sentences. Linguists therefore often record prosodic and paralinguistic features, including pauses and perhaps falling or rising intonation that help to structure spoken utterances; vocal characteristics such as loudness or voice quality; and aspects of delivery such as hesitation and false starts. All of these may be relevant to the interpretation of an interaction. As suggested above, however, the features transcribed will depend on the reasons for making the transcription, and the eventual analysis envisaged. As an illustration, Figure 15.1 comes from research looking at the effects of an educational intervention designed to encourage primary school children to explore ideas more effectively.

Of interest to the original researchers is the fact that the children are asking each other for opinions and ideas to help address a scientific problem. These and other features are evident throughout the longer transcript from which this brief extract is taken. Written conventions such as punctuation are seen as compatible with this focus, and may even help identify structures such as questions, which are of interest.

I have retranscribed this extract in Figure 15.2. This is a detailed transcript that includes some features of spoken language – repetition and incomplete utterances, brief pauses, some aspects of voice quality. A right-hand column is used for additional information or explanation. I was interested in the negotiation of social relations between these and other children (see Swann, 2007). It is relevant here, for instance, that

Ross's turn 2 is uttered in a smiley voice (the children are actually rehearsing something they have been through before, and Ross refers back to this humorously rather than giving Alana the answer she expects). Alana, at turn 3, smiles to show she gets the joke while also correcting Ross. She experiences some brief dysfluency before bringing the conversation back on track towards the end of her utterance. This produces a serious response from Ross. Interpersonal work at this level of detail is harder to analyse without relatively detailed transcription.

Figure 15.1
Transcript of science talk using written conventions

In a science lesson on light, three children, Alana, Ross and Dijek, are considering how many sheets of tissue paper it would take to block out light. Dijek has said ten, and given a reason, and Alana turns to ask Ross for his opinion.

1	Alana:	(*To Ross*) Why do you think it?
2	Ross:	Because I tested it before!
3	Alana:	No, Ross, what did you think? How much did you think? Tissue paper. How much tissue paper did you think it would be to block out the light?
4	Ross:	At first I thought it would be five . . .

Note: This is an extract from a longer transcript, with turn numbering added.

(Source: Mercer et al. 2004: 369[1])

Figure 15.2
Detailed transcription of science talk indicating some features of spoken interaction

1	Alana:	why do you think it	To Ross
2	Ross:	because I tested it before	Smiley voice
3	Alana:	<u>no (.) Ross</u> what no what did you think how much did you think tissue paper (.) <u>how much tissue paper</u> did you think (.) it would be (.) to block out the light	<u>Smiling</u> <u>Head movement,</u> <u>vocal emphasis</u>: fresh start after disfluency?
4	Ross:	at first I thought it would be five . . .	

Note: See Figure 15.4 for transcription conventions.

Figure 15.3 is a longer extract of transcribed talk, showing additional transcription conventions. This comes from one of a series of English lessons in a secondary school in Denmark, near Copenhagen (Dam and Lentz, 1998). The transcript begins with brief notes to contextualize the interaction.

Use of punctuation represents a trade-off between legibility and accessibility of the transcript and what might be a premature and impressionistic analysis of the data. It is probably best, at least initially, to make limited use of conventional punctuation before deciding whether and how to punctuate as in Figure 15.1. Figures 15.2 and 15.3 indicate how, alternatively, the transcriber may begin to add features that are characteristic of spoken interaction. Figure 15.4 illustrates a simple set of conventions used in these and other transcripts. More detailed sets of conventions are also available, allowing transcribers to record, for example, intakes of breath, increased volume, stress, syllable lengthening etc. (see, for instance, the widely used conventions devised by the conversation analysts Sacks et al., 1974).

Figure 15.3

Transcription of small group talk illustrating transcription conventions

A class of 15-year-old mixed-ability students is carrying out a project on 'England and the English'. The extract shows a group of students, two girls and two boys, beginning to plan what to do for their homework. The students are seated round a table, the girls opposite the boys.

		Transcription	**Notes**
1	G1:	What are we going to do at home (.) any ideas	addresses group directly
2	B1:	Yes (.) I take <u>this</u> (.) I take this ((general laughter)) yes yes I take it mmh and I see and I see if there's something I can use (.)	refers to book, holds up
3	G1?:	We can use	
4	B1:	We can use	
5	B2:	So what (would) we do (xxxxxx) read it at home (.) the questionnaire [(.) read it at home	question towards girls?
6	B1:	[(xxxxxxxx) [. . .]	
7	G2:	Maybe I can get some materials for this	
8	G1:	From (xxxxx) (mother)	
9	G2:	Yes	
10	B1?:	from where	
11	G2:	from my mother (.) from the travel agency	

Note: G = girl; B = boy. For other transcription conventions see Figure 15.4.

(Source: Swann 2001: 332)

On a practical level, detailed transcription is time-consuming. Edwards and Westgate (1994) suggest that every hour's recording may require 15 hours for transcription. I find that I can make a rough transcript far more quickly than this, but a detailed transcript may take longer. As a compromise, researchers sometimes begin with a rough transcript of data, then select certain episodes for more detailed transcription and analysis.

[maybe three [I have got	square brackets indicate overlapping speech
A: you know// B:// come off it	latching (//) indicates a turn that follows rapidly after another with no perceptible gap; a single slash (/) is sometimes found.
(that's right)	brackets indicate the transcription of these words is uncertain
(xxxxx)	utterance that is impossible to understand, and cannot be transcribed
(.)	a brief pause
(1.0)	a longer pause of 1 second or more – timing given in seconds
((laughter))	may refer to non-speech element such as laughter, a cough etc; may also be used to describe the voice quality of the following word – e.g. ((whispered))
COME BACK	as an alternative to double brackets, special formats may be used to indicate features such as loudness or emphasis
come back	a further option is to underline a word or phrase and specify how this is articulated, or any other feature of interest, in a separate right-hand column
[. . .]	excision: some data omitted

Figure 15.4 A simple set of transcription conventions

In order to protect the anonymity of speakers they are usually given pseudonyms as in Figures 15.1 and 15.2. Alternatively, they may be referred to as S, for 'speaker' (S1, S2 etc.); or aspects of their role or identity may be indicated, e.g. G for 'girl' (G1, G2 etc. as in Figure 15.3); or T for teacher and S1, S2 etc. for students.

Representing languages, varieties and styles

The transcripts in Figures 15.1–3 come from contexts in which only one language, English, is being used. Several conventions exist to record the use of different languages, or language varieties, or switching between language varieties. Researchers publishing in English sometimes represent other languages in translation, using a convention such as bold type or italic. Alternatively the original language may be retained with translation. Languages that do not use roman script may be represented in their original

Figure 15.5 Transcript illustrating alternation between English and Tamil

Extract from an English lesson in a school in Jaffna, Sri Lanka.

Teacher:	What did I give for homework yesterday?
Student 1:	Page forty.
Teacher:	Okay, take them out, I want to correct your work first. (*Goes towards Student 2*)
Student 2:	**Naan ceiya marantuTTan**, Miss. 'I forgot to do it' (Teacher continues in English)

Note: English is in plain text, Tamil in bold. An English translation is given below the Tamil.

(Source: Canagarajah 2000: 204)

form and/or in transliteration. The latter strategy is adopted by Suresh Canagarajah in a study of the use of English and Tamil in Sri Lanka (see Figure 15.5).

Canagarajah is interested here in the use of English and Tamil for different purposes. Transcriptions of classroom interaction provide evidence of the way speakers switch between languages. In this case, a student who has forgotten his homework uses Tamil in a bid to establish solidarity with the teacher, appealing to her identity as a fellow Tamil speaker. The teacher rejects this, upholding institutional norms by continuing in English. Canagarajah argues more generally that speakers use codeswitching to negotiate hybrid postcolonial identities in the classroom and in other contexts.

It is more difficult to decide how to represent language varieties closely related to English, or different varieties of English, that do not have a conventional orthography. Figure 15.6 comes from Ben Rampton's study of language crossing (defined as 'the use of a language which isn't generally thought to "belong" to the speaker', Rampton, 2006: 131).

Figure 15.6

Representing crossing into 'stylised Asian English'

Participants and setting: At the start of the school year, Mohan (15 years, male, Indian descent, wearing radio-microphone), Jagdish (15, male, Indian descent) and Sukhbir (15, male, Indian descent) are in the bicycle sheds looking at bicycles at the start of the new academic year. Some new pupils run past them.

1	SUKH	STOP RUNNING AROUND YOU GAYS (.)
2	SUKH	[((laughs))
3	MOH	((using a strong Indian accent for the words in bold:))
		[**EH** (.) **THIS IS NOT MIDD(LE SCHOOL**) no more (1.0) this is a respective (2.0)
4	ANON	(school)
5	MOH	school (.) yes (.) took the words out my mouth (4.5)

Note: bold type is used for instances of crossing that are of interest.

(Source: Rampton 2006: 135)

When Sukhbir's remonstration with some younger pupils (Turn 1) has no effect, Mohan continues, switching from his normal accent into what Rampton terms 'stylized Asian English'. Rampton notes that stylized Asian English is 'stereotypically associated with limited linguistic and cultural competence . . . and by implication the switch suggests the pupils are irresponsible or lacking in self-control' (2006: 135). In this version of the transcript, produced for a non-specialist audience, Rampton represents the switch (and other instances of crossing) in bold, along with an indication that this involves the adoption of a strong Indian accent. He does not, however, attempt to represent the accent itself. In the main report of his research, Rampton (1995/2005: 149) uses an alternative convention, showing switches in both standard spelling and the International Phonetic Alphabet, which provides a more technically accurate representation of pronunciation. For example:

EH (.) THIS IS NOT MIDD(LE SCHOOL)
aɪ   dɪs   ɪz nɒtʰ mɪd

Such representations assume some phonetic understanding on the part of readers – for instance that readers will understand that [ɳ ʈ ɖ] represent 'retroflex' sounds, produced when the tip of the tongue bends back behind the alveolar ridge. These sounds are found in many Indian languages and also in Indian English. Transcriptions sometimes adopt 'one-off' conventions for pronunciation features that are the focus of attention, for example, % to represent a glottal stop in words such as *par%y*, or *invi%e* (Sebba 1993: 19). Alternatively the International Phonetic Alphabet may be used selectively for individual words, as in 'Its tail is short and [bɪʃ i]' (where a young learner of English pronounces *bushy* to rhyme with *fishy*). Some researchers adopt non-standard orthography throughout a transcript in an attempt to indicate pronunciation – for example, *I wz gonna, probly's, liddle*, although such conventions are not always phonetically motivated – for example, in the case of *laffing* for *laughing*, or the *z* in *iz* for *his*. Such practices are controversial. It is argued that non-standard orthography is not always used consistently, does not accurately reflect pronunciation, and risks representing speakers, or certain speakers (working-class speakers, children, non-native speakers) as somehow deviant or incompetent (see discussion in Bucholtz, 2000; and Roberts, 1997; and an earlier debate between Fine, 1983 and Preston, 1982, 1983 on the use of non-standard orthography in folklore texts).

Laying out a transcript

The examples above adopt what I shall term a 'standard' transcription layout, with speaking turns following one another in sequence. While this is the most common layout there are also alternatives. Transcript layouts tend to foreground certain aspects of an interaction – for example turn-taking patterns, particular types of contribution.

Figures 15.7 and 15.8 illustrate alternative layouts for a transcribed conversational narrative, a story about a bird's nest recounted by 11-year-old Lee, in conversation with his friend Geoffrey and a researcher, Janet Maybin. Figure 15.7 uses a standard layout, representing the story as embedded in ongoing conversation, sparked off by a comment from Geoffrey and prompting further conversation on this theme. In Figure 15.8, from a different publication, Maybin is interested in the poetic quality of the narrative. She abstracts this from the interaction and transcribes it as a series of lines and verses (following Hymes 1996).

An alternative to a standard layout sometimes used in transcribing children's speech is a 'column' layout, in which each speaker is allocated a separate column for their speaking turns. Figure 15.9 illustrates this layout – this is a retranscription of Figure 15.3.

In group talk it's often interesting to look at the role taken by different students. Column transcripts make it easier to track one speaker's contributions – the number and type of contributions they make, the topics they focus on, or whatever else is of interest. In this case, Girl 1 seemed to play an organizing or chairing role – for example, by asking for ideas from the rest of the group; by 'correcting' Boy 1, reminding him that his work is for the group as a whole (line 13); and by completing Girl 2's turn (line 24). A column transcript would help an analyst track this type of behaviour, to see if Girl 1 maintained this role or if it was also taken on by other students.

The standard transcription layout suggests a connected sequence, in which one turn follows on from the preceding one. This does seem to happen in the extract transcribed

An earlier interactional theme of responding to animals in distress is taken up again by Lee in this extract.

Geoff	Since I started drawing birds, like in Miss Clark's class I had to draw that parrot, right the big parrot about that big
Lee	/ I drew the man, didn't I?
Geoff	Since I drew that, whenever I started getting bored, I went upstairs, got my paper, and drew a couple of birds, tiny ones. I used, whenever I went over me uncle's house, I used to take a couple of pieces of paper and some felts like and draw all these birds parrot
Lee	/Yesterday I was on, I was walking with my mum, we walked past this bush, and there was this nest and it was fallen down on the floor, and I goes 'Mum look, there's a nest on the floor', and I goes 'Mum can I go and have a look at it?' and I went over there and there was four baby chicks in it, little chicks, I think they were willow warbler and my mum said 'Climb up and put them back in the tree', so and I had some bread, eaten some bread, so I fed it bits of bread, cause she had to go to the phone, and em she waited and I put it back up in the tree and its mum's with it now. Yea, cause someone, someone had pulled the nest down, out of the tree
Geoff	I know this kid called Richie Binns who knocked a nest down on purpose [. . .]

(Source: Maybin 2006: 127–8)

Figure 15.7
Transcription of a conversational narrative: standard layout

(1)	Yesterday I was on, I was walking with my mum,
(2)	we walked past this bush,
(3)	and there was this nest
(4)	and it was fallen down on the floor,
(5)	and I goes "Mum look, there's a nest on the floor",
(6)	and I goes "Mum can I go and have a look at it?"
(7)	and I went over there
(8)	and there was four baby chicks in it, little chicks,
	[. . .]

Note: 'Lines are identified rhythmically and correspond to [narrative] clauses (treating line 1 as including a false start). Verses consist of two sets of paired lines linked through repetition and parallelism, each new verse also moving the story on' (Maybin and Swann, 2007: 507). These conventions, it is argued, reveal the poetic quality of the narrative.

(Source: Maybin and Swann 2007: 507)

Figure 15.8
Transcription of a conversational narrative: poetic layout

in Figures 15.3 and 15.9 but it is not always the case. In young children's speech, for instance, speaking turns may not follow on directly from a preceding turn. Column transcripts do not make the same assumptions about sequencing and connections between turns, so may be useful for this kind of talk. At issue, however, is the allocation of columns to speakers. Because of factors such as the left–right orientation in European scripts, and associated conventions of page layout, we may give priority to information located on the left-hand side. Ochs (1979) points out that, in column transcripts of adult–child talk, the adult is nearly always allocated the left-hand column, suggesting

	G1	G2	B1	B2	Notes
1	What are we going				addresses group
2	to do at home (.)				directly
3	any ideas				
4			Yes (.) I take		refers to book,
5			this (.) I take		holds up;
6			this (.) yes yes		general
7			I take it mmh and		laughter around
8			I see and I see		here
9			if there's		
10			something I can		
11			use (.)		
12					
13	We can use (?)				
14			We can use		
15				So what (would)	question
16				we do (xxxx) read	towards girls?
17				it at home (.)	
18				the questionnaire	
19			(xxxxx)	(.) read it at	
20				home	
	[. . .]				
21		Maybe I can get			
22		some materials			
23		for this			
24	From (xxx)				
25	(mother)				
26		Yes			
27			from where (?)		
28		from my mother			
29		(.) from the			
30		travel agency			

Note: (?) indicates a guess at a speaker; in this case, I have numbered lines not turns; this makes it easier to refer to any overlapping speech.

(Source: Swann 2001: 333)

Figure 15.9   Transcription of small group talk: column layout

they are the initiator of the conversation. In Figure 15.9 I began with Girl 1, probably because she spoke first, but I also grouped the girls and then the boys together. This may be useful in research attending to gender issues, but Ochs's comment is a further reminder that such decisions are not neutral: they may have an ideological basis, and they may suggest certain readings or interpretations of data.

Accounts of conversational turn-taking have often assumed that one person talks at a time (e.g. Sacks et al., 1974). This is not always the case, however, particularly in more informal discussion where there may be considerable amounts of overlapping talk and where speakers frequently complete one another's turns. In her analysis of informal

Figure 15.10
Transcription of
group talk: stave
layout

1	Bel	Right/anything else?/everyone [have a think/right/
	Jan	[everyone have a think
	Lou	
	Rosa	

2	Bel	
	Jan	about their important memories/
	Lou	
	Rosa	

3	Bel	I've got one (.)/right I remember (.)
	Jan	
	Lou	
	Rosa	

4	Bel	[((laughs)) Jan AGAIN/
	Jan	I've got this important [memory of school was-/I got
	Lou	
	Rosa	

5	Bel	
	Jan	[this effort trophy at middle school (.)/
	Lou	[Jan again/ yeah?/
	Rosa	

6	Bel	
	Jan	and I-/oh and I were-/and I was dead chuffed/I thought
	Lou	
	Rosa	

7	Bel	
	Jan	it were great/ an effort trophy?/ it
	Lou	I got one of them/ yeah/
	Rosa	

8	Bel	were great weren't it?/
	Jan	[it were great/
	Lou	[at the fourth year of juniors/
	Rosa	

Note: A slash (/) represents the end of a tone group; a question mark indicates the end of a tone group analysed as a question.
Staves are numbered and separated by horizontal lines; all the talk within a stave is to be read together, sequentially from left to right.

Transcript adapted from Davies' original. Davies follows Coates in representing, within a stave, only those students who are speaking. The version above includes all students, illustrating that Rosa does not speak in this sequence. Rosa may have been contributing non-verbally, and she speaks later in the discussion.

(Source: adapted from Davies 2000: 290)

talk amongst women friends, Jennifer Coates developed a method of transcription in which she used a 'stave' layout (by analogy with musical staves) to represent the joint construction of speaking turns (see, for instance, Coates, 2006). Stave transcription may also be adopted to illustrate highly collaborative talk in institutional contexts such as education. Figure 15.10 comes from a study made by Julia Davies (2000) of English lessons in three secondary schools in Sheffield, in the north of England. Davies was particularly interested in gender issues – in how girls and boys worked together in single-sex and mixed-sex groups. Figure 15.10 shows a group of four teenage girls reflecting on their earlier experiences of school. Davies found (like Coates) that the girls' talk was particularly collaborative (e.g. it contained overlapping speech, joint construction of turns and several indicators of conversational support).

The layout selected for a transcript will reflect certain research interests and analytical priorities. Here I have tried to show how different layouts highlight certain aspects of talk and play down others, and may therefore predispose the analyst/reader towards certain readings or interpretations.

Multimodal transcription

Many of the transcripts above include conventions to represent non-verbal information that may contribute to the meaning of an utterance: features such as pauses, loudness or emphasis, laughter, aspects of voice quality. Transcripts may also use an additional (usually right-hand) column for such information, or to indicate activities that accompany speech (e.g. a student holding up a book in Figure 15.3). In all of these cases, verbal language is the main focus of attention and other features are analysed as ancillary or supporting elements. Conventions also exist, however, to represent a range of communicative modes more systematically. These do not simply reflect alternative transcriptions: they are also underpinned by theories of communication that take account of the combination of different modes in producing meaning. In relation to the analysis of classroom interaction, for instance, Jewitt and Kress comment:

We proceed on the assumption that representation and communication always draw on a multiplicity of modes, all of which contribute to meaning. We focus on means for analysing and describing the full repertoire of meaning-making resources which students and teachers bring to the classroom (actional, visual, spoken, gestural, written, three-dimensional, and others, depending on the domain of representation), and on developing means that show how these are organised to make meaning. That is, we focus on a multimodal approach to classroom interaction.

(Jewitt and Kress, 2003: 277)

Multimodal transcription is a highly complex process. Norris (2004) describes a step-by-step process that involves the separate transcription of spoken language, proxemics (distance between speakers), posture, gesture, head movement, gaze, music (i.e. background music that speakers seem to respond to), and print (participants' use of print media), followed by the integration of these dimensions to produce a complete transcript. 'Transcription' of visual elements involves the selection and assembly of video stills representing relevant activity – for example, initial posture followed by each postural change – time-coded to identify their exact location in the interaction. Figure 15.11 is an

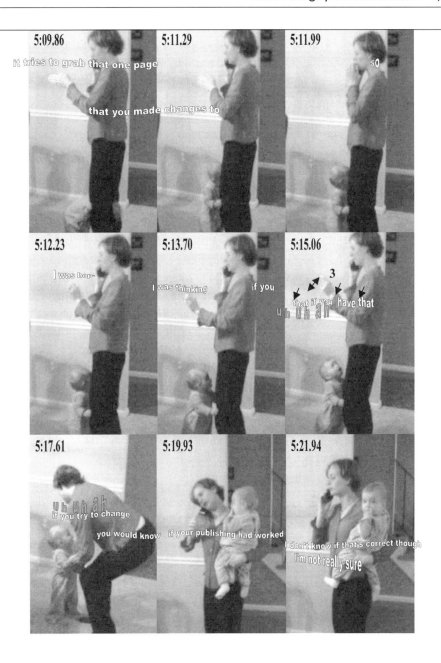

Figure 15.11
Multimodal transcript including video stills

Note: in the transcription of speech, rising and lowering of intonation is represented by curves, pitch by size and boldness of letters, pauses by spaces between letters or utterances, overlap by closeness/touching of utterances. The time code represents minutes: seconds. hundredths of a second.

In photographs, speaker's faces are sometimes blurred to protect their anonymity, but Norris's informants have given permission for their photographs to be used.

(Source: Norris 2004: 76)

extract from Norris's final (integrated) transcript of a web designer working at home, talking to a client on the phone while also looking after her daughter. In this case, arrows have been superimposed to indicate the direction of a gesture (at 5:15.06). Verbal language is also superimposed on the image sequence. A separate document contains observations on the overlap between different modes across this sequence of images. The relative salience of visual information tends to de-emphasize the verbal component in this and similar transcripts. Norris argues, however: 'we are not taking away the importance of spoken language, but rather accentuating the other communicative modes that are as essential in interaction as spoken language' (2004: 65).

It is possible to make simpler and/or more selective transcripts that indicate the integration of different communicative modes. Features that are closely integrated with speech may be represented graphically in the transcript (above, below or next to the lines of speech). The inclusion of several features (the various dimensions identified by Norris, for instance) may make a transcript hard to read, but it is possible to focus on aspects that are of particular interest. The transcript in Figure 15.12 indicates a teacher's gaze towards female and male students in a primary school classroom. The full transcript from which this is extracted shows that the teacher's gaze is more frequently directed towards the boys at critical points in the interaction, such as when a question is to be answered.

The transcript conventions discussed earlier in this chapter may also be adapted to include a greater degree of non-verbal information. Figure 15.13 shows how Jewitt and Kress (2003) use 'speech' and 'action' columns to transcribe a teacher's explanation of blood circulation in a science lesson. Jewitt and Kress also provide photographs of a diagram drawn by the teacher and of a model of the upper part of the human body that he uses in his explanation.

Figure 15.12
Representation of teacher's gaze towards female and male students

Teacher:	If you have a pendulum (.) which we established last week was a weight a mass (.) suspended from a string or whatever (.) and watch I'm holding it with my hand so it's at rest at the moment (.) what is it that makes the pendulum swing in a downward direction for instance till it gets to there? (.) [just watch it
Matthew:	[Gravity
Teacher:	What is it Matthew?
Matthew:	Gravity
Teacher:	[Yes (.) now we mentioned gravity when we
Boy:	[(xxxxx)
Teacher:	were actually doing the experiments but we didn't discuss it too much (.) OK so it's gravity then that pulls it down (.) what causes it to go up again at the other side?
Boy:	[Force the force
Boy:	[The string miss

Note:	pendulum – solid underlining = gaze to girls
	hand – broken underlining = gaze to boys
	? = utterance analysed as a question

(Source: Adapted from Swann 1989/1998: 185–96)

	Speech	Action
Figure 15.13 Representation of speech and action in a science lesson	Now if we look at that on our model you can actually see here the heart has four main blood vessels okay now . . . [. . .]	Places model on front desk stands behind model, arms in front picks up heart, points at heart puts heart back in model [. . .]

(Source: Jewitt and Kress 2003: 283)

Guy Cook (1995), in a paper provocatively subtitled 'transcribing the untranscribable', points to two broad problems in the representation of non-verbal information. One has to do with the potential infinity of detail that might be included in ever more delicate transcripts; the other concerns the potential for infinite expansion: once transcription goes beyond words, it is not clear where it should stop – what should count as relevant non-verbal information. In practice, researchers are necessarily selective in this as in other aspects of transcription. All transcription involves choices, related to particular research interests, disciplinary priorities, theories, ideologies. As Bucholtz (2000) argues, transcription therefore requires a degree of reflexivity and an acknowledgement of the affordances and limitations of the particular choices made.

Note

1   These data come from a research project funded by the Nuffield Foundation, and led by Neil Mercer, University of Cambridge. I am grateful to Neil Mercer and the research team for permission to reanalyse data from the project.

References

Bucholtz, M. (2000) 'The politics of transcription', *Journal of Pragmatics*, 32: 1439–65.
Canagarajah, A.S. (2000) 'Constructing hybrid postcolonial subjects: codeswitching in Jaffna classrooms' in M. Heller and M. Martin-Jones (eds) *Voices of Authority: education and linguistic difference*, London: Ablex.
Coates, J. (2006) *Women Talk: conversation between women friends*, Oxford/Cambridge, Mass: Blackwell Publishers.
Cook, G. (1995) 'Theoretical issues: transcribing the untranscribable' in G. Leech, G. Myers, and J. Thomas (eds) *Spoken English on Computer: transcription, mark-up and applications*, London: Longman.
Dam, L. and Lentz, J. (1998) *It's up to yourself if you want to learn: autonomous language learning at intermediate level* (Video and print), Copenhagen: DLH.
Davies, J.A. (2000) 'Expressions of Gender: an enquiry into the way gender impacts on the discourse styles of pupils involved in small group talk during GCSE English lesson, with particular reference to the under-achievement of boys'. Unpublished thesis, University of Sheffield.
Edwards, A.D and Westgate, D.P.G. (1994, 2nd edn) *Investigating Classroom Talk*, London: Falmer Press.

Fine, E. (1983) 'In defense of literary dialogue: a response to Dennis R. Preston', *Journal of American Folklore*, 96 (381): 323–30.

Hymes, D.H. (1996) *Ethnography, Linguistics, Narrative Inequality: towards an understanding of voice*, London: Taylor and Francis.

Jewitt, C. and Kress, G. (2003) 'A multimodal approach to research in education', in S. Goodman, T. Lillis, J. Maybin and N. Mercer (eds) *Language, Literacy and Education: a reader*, Stoke on Trent: Trentham Books in association with the Open University.

Maybin, J. (2006) *Children's Voices: talk, knowledge and identity*, Basingstoke, Hants/New York: Palgrave Macmillan.

Maybin, J. and Swann, J. (2007) 'Everyday creativity in language: textuality, contextuality and critique', in J. Swann and J. Maybin (eds) Special Issue of *Applied Linguistics* on *Language Creativity in Everyday Contexts*, 28 (4): 497–517.

Mercer, N., Dawes, L., Wegerif, R. and Sams, C. (2004) 'Reasoning as a scientist: ways of helping children to use language to learn science', *British Educational Research Journal*, 30 (3): 359–77.

Norris, S. (2004) *Analyzing Multimodal Interaction: a methodological framework*, New York/London: Routledge.

Ochs, E. (1979) 'Transcription as theory', in E. Ochs and B.B. Schieffelin (eds) *Developmental Pragmatics*, London: Academic Press.

Preston, D.R. (1982) 'Ritin' fowklower daun rong: folklorists' failures in phonology', *Journal of American Folklore*, 95 (377): 304–16.

Preston, D.R. (1983) 'Mowr bayud spellin': a reply to Fine', *Journal of American Folklore*, 96 (381): 330–9.

Rampton, B. (1995, 2005, 2nd edn) *Crossing: language and ethnicity among adolescents*. Manchester: St Jerome Press.

Rampton, B. (2006) 'Language crossing', in J. Maybin and J. Swann (eds) *The Art of English: everyday creativity*. Basingstoke, Hants: Palgrave Macmillan in association with the Open University.

Roberts, C. (1997) 'Transcribing talk: issues of representation', *TESOL Quarterly*, 31 (1): 167-72.

Sacks, H., Schegloff, E.A. and Jefferson, G. (1974) 'A simplest systematics for the organization of turn-taking for conversation', *Language*, 50 (4): 696–735.

Sebba, M. (1993) *London Jamaican: language systems in interaction*, London: Longman.

Swann, J. (1989) 'Talk control? An illustration from the classroom of problems in analysing male dominance of conversation', in J. Coates and D. Cameron (eds) *Women in their Speech Communities*, London: Longman. Edited version reprinted in J. Coates (ed.) (1998) *Language and Gender: a reader*, Oxford: Blackwell Publishers.

Swann, J. (2001) 'Recording and transcribing talk in educational settings', in C.N. Candlin and N. Mercer (eds) *English Language Teaching in its Social Context*, London: Routledge.

Swann, J. (2007) 'Designing "educationally effective" discussion', *Language and Education*, 21 (4): 342–59.

Introduction to chapter 16

This chapter is one of three that focus on methods of carrying out research in Applied Linguistics and it is also one of several that talk about using corpus data as an aid in studying language. Unlike the other 'corpus' chapters, though, this one concentrates on spoken language and on a feature of spoken English (the word *like*) that is much more frequent in spoken English than in written English. The key concepts introduced in this chapter are: spoken corpus, word frequency, discourse marker and vague language.

The background to this chapter

A corpus is a collection of texts that are stored electronically. The texts may be written or spoken, but spoken texts have to be transcribed to go into a corpus. Specialized software is used to investigate corpora. This software usually does tasks such as counting the instances of a given word or structure, finding phrases that occur frequently, identifying collocations, and comparing one kind of text with another. Corpora are now a very popular way of investigating language and several chapters in this book have referred to them.

Corpora have been used to study language since the 1960s. In the early days they were used mainly to test hypotheses about a language (e.g. does a particular structure really exist?) and to measure the relative frequency of two language features (e.g. is the present tense or the past tense more frequent?). Nowadays, however, researchers are more likely to look at a corpus to develop new ideas about language than to measure the frequency of old concepts. The researchers who have specialized in spoken English in particular stress the unforeseen ways in which speech is different from writing. They also question the reliability of grammars of English that are based on writing rather than speech.

Most researchers investigating corpora use a number of techniques that take both a broad view (processing the corpus as a whole) and a narrow view (looking at individual instances of a word in use). Adolphs illustrates some of these techniques in this chapter. For example, she uses a simple list of words, ordered from most to least frequent, to demonstrate that her chosen word, *like*, is much more frequent, relatively, in spoken than in written English. She also uses measurements of collocation (see Chapter 2 by Oakey for an explanation of this) to demonstrate which other words occur frequently close to *like*, and so to strengthen her argument that *like* is used in the context of vague language. Adolphs is also able to give a general sense of the most frequent uses of *like*. To see these she will have looked quickly at all the examples of *like* in her corpus. One way to do this is to use concordance lines. Concordance lines show each instance of the chosen word with a few words on either side. For a more detailed study, Adolphs picks some representative examples of *like* and examines their place in each individual conversation more closely.

Adolphs mentions some of the features of spoken English that have been identified by her and her colleagues. One is the prevalence of vague language, that is, expressions such as *sort of* or *and things like that* that make information less rather than more precise. The function of vague language often seems to be to make a statement or question less assertive or aggressive rather than to indicate a lack of precise knowledge. For example, here is an extract from an interview with a young girl; the interviewer is asking the girl about her father:

> Has he got any particular wishes? Is he **sort of** trying to encourage you to go in any direction?

In terms of the question itself, there would be little difference if the speaker left it out:

> Is he trying to encourage you to go in any direction?

However, the second version of this may sound a little like an accusation – the father is interfering too much. The original version, with *sort of*, sounds less accusatory.

Another phenomenon mentioned by Adolphs is creativity in spoken language. Carter (2004) notes that, although we often think of creativity in language as belonging to poets and other literary writers, ordinary speakers are often creative too. The example quoted by Adolphs is the expression *an anti anti social chair*. She points out that this breaks the norms of use in two ways. First, 'anti-social' is an expression usually used of people or their behaviour, not of objects (e.g. *I think it* [throwing litter] *is the most anti-social thing that anybody ever does*). Second, using *anti* to negate *anti-social* is extremely unusual, if not unique in this instance. Thus, the speaker, in using this expression to indicate 'I became a very sociable person because I sat in that chair', is being very creative.

Finally, Adolphs devotes most of the chapter to the study of a discourse marker, *like*. A discourse marker is a word or phrase whose function is best described in terms of its role in an interaction rather than in terms of grammatical word class. Two roles for *like* are identified here: as a marker of direct speech (as in *she was like 'I don't want to go there'*); and as a preposition (arguably) whose main function is to link together two utterances in the conversation. Both uses are highly colloquial and unlikely to be found in teaching materials. Researchers who are investigating language from the point of view of written grammar may not think to look for them but they can be discovered by detailed study of spoken language.

Focusing on the argument

This chapter uses relatively few examples of a single word to illustrate points about using a corpus to study spoken English. Talking about one apparently insignificant word could appear trivial, but the chapter avoids this by linking this study into a much wider context. The chapter begins, not just by describing the CANCODE corpus (© Cambridge University Press) but by arguing for its unique value in a research field that is dominated by corpora of written language. The word *like* is selected for study, not just because it is frequent, but also because it illustrates a number of larger points that Adolphs wishes to make. These include points about spoken English itself – it uses creativity, vague language, direct speech and discourse markers. They also include points about what it means to do research into a language, and the challenges posed by researching something as ephemeral as speech.

Adolphs ends by posing a question: how much information about spoken language can be made available to learners, and in what contexts? It is interesting that she poses this as a question rather than as advice. She recognizes that it may not be easy for teachers to accommodate findings about conversational English into their materials or their coursebooks, and that to do so may involve looking not only at what is taught but also how it is taught.

A language tip

This chapter uses the words *corpus* and *corpora*, which can be confusing. The first is the singular form of the noun; the second is the plural. In these sentences, Adolphs uses the singular *corpus*:

> A computerized language **corpus** is a principled collection of texts stored in electronic format. We can learn more about the language in a **corpus** by using software designed to make patterns of language accessible.

In these sentences, she uses the plural *corpora*:

> Most language **corpora** are assembled with the aim of making statements about language which can be statistically supported. . . . There is a general tendency for written language to predominate in computerized **corpora** because such data are so much easier to collect.

Another word which is often confused between singular and plural is *data*. Originally this was a plural word with a singular form *datum*. Nowadays, however, *datum* is very rarely found. Many people would still consider *data* to be plural and would use it, as Adolphs does, with a plural verb, for example, *The spoken data were recorded . . .* Increasingly, however, *data* is found being used as if it was a singular noun, for example, *Last year, data was collected . . .* On balance, this singular use is probably best avoided in formal writing as some people would consider it incorrect.

To think about

1 Adolphs says that corpus studies can be quantitative and/or qualitative. Which of the examples she gives are quantitative and which are qualitative?

2 What do you think about the uses of *like* that Adolphs presents in this chapter? Do you regard them as 'incorrect'? Or as good, colloquial English? How would you use this information with learners?

3 From the evidence in this chapter, do you think that using a corpus tells you things about English that you did not know before?

CHAPTER 16

Using a corpus to study spoken language

Svenja Adolphs

The aim of this chapter is to explore the contribution corpora can make towards the study of spoken language. To this end, examples from the five-million-word Cambridge and Nottingham Corpus of Discourse in English (CANCODE) are examined.[1] The spoken data were recorded in a wide variety of mostly informal settings across the islands of Britain and Ireland and then transcribed and stored in computer-readable form. This chapter focuses on a particular example, the word *like*, in order to illustrate the relationship between language and discourse as it emerges from the corpus data used for this study.

What is a corpus of spoken language?

A computerized language corpus is a principled collection of texts stored in electronic format. We can learn more about the language in a corpus by using software designed to make patterns of language accessible. Corpus linguistics is both a tradition and a methodology that is concerned with this process. Biber et al. (1998: 4) describe corpus linguistics as follows:

- it is empirical, analysing actual patterns of use of a language in natural texts
- it utilizes a large and principled collection of natural texts, known as a 'corpus', as the basis for analysis
- it makes extensive use of computers for analysis, using both automatic and interactive techniques
- it depends on both quantitative and qualitative analytical techniques.

Most language corpora are assembled with the aim of making statements about language which can be statistically supported. They are invaluable in the construction of authentic reference materials such as dictionaries for learners of English for example. There is a general tendency for written language to predominate in computerized corpora because such data are so much easier to collect.

However, the past two decades have seen major advances in the development of spoken corpora including, for example, the Cambridge and Nottingham Corpus of Discourse in English *CANCODE* (McCarthy 1998), the Limerick Corpus of Irish English *LCIE* (Farr et al. 2004), the Hong Kong Corpus of Spoken English *HKCSE* (see Cheng and Warren 1999, 2000, 2002), the Michigan Corpus of Academic Spoken English *MICASE* (Simpson et al. 2000), and the Corpus of Spoken Professional American English *CSPAE*. There is also a growing interest in the development of spoken corpora of international varieties of English and other languages, as well as of learner language (e.g. De Cock et al. 1998).

Research outputs based on such corpora of spoken language-in-use are wide-ranging and include, for example, descriptions of spoken versus written lexis and grammar (e.g. Biber et al. 1999; Carter and McCarthy 2006), discourse particles (Aijmer 2002), courtroom talk (Cotterill 2004), media discourse (O'Keeffe 2006) and health care communication (Adolphs et al. 2004).

The analysis of written corpora often focuses on frequency information and concordance outputs. In addition to the use of such methods, spoken corpus analysis tends to benefit from an approach that goes beyond the clause boundary. A number of studies start with the exploration of concordance and frequency outputs and use these as a point of entry for subsequent analysis of discourse level features (see, for example, McCarthy 1998). This approach will be illustrated in the sample analysis below.

Developing research and classroom applications: the example of *like*

One of the key contributions that spoken corpus analysis can make in relation to language description is to help us identify features of spoken English which have been largely neglected and remained under-explored due to a long tradition of using exclusively written data as the basis for descriptions of the English language. The analysis below explores some examples of the word *like* which are more typical of its usage in spoken discourse.

Word frequencies

An analysis of word frequencies in different corpora can be a useful first step to get a general idea of the texts in the corpus.

Adolphs (2006: 41) shows the ten most frequent words in the written part of the British National Corpus compared with the spoken CANCODE corpus. While there is a certain amount of overlap between the two corpora in terms of the most frequent items, there are a number of differences which highlight the fact that one corpus contains written language samples while the other consists solely of spoken language. In particular the personal pronoun 'I' and the signal of active listenership 'Yeah', which feature among the most frequent items in the CANCODE corpus but are absent from the written data, indicate the difference in mode.

The word *like* is the twenty-third most frequent item in the CANCODE corpus and occurs with an overall frequency of 31,743 instances. It is five times more frequent in spoken than in written English. The high frequency of occurrence in the spoken language of this item suggests that it carries a number of additional functions in speech compared with its uses in writing. In order to fully illustrate the meaning of items such as this one, it is important to go beyond the sentence which still remains the main unit in descriptions of lexis and grammar in reference material about the English Language. When we study the word *like* in the CANCODE corpus, it is therefore important to consider stretches of discourse which capture the nature of the interaction across speaking turns.

In addition to the traditional grammatical roles of *like* as a preposition, conjunction, common verb and suffix, an analysis of spoken corpus data illustrates that it often fulfils the function of a discourse marker. It is this function which is the focus of the following analysis.

Frequency rank	BNC (written)	CANCODE (spoken)
1	The	The
2	Of	I
3	And	And
4	A	You
5	In	It
6	To	To
7	Is	A
8	Was	Yeah
9	It	That
10	For	Of

Table 16.1
Top 10 frequent items in the BNC and CANCODE

Like as discourse marker

When *like* is used as a discourse marker, it often functions to mark direct speech in speech reporting episodes. In addition, *like* is often used to suggest points of comparison or exemplification even if those comparisons and examples are not actually drawn upon. These two functions will be examined in more detail below.

Speech reporting

One of the more frequent uses of *like* in spoken English is to mark direct speech. This is a relatively recent phenomenon but it is extensive, the corpus reveals, in the speech of younger speakers. The use of *like* in this way is not quite (yet) an example of spoken standard English. *Like* stands in the place of '*said that* plus quoted speech'. As such it often introduces speech reports. In his study of CANCODE data McCarthy (1998: 161) finds that 'in the narrative texts in the CANCODE corpus, speech reports are overwhelmingly direct speech, and with reporting verbs in past simple (*said, told*) or historical present *says*'. One of the reasons for this is to add to the 'vividness' and 'real-time staging' (ibid.) of the discourse. Furthermore, representing the speech as a direct quotation adds to the authenticity of a narrative. The extract below, drawn from the CANCODE corpus, illustrates this. It involves the recount of a narrative and is drawn from a conversation between three female friends in their twenties. The conversation centres around an inflatable ('blow-up') chair.

Extract 1

> <S02> I was having this hideous party last weekend and there was a blow up chair so I sat in it for a bit. I was feeling really antisocial and just really wanted to go home. And Jane and Benny had made me come cos it's this Denise and oh er she's a hairdresser and she had a lot of hairdressery friends. All dressed really smartly and standing round not saying anything.
> <S01> Jane is?
> <S02> No Jane's friend Denise.
> <S01> Oh right.
> <S02> So Jane made me come because she she she'd agreed to go and so she was **like** "I don't want to go there and there are all these hairdressers and me and Benny."
> [laughter]
> <S02> And that was that. It was really shit and I wish I hadn't agreed to do it. Sat in the chair. After five minutes I was **like** "Yeah. Party" and singing. Making suggestions [laughter]
> <S02> Suddenly became the life and soul after sitting there.
> <S01> Barmy.
> [laughter]
> <S01> An anti anti social chair. Maybe I'll get one.
> [laughs]
> <S01> They're just so ugly.
> <S03> They are hideous.

The word *like* is used here to report the speech of other people, as well as that of the speakers themselves. The goal of the conversation is to entertain the other speakers and to keep the conversation flowing. There is, as has been noted, almost a display or performance element to what is quoted by means of *like*, so that *like*, certainly much more than a plain 'said', serves to dramatically highlight what follows and sets the stage for a speech report which is marked by its quotability, especially by its intensity and by the very prosodic contours which are reproduced. Other elements that add to this goal and to the vividness of the conversation are the use of strong evaluative statements ('It was really shit', 'they are hideous') and the embedding of creativity in the narrative ('An anti anti social chair'). The latter is achieved through the use and part repetition of 'anti social' in relation to an inanimate object.

Comparison and exemplification
The next extract from the CANCODE corpus illustrates another function of the word *like* which we commonly find in the spoken corpus data. The conversation below takes place between two cleaners in a hall of residence. The item *like* here introduces a new element into the discourse flow which prompts further elaboration. Its function is to compare the situation that is being discussed (Lynsey and Agnes's job) with a similar situation (Alice's job). This, in turn, extends the discussion in a particular direction.

Extract 2

> \<S1\> Ah it's a bit dicey cos there's a lot of people going round at the minute. You
> know what with Adam checking the lights and+
> \<S2\> Yeah.
> \<S1\> + checking curtains. Mind you I had to laugh cos I went over there And
> Lynsey and bloody Agnes are sitting in the bloody porter's lodge talking. I thought
> You've got a good sodding job.
> \<S2\> [unintelligible] find you summat to do.
> \<S1\> Oh **like** what Alice's doing?
> \<S2\> Well she's wip= she's re-cleaning what she cleaned the other week+
> \<S1\> [unintelligible]
> \<S2\> +from what I saw of her yesterday.
> \<S1\> I can't see the point can you.
> \<S2\> No. It's so boring.

In the next extract *like* is used in a similar way and is again preceded by 'oh' and refers
back to the information presented in the preceding turn, marking the collaborative
nature of the discourse at hand. In this conversation two members of a family are
chatting. The first use of *like* in this extract functions to express the similarity between
two objects in order to establish a closer description of a particular point of reference.
This is done collaboratively with speaker \<2\> extending and refining the description
advanced by speaker \<1\>. The second use of *like* again expresses similarity and
functions to suggest a point of comparison although this time the point of reference
is contained within the speaker's utterance and does not extend the previous discourse.

Extract 3

> \<S1\> This was just There was a nice little c= little like a little house cafe erm of
> home-made things and we had to have a lunch there you know. Just er They were
> doing these toasties you know where you put it in a toaster and put it down and put
> a filling in the toaster. Erm
> \<S2\> Oh **like** waffle type things.
> \<S1\> Yes. And we had our lunch there and you could walk through this cafe and
> then into this big mill. And erm I got two two packs. One was three hundred grams
> and it was two ninety nine and the other one was three hundred grams and it was
> one ninety nine but it wasn't wool it was silky. It was a silky thing. Erm I I've
> \<S2\> Oh Chrissy got some stuff. It was **like** ribbon that she got.
> \<S1\> Oh yes this is the up and coming thing this ribbon.

One of the reasons why the word *like* cannot easily be described with reference to single
utterances is that there are a number of features in the extended stretch of conversation
which are important markers of spoken language and reinforce the function of *like* in
this context. For example, *like* co-occurs here with a number of markers of vague
language and other discourse markers, including *just, home-made things, you know,*

waffle type things and some stuff. Vague language (see Adolphs et al. 2007; Channell 1994) softens expressions so that they do not appear too direct or unduly authoritative and assertive. When we interact with others there are times when it is necessary to give accurate and precise information; in many informal contexts, however, speakers prefer to convey information which is softened in some way or which is purposefully imprecise, although such vagueness is often wrongly taken as a sign of careless thinking or sloppy expression.

Table 16.2 shows the 15 most frequent collocates of the word *like* in the CANCODE corpus. Using the C-Score, a measure to calculate the level of attraction between the word *like* and other words in the corpus, the output thus generated illustrates the strong patterning with the kinds of vague language and discourse markers discussed above (e.g. *things, just, stuff, anything, something, (you) know*).

Table 16.2
Fifteen most frequent collocates of *like* in the CANCODE corpus

	Word	C-Score
1	that	2.38
2	things	2.02
3	it	1.79
4	something	1.78
5	you	1.58
6	looks	1.50
7	to	1.23
8	just	1.15
9	this	0.84
10	don't	0.79
11	know	0.74
12	would	0.48
13	stuff	0.46
14	anything	0.42
15	sounds	0.26

Deictic reference markers (*this, these*) which underline the shared context and shared knowledge of the participants also abound in the extract above (e.g. *these toasties, this café, this ribbon*). It is interesting to note that *like* shares the same communicative territory as vague language markers, discourse markers and reference markers. The corpus also reveals that in terms of social interaction *like* has a particular provenance in more informal encounters. In CANCODE there is a significantly lower count of uses of *like* as a discourse marker in the more formal contexts.

Conclusion

The analysis in this chapter has illustrated the use of a corpus to study spoken language. Two functions of the word *like* have been discussed which tend to appear more frequently in spoken discourse than in written discourse. A corpus of spoken English can provide evidence of frequency distribution, as well as discourse level features that co-occur with individual words that are being investigated. Spoken corpora that are carefully categorized in terms of different contextual configurations can also provide evidence for word distribution across different contexts. The specific uses of *like* discussed above are associated mainly with casual conversation between people who know each other well. As a result we need to address the *applied* linguistic question of how far this kind of information can be useful in terms of reference material of English. How much information do learners needs concerning contextual usage or are the broad categories of spoken and written sufficient for most purposes? A grammar of English which is corpus-informed, based on both written and spoken examples and which illustrates the extent to which *like* functions across sentence boundaries and across speaking turns needs to find appropriate ways of highlighting such features for learners of English. Further evidence from spoken and written corpora is required to support this process. The new uses of the word *like* discussed above especially in relation to speech reporting functions also mean that it is important to keep updating spoken corpora on a regular basis to capture new and emerging patterns of use.

Acknowledgements

I am grateful to Ronald Carter for comments on an earlier draft of this paper.

Note

1   The corpus was developed at the University of Nottingham, UK between 1994 and 2001, and was funded by Cambridge University Press ©, with whom sole copyright resides.

References

Adolphs, S. (2006) *Introducing Electronic Text Analysis: A Practical Guide for Language and Literary Studies.* Abingdon and New York: Routledge.

Adolphs, S., Atkins, S. and Harvey, K. (2007) 'Caught between professional requirements and interpersonal needs: vague language in health care contexts'. In J. Cutting (ed.) *Vague Language Explored.* Basingstoke: Palgrave Macmillan, 62–78.

Adolphs, S., Brown, B., Carter, R., Crawford, P. and Sahota, O. (2004) 'Applying Corpus Linguistics in a health care context'. *Journal of Applied Linguistics* 1: 9–28.

Aijmer, K. (2002) *English Discourse Particles: Evidence from a Corpus.* Amsterdam and Philadelphia: John Benjamins.

Biber, D., Conrad, S. and Reppen, R. (1998) *Corpus Linguistics: Investigating Language Structure and Use.* Cambridge: Cambridge University Press.

Biber, D., Johansson, S., Leech, G., Conrad, S. and Finegan, E. (1999) *Longman Grammar of Spoken and Written English.* London: Pearson.

Carter, R. (2004) *Language and Creativity: The art of common talk.* London and New York: Routledge.

Carter, R. and McCarthy, M. (2006) *The Cambridge Grammar of English.* Cambridge: Cambridge University Press.

Channell, J. (1994) *Vague Language.* Oxford: Oxford University Press.

Cheng, W. and Warren, M. (1999) 'Facilitating a Description of Intercultural Conversations: The Hong Kong Corpus of Conversational English'. *ICAME Journal* 23: 5–20.

Cheng, W. and Warren, M. (2000) 'The Hong Kong Corpus of Spoken English: Language learning through language description'. In L. Burnard and T. McEnery (eds), *Rethinking Language Pedagogy from a Corpus Perspective: Papers from the Third*

International Conference on Teaching and Language Corpora. Frankfurt am Main: Peter Lang, 132–44.

Cheng, W. and Warren, M. (2002) '// ↘↗beef ball // → you like //: The Intonation of Declarative-Mood Questions in a Corpus of Hong Kong English'. *Teanga* 21: 151–165.

Cotterill, J. (2004) 'Collocation, Connotation and Courtroom Semantics: Lawyers' Control of Witness Testimony through Lexical Negotiation'. *Applied Linguistics* 25: 513–537.

De Cock, S., Granger, S., Leech, G. and McEnery, T. (1998) 'An automated approach to the phrasicon of EFL learners'. In S. Granger (ed.), *Learner English on Computer*. London: Longman, 67–79.

Farr, F., Murphy, B. and O'Keefe, A. (2004) 'The Limerick Corpus of Irish English: Design, description and application'. *Teanga* 21: 5–29.

McCarthy, M. (1998) *Spoken Language and Applied Linguistics.* Cambridge: Cambridge University Press.

O'Keeffe, A. (2006) *Investigating Media Discourse.* London: Routledge.

Simpson, R., Lucka, B. and Ovens, J. 2000. 'Methodological challenges of planning a spoken corpus with pedagogical outcomes'. In L. Burnard and T. McEnery (eds), *Rethinking Language Pedagogy from a Corpus Perspective: Papers from the Third International Conference on Teaching and Language Corpora*. Frankfurt am Main: Peter Lang, 43–9.

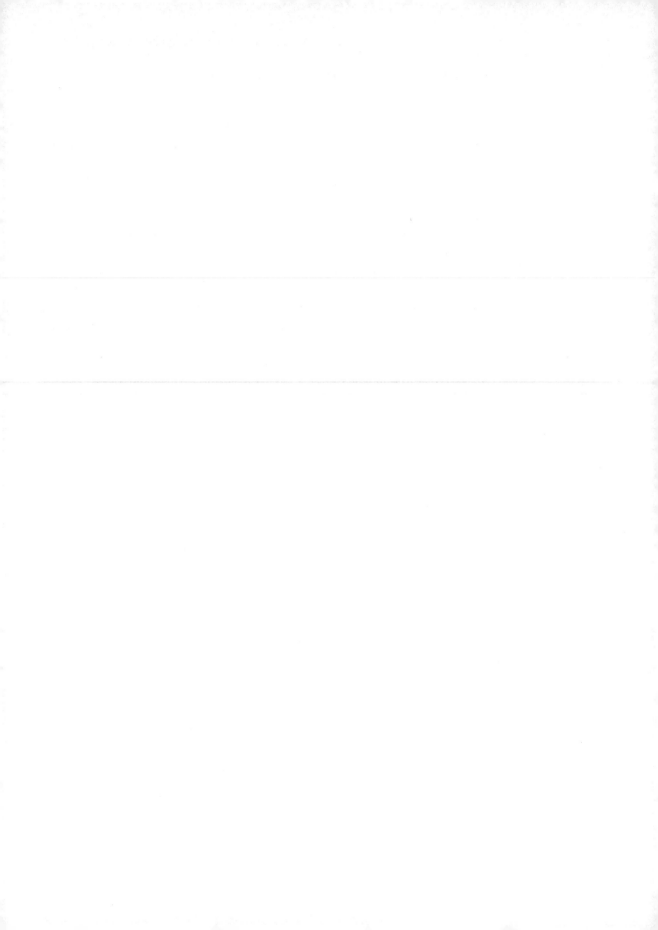

V Skills of interpretation

Introduction to chapter 17

This chapter is the first of our 'study skills' chapters. It focuses on noun phrases, which are a key ingredient of academic writing. Often, noun phrases in this kind of writing are very long and include a lot of information. Interpreting and processing that information can be difficult.

Here is an example, from chapter 2 of this book, with two long noun phrases underlined:

This chapter describes <u>the insights into collocation which can be obtained using two different methodological approaches</u>, and then discusses where collocation may sit between <u>the conflicting demands of creativity and conformity in English language use</u>, first as a native language and then as an international lingua franca.

The first noun phrase can be explained like this:

- there are insights into collocation
- we can obtain these insights in two ways
- those two ways use different methods
- (the rest of the chapter will tell us what these two methods are)

The second may be explained like this:

- people should use English in a creative way
- they should also use English in a way that conforms to rules
- these two needs create conflict
- (the chapter will tell us something about collocation and this conflict)

Long noun phrases very often relate to abstract concepts: insights, collocation, demands, creativity, conformity and so on. Understanding academic writing in English depends on being able to understand these concepts and to see how they relate to each other. This chapter offers a way of thinking about the long noun phrases that you meet in this book and elsewhere. This in turn will help you to understand sentences that appear to be very difficult.

CHAPTER 17

Understanding noun phrases

David Oakey

Writers of Applied Linguistics texts, like other writers of academic English, need to express what they mean very precisely. In the case of nouns, it is very unusual for one noun to express a precise enough meaning on its own: the noun *language* has a general meaning which may not be specific enough to say what the writer wants to mean. Similarly, many of the things which writers talk about are too complicated to be expressed by a single word. The meaning of *learning a language* cannot be expressed in a single word, neither can *teaching and learning a language*. It is easier to understand Applied Linguistics writing if you understand how writers combine nouns with other words to make precise meanings. Look at the following:

- second language

- second language acquisition

- second language acquisition research

- second language acquisition research and task-based instruction.

These are all examples of noun phrases: combinations of two or more words which mean one thing and act like one noun in a clause or sentence. The English used by writers in Applied Linguistics contains many long noun phrases because the meanings of objects, facts, ideas and opinions in the subject are too complicated for a single word.

Head nouns

The most important word in a noun phrase is the head noun: the key to its meaning. It is sometimes difficult to work out which word in a noun phrase is the head noun because of the way the noun phrase has been put together. When you are reading an academic English sentence you may recognize every single word in a noun phrase, but you may find the whole phrase difficult to understand because you do not know which word is the head noun. The head noun is in bold in the following noun phrases:

- second **language**

- second language **acquisition**

- second language acquisition **research**

- second language acquisition **research** and task-based **instruction**.

The head noun here is the general meaning of the noun combination. The other words make its meaning more specific and therefore more precise.

There are several ways to combine nouns with other words to form noun phrases:

- **compounds**

  two or more nouns next to each other, such as:

  <u>language acquisition</u> and <u>language acquisition research</u>

- **prepositions**

  words like *for, from, in, of,* such as:

  models <u>of</u> the communication process

- **conjunctions**

  words like *and* and *or*, such as:

  devices <u>and</u> conventions

- **gerunds**

  verbs which end in *-ing* but act like a noun, such as:

  cultural <u>stereotyping</u> and <u>learning</u> a second language

- **adjectives**

  words which add more information before a noun, such as:

  <u>second</u> language or <u>intercultural</u> communication methodologies

- **relative clauses**

  verb groups which add more information after a noun, such as:

  an area <u>that</u> needs investigation.

Noun phrases often contain more than one of the above at the same time.

Activity 1	Identifying the head noun in a noun phrase

The following noun phrases are all used in chapters in this book. Underline the head noun in each one:

1   language use

2   language learners

3   users of the language

4   learning a second language

5 the language learning process

6 the role of the language teacher

7 second language learner attitudes

8 second language research projects

9 the importance of spoken language

10 English language learning contexts

11 models of second language learning

12 doing research into spoken language

13 second language acquisition research

14 the psychology of the language learner

15 different varieties of the target language

16 a prestigious standard form of the language

17 language use across varieties and situations

18 the structure of the language of the source text

19 the findings of research into second language acquisition

20 new and different ways of thinking about language teaching

21 individual users' intuitive knowledge of the language system

22 the information processing model of foreign language learning

23 cultural politics within international English language education

24 applied linguistics outside the context of the language classroom

25 theoretical bases of communicative approaches to second language teaching and testing

Noun phrases with relative clauses

Relative clauses with relative pronouns

More information is added to noun phrases in one or more relative clauses. These usually begin with a relative pronoun such as *which, who,* or *that. A* relative clause giving more information about a head noun in a noun phrase might in turn contain a second noun phrase. This second noun phrase may in turn contain another relative clause giving more information about the head noun of the second noun phrase. A lot of information can be embedded in noun phrases this way, and, since there is no limit to this process, they can become long and dense. The head noun is in bold in the following noun phrases, while the relative pronoun is underlined:

* **students** who plagiarize

- **consumers** who speak a first language which is not English

- a complex **process** which cannot be controlled by the teacher

- **people** who have learnt a language under conditions that would seem to be impossible

- **people** who either do not share another language or who do understand each other's language but who prefer to communicate in a third language – English – which does not give either of them an advantage over the other.

Non-finite relative clauses without relative pronouns

Other relative clauses add information to the head noun with a non-finite verb form. This could be an *-ing* form such as *being, relating,* or *focusing,* or a past participle such as *focused, identified* or *discussed.* The head noun is in bold in the following noun phrases, while the -ing form or past participle is underlined:

- the **area** being researched

- the key **concepts** introduced in this chapter

- **activities** arising from globalization processes

- the **opportunities** offered by a task-based approach to language teaching.

Activity 2	Identifying the head noun in noun phrases containing relative clauses

The following noun phrases are all used in chapters in this book. Identify the head noun in each one, plus any -ing forms, past participles, or relative pronouns which are used to add the extra information:

1 the topic being investigated

2 collocations marked with a '+'

3 a web designer working at home

4 classes focusing on speaking skills

5 texts and spoken data produced by native speakers

6 the 20 semantic categories identified by Francis *et al.*

7 the transcript conventions discussed earlier in this chapter

8 the methodology emerging from the cultural chauvinism argument

9 the challenges posed by researching something as ephemeral as speech

10 cross-borders migration arising from civil war and economic disparities

11   controversies surrounding the introduction of CLT in non-Western countries

12   the emergence of new varieties of English associated with communities of English-users

13   behaviour considered 'exceptions' to the stereotype in the cultural description methodology

14   a quick check of a small sample of applied linguistics articles published in academic journals

15   a distinction between societies oriented towards the 'individual' and those that prioritize the 'collective'

16   two necessary characteristics of the language learning process relating to the nature of language as system

17   chapters dealing with topics in applied linguistics that do not relate directly to language teaching

18   advertisements aimed at consumers who speak a first language which is not English and who may in some instances not understand English

19   research looking at the effects of an educational intervention designed to encourage primary school children to explore ideas more effectively

20   nominalized forms that are standard technical terms associated with different areas of applied linguistics which even the less successful writers use comfortably

Noun phrases in long sentences

We have seen how noun phrases in Applied Linguistics can become very long. Long noun phrases can also cause problems when they are used together in sentences. Even simple sentences can become very long and difficult to read:

1   X is lower than Y.

2   the highest frequency in a low-rated dissertation (21.2 per thousand) is lower than the lowest frequency in a high-rated dissertation (26.7 per thousand).

Sentence 1 (5 words long) and sentence 2 (23 words long) have the same simple grammatical structure (X is lower than Y), but sentence 2 uses longer noun phrases and is therefore much longer and harder to read.

One other reason why sentences in Applied Linguistics are long is that the writer includes a list of items as examples or reasons. The sentence often contains a general noun like *issue, concept* or *factor,* and the list of noun phrases are all examples of this more general noun.

A number of key concepts are introduced in this chapter, including globalization, new varieties of English, English as a Lingua Franca, and the contrast between 'centre' and 'periphery'.

| Activity 3 | Making sense of lists of noun phrases |

Each of the sentences below contains a list. Identify the general noun in the sentence, and then work out how many items there are in each list. For each item, identify the head noun and the way the writer has added extra information to it.

1   The key issues introduced in this chapter are: the characterization of cultures; critical applied linguistics; and inter-cultural communication.

2   It discusses three key issues: Communicative Competence, Communication used in classroom teaching, and controversies surrounding the introduction of CLT in non-Western countries.

3   There are many factors influencing language learners and teachers: teaching methods, the learners' motivation, the community of the institution in which the learning takes place, and the role of the language being learnt in the community of which teachers and learners are a part.

4   Research outputs based on such corpora of spoken language-in-use are wide-ranging and include, for example, descriptions of spoken versus written lexis and grammar (e.g. Biber et al. 1999; Carter and McCarthy 2006), discourse particles (Aijmer 2002), courtroom talk (Cotterill 2004), media discourse (O'Keeffe 2006) and health care communication (Adolphs et al. 2004).

5   However, the past two decades have seen major advances in the development of spoken corpora including, for example, the Cambridge and Nottingham Corpus of Discourse in English CANCODE (McCarthy 1998), the Limerick Corpus of Irish English LCIE (Farr et al. 2004), the Hong Kong Corpus of Spoken English HKCSE (see Cheng and Warren 1999, 2000, 2002), the Michigan Corpus of Academic Spoken English MICASE (Simpson et al. 2000), and the Corpus of Spoken Professional American English CSPAE.

6   Norris (2004) describes a step-by-step process that involves the separate transcription of spoken language, proxemics (distance between speakers), posture, gesture, head movement, gaze, music (i.e. background music that speakers seem to respond to), and print (participants' use of print media), followed by the integration of these dimensions to produce a complete transcript.

| Activity 4 | Inventing noun phrases |

Try to make some simple noun phrases from the words in the table below. They can be as short or as long as you like. Use grammatical words like by, and, of, the, a/an, to, on, in, and into if necessary.

writing	English	speaking	analysis	communication
learners	world	research	focusing	acquisition
students	teachers	language	using	

Example   learners of English; the analysis of writing by learners of English

Introduction to chapter 18

This is the second of the 'study skills' chapters. It relates to an important issue: how writers report what other people have said. This is important for a number of reasons. For example:

- Academic writers (including students) have to 'report' all the time, as many of their facts and ideas will come from other people.
- Academic readers have to understand the different ways that reporting can be done, and what they mean.
- Some quite subtle messages can be given out by how reporting is done, and it is important to understand what these are.

Here is an illustration, from chapter 12 of this book. I have simplified the sentence a bit:

> *Kumaravadivelu (2007: 65–9) maintains that cultural stereotypes underpin US notions of cultural assimilation.*

Here we are presented with an idea ('cultural stereotypes underpin US notions of cultural assimilation') and we are told who this idea belongs to (Kumaravadivelu). We also know that Kumaravadivelu presented this idea as something he definitely believed. We are less sure whether the writer of chapter 12 agrees with Kumaravadivelu or not. All of this can be changed by altering the sample sentence. Here are four examples:

1. *Cultural stereotypes underpin US notions of cultural assimilation (see Kumaravadivelu 2007: 65–9).*
   - This means that the idea ('cultural stereotypes . . .') is generally accepted and no longer has to be argued. Kumaravadivelu talks about the idea but may not be the person who first thought of it.

2. *Kumaravadivelu (2007: 65–9) hypothesized that cultural stereotypes underpin US notions of cultural assimilation.*
   - This means that Kumaravadivelu was not certain about this idea. Using the word *hypothesized* instead of *maintains* tells us this.

3. *Kumaravadivelu (2007: 65–9) points out that cultural stereotypes underpin US notions of cultural assimilation.*
   - This means that the writer of chapter 12 definitely agrees with Kumaravadivelu and accepts his idea as definitely true. The verb *points out* tells us this.

4. *Kumaravadivelu (2007: 65–9) claimed that cultural stereotypes underpin US notions of cultural assimilation.*
   - In this version the writer uses *claimed* in the past tense. This suggests that the writer does not agree with Kumaravadivelu.

It is important to recognize that none of these reports would be 'wrong' but that the writer of chapter 12 has to use the version that accurately presents his view of Kumaravadivelu's idea.

CHAPTER 18

Identifying and reporting other people's point of view

David Oakey

Any piece of academic writing is the end result of a process of thought and research by one or more writers. The writers of the chapters in this book have all combined their ideas and opinions with the previous work of other authors:

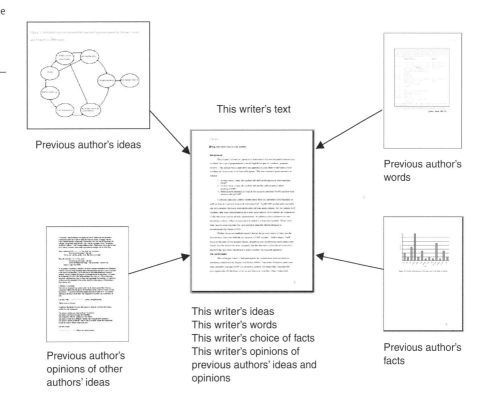

Previous author's ideas

This writer's text

Previous author's words

Previous author's opinions of other authors' ideas

This writer's ideas
This writer's words
This writer's choice of facts
This writer's opinions of previous authors' ideas and opinions

Previous author's facts

In your own academic writing, you will need to use information from other authors to show your reader that:

- you have read a wide variety of texts in your subject
- you understand your subject and are familiar with important research in the field
- you agree or disagree with other people's facts, ideas, and opinions
- you can support your own ideas and opinions with previous work.

In your writing you must show the difference between your work and other people's work. If you use other people's work without showing this difference correctly, your readers may think you have copied it dishonestly. You risk being accused of plagiarism, a very serious academic offence. This section will show how the writers of the chapters in this book have used other people's work. It will help you use other people's work in your own academic writing in an appropriate way.

Verbs for reporting what people have said

| Activity 1 | Identifying reporting verbs |

Find the verbs used by the writer of the paragraph below to bring the ideas of previous authors into his text:

The real world dynamics that challenge a stable or context-free definition of communicative competence have given rise to a number of alternative views. For example, Alptekin (2002) argues that Canale and Swain's native speaker grammatical competence is an inappropriate aim in contexts where students are more likely to use English with other non-native speakers. Alptekin suggests that a more appropriate aim is the kind of linguistic competence developed by successful learners of English. Smith (2002) proposes that exploring patterns of communication in social networks can help define communicative competence for groups of individuals. Moreover, Leung suggests that we should go back to the ethnographic bases of Hymes' (1972) original formulation of communicative competence, arguing that language educators should 're-engage with the socially dynamic uses of English and continually re-work the contextual meaning of the concept' (Leung 2005: 138).

The grammar of reporting verbs

There are several main patterns for reporting verbs when the author is the subject of the verb:

a) **Verb + Noun**
Chilton and Schäffner (1997: 222) point out examples such as *the opposition's claims were shot down in flames*, in articles about politics.

b) **Verb + that**
Krashen holds that the learned system has no influence on the acquired system – there is no leakage, no permeability between the two.

c) **Verb + 'wh' word**

In this chapter Adrian Holliday <u>suggests how</u> someone visiting or working in another country might respond to such stereotypes.

d) **Verb + Noun + as + Noun**

The Compact Oxford Dictionary <u>defines stereotype as 'a preconceived and over-simplified idea of the characteristics which typify a person or thing'</u>.

The grammar patterns of the more common reporting verbs are summarized in the table below:

Table 18.1

Verb + noun	Verb + *that*	Verb + + 'wh' word	noun + *as* + noun	
☑			☑	analyze, categorize, characterize, classify, define, interpret, refer to, see, view
☑				assess, call, call for, carry out, cite, compare, conduct, criticize, integrate, list, look at, mean, offer, outline, provide, reiterate, review, term
	☑			argue, claim, comment, conclude, feel, hold, maintain, state, think
☑	☑			assume, find, imply, propose
☑		☑		ask, describe, discuss, distinguish, evaluate, examine, explore, focus on, identify, investigate, question, measure, study, survey, talk about, test
☑	☑	☑		believe, confirm, demonstrate, discover, emphasize, explain, indicate, mention, note, observe, point out, recognize, remark, report, reveal, say, show, stress, suggest, write

Two of the above verbs, *carry out* and *conduct*, perform particular research tasks and so are used with particular nouns:

carry out	research, task, activity, experiment, study, analysis, investigation, work, project
conduct	research, interview, study, experiment, analysis, evaluation, meeting, observation, survey

| **Activity 2** | **Identifying patterns of reporting verbs** |

Look at the examples below. Identify the reporting verb, its grammar pattern, and whether it is reporting what the author said or did. The first example is done for you:

1   Labov (1972) states that lower middle class women often endorse this type of shift.
    Verb: *state*   Pattern: V + *that*   Reports: something the author said

2   Willis and Willis (2007) offer ways to generate a varied sequence of tasks arising from a chosen topic.

3   Edwards and Westgate (1994) suggest that every hour's recording may require 15 hours for transcription.

4   Sakaguchi (2002) investigated the language of drinks cans sold from street kiosks and machines in Japan.

5   Savignon (1991) defined CLT as involving negotiation, interpretation and expression of meaning in the target language.

6   Halliday and Hasan (1985) use the term 'register' to refer to different kinds of spoken and written language that are found in different contexts.

7   For example, Chilton and Schäffner (1997: 222) point out examples such as *the opposition's claims were shot down in flames*, in articles about politics.

8   Adolphs (2006: 41) shows the ten most frequent words in the written part of the British National Corpus compared with the spoken CANCODE corpus.

9   Kim (2005: 108) also notes that Hofstede's model 'forced a single bipolar dimension of individualism and saw collectivism as an absence of individualism' that was derived from the need to negatively Other 'barbarians'.

10 Kumaravadivelu (2007: 65–9) maintains that cultural stereotypes which are believed to be egalitarian by their users are an influential underpinning of US notions of cultural assimilation which in turn impose ethnocentric cultural viewpoints.

Reporting what people have said: the different 'voices' in a text[1]

You can learn a lot about a writer's point of view by noticing the way they report the work of previous authors. The writer may agree with the previous author, or may have a neutral point of view.

- *point out* and *show* mean that the writer agrees with the previous author's idea

- *suggest* and *argue* mean that the writer is neutral, and does not agree or disagree with the previous author's idea

Imagine a student writer is writing an essay on spoken discourse and reads the chapter in this book by Koester. The student decides to use the statement underlined below:

Note that the elements occur as adjacency pairs, e.g. 'summons – answering summons', or as sequences, e.g. 'initial enquiries', which consists of two reciprocal adjacency pairs. <u>The first 'hello' in a telephone call is not actually a greeting, but answers the summons (the ringing of the phone).</u> In face to face conversations, summons are not usually necessary, unless calling to attract the other person's attention.

Below are nine sentences showing the different ways the student writer can bring Koester's statement into his or her essay. Each sentence uses the underlined statement by Koester but in a slightly different way:

1   'The first "hello" in a telephone call is not actually a greeting, but answers the summons' (Koester 2009: 23).

2   Koester (2009: 23) argues that 'the first "hello" in a telephone call is not actually a greeting, but answers the summons'.

3   Koester (2009: 23) points out that 'the first "hello" in a telephone call is not actually a greeting, but answers the summons'.

4   Koester (2009: 23) claims that 'the first "hello" in a telephone call is not actually a greeting, but answers the summons'.

5   As Koester (2009: 23) points out, 'the first "hello" in a telephone call is not actually a greeting, but answers the summons'.

6   According to Koester (2009: 23), 'the first "hello" in a telephone call is not actually a greeting, but answers the summons'.

7   The first 'hello' in a telephone call is not actually a greeting, but answers the summons.

8   The first 'hello' in a telephone call is not actually a greeting, but answers the summons (Koester 2009).

9   'Hello' when initially used in a phone conversation is a response to the call, rather than a greeting (Koester 2009).

Each sentence brings Koester's statement into the student's essay, but the reader gets a slightly different idea about the writer's point of view in each one. The writer may agree with it, or be neutral about it. The sentences also contain different numbers of Koester's and the student's words. This has an effect on the 'voice' heard by the reader. A sentence containing mostly the student's words contains more of the student's 'voice', while a sentence containing more of Koester's words contains more of her 'voice'. If a sentence begins with Koester's name as the subject, her voice is dominant. If a sentence has her name in brackets at the end, then the writer's voice is dominant.

Activity 3   The writer's point of view and 'voice'

Look at the differences in each sentence (1–9 above) and decide how they affect the writer's opinion and the "voice" heard by the reader. Fill in the table. Which sentences might cause problems for the writer?

Table 18.2

	Statement	words in the text	writer's opinion of the statement	'voice' heard by the reader
1	author's	author's	neutral	mostly author
2	author's	author's	neutral	author more than writer
3	author's	author's	agrees	author more than writer
4				
5				
6				
7				
8				
9				

Notice that the writer of sentence 7 above is in danger of being accused of plagiarism. Since the writer does not include any reference to the work of Koester in this sentence, the reader believes it is all the writer's own work, which it is not. The acceptability of sentence 8 is debatable. The writer has included a short reference to the source, but has used exactly the same words as the author. Many people would consider this plagiarism.

Activity 4	Identifying writers' points of view and 'voice'

In the examples below the writer has used the work of a previous author. Identify the statement, whose words are in the text, the writer's opinion of the claim, and whose 'voice' is heard most by the reader The first two examples are done for you:

1 Some researchers maintain that collocation is central to language production (Sinclair 1991; Hunston and Francis 2000).
Claim: collocation is central to language production
Words in the text: writer's
Writer's opinion of the claim: neutral (*maintain* is the reporting verb)
'Voice' heard by the reader: mostly writer's

2 According to Lamie (2001), for example, one criticism of recording interviews is the uneasiness a participant may feel in response to being recorded.
Claim: one criticism of recording interviews is the uneasiness a participant may feel in response to being recorded
Words in the text: writer's
Writer's opinion of the claim: neutral (the structure is *according to X*)
'Voice' heard by the reader: mostly writer's

3 Table 1 suggests the existence of what Cruse (ibid.) calls 'semi-systematic collocational restrictions' which act on *purse* and other near-synonyms.

4 *Da* is a discourse particle, and as Allen et al. remark (1995: 366), 'it is not always possible to provide a literal translation' into English for words of that class.

5 Chen and Foley (2004) have demonstrated that there is a similar link between higher proficiency in the use of nominalization in the L2 and academic success.

6 According to Berg (1995), this is an important step to ensure the suitability of research instruments and to help check for researcher bias in the interview questions.

7 As Bucholtz (2000) argues, transcription therefore requires a degree of reflexivity and an acknowledgement of the affordances and limitations of the particular choices made.

8 A study of telephone dialogues in a selection of English language textbooks (Wong 2002) revealed that the opening sequences bore little resemblance to those of natural conversations.

9 Seedhouse (2004), who uses CA to investigate classroom language, argues that the classroom has its own 'interactional architecture' which differs from that of language outside the classroom.

10 As Bogdan and Biklen (1998) noted, the accuracy with which the transcribing of interviews is done influences how easy it is to work with the reported data from the interview participants.

11 In his study of CANCODE data McCarthy (1998:161) finds that 'in the narrative texts in the CANCODE corpus, speech reports are overwhelmingly direct speech, and with reporting verbs in past simple (*said, told*) or historical present *says*.'

12 Katsaridi (2003) looked at shop signs in streets in Athens and found that English was used to create a perception in potential Greek customers that the shop sold high-quality goods and that they, the customers, belonged to the social group that would buy such high-quality products.

13 As Bucholtz (2000) argues, transcription therefore requires a degree of reflexivity and an acknowledgement of the affordances and limitations of the particular choices made.

14 Citing the work of social theorist Browne (2006), Waters defines political correctness as a hegemonic force which has become dominant in English-speaking Western society and creates the impression that everyone is either an 'oppressor' or a 'victim' (Waters 2007b: 354).

You will be able develop your own voice as an academic writer more easily if you can control the way you present information from previous authors in your own work. It is therefore important for you to learn to use these different ways of reporting appropriately. Your voice will be lost in a 4,000 word essay if you only begin sentences with the name of a previous author.

Note

1 Adapted from Groom, N. (2000) 'Attribution and averral revisited: three perspectives on manifest intertextuality in academic writing', in Thompson, P. (Ed.) *Patterns and Perspectives: Insights into EAP writing practice*. Reading: CALS.

VI Skills of expression

Introduction to chapter 19

This is the first of two chapters that focus on skills that are important for expressing yourself in academic writing. It deals with the difficult topic of saying what you think about the things that you have read, that is, whether you agree or disagree with the ideas you are talking about.

It is often difficult, when we are reading about something new, to have a clear idea of our own opinion. We may find that we automatically agree with something we read because it is presented in a persuasive way. Or, we may find that we instinctively disagree, because what we read contradicts what we have always believed or what we have always done. It is important to 'keep an open mind' at the beginning but it is also important in the end to form a view that we are ready to defend. Often we have to read several conflicting ideas before we have a definite sense of which ones we agree with and why.

Having decided which ideas we agree with, it can be difficult to know how to express that in an appropriate way. Simply saying that an idea is correct may not be sufficient and we may need to find evidence for our support. Disagreeing can be even more difficult, especially if we want to avoid sounding arrogant or more knowledgeable than we really are. In general, the problem is how to be 'personal' while at the same time being 'professional': how to have a voice that is distinctive but also academic.

This chapter gives several examples, from this book, of writers agreeing or disagreeing with others, or indeed of keeping an open mind. Recognizing the writer's voice in what we read can be a great help in expressing our own.

CHAPTER 19

Finding your voice

David Oakey

Many facts and ideas in Applied Linguistics are disputed because academics have different theoretical positions, hold opposing philosophical beliefs, or support conflicting methodological approaches. If you are studying Applied Linguistics at MA level you will need to express an opinion about previous authors' work. You will find that if you only repeat in your essays the work of the authors you have read, you will not get a good mark. It is much easier to write about something if you have formed an opinion about it. Having an opinion also makes it easier to identify authors whose work you agree with, and other authors whose work you disagree with.

Writers often develop their own ideas and opinions by responding to the ideas and arguments of previous authors. The first response to a previous author by a writer is for the writer to choose to include the previous author's work in the writer's text. This shows that the writer considers the author's work to be important to the topic. The second response is to report what the previous author said. This can be a direct quotation using the previous author's words, or the reporting can be indirect, in the form of a summary in the writer's words. The writer's third response is to show his or her opinion of the previous author's work.

An example of this is in the chapter by Kennedy. He decides that the 'three circles' model proposed by Kachru in 1985 is important for his text. He summarizes Kachru's model by describing the inner, outer and expanding circles in his own words:

Let us look at the roles of English in different areas of the world. Kachru (1985) suggested three concentric 'circles' of English language users, an inner circle, an outer circle, and an expanding circle. The inner circle consists of speakers of English as a first language, e.g. from UK, North America, New Zealand and Australia. Outer circle speakers use English as a major additional language primarily for use within their nation. Many of the former British colonies in Africa and Asia (e.g. Kenya, Nigeria, India) fall into this category with English playing a major role since independence. The third, expanding circle increases year on year as more nations and the people within them realize the need for English for international communication (e.g. Brazil, Spain, Thailand).

Kennedy's opinion of Kachru's model is balanced. He thinks that the model was useful when Kachru first suggested it, as Kennedy writes in the next paragraph:

The valid point Kachru was making at the time was that the direction of sociolinguistic influence (reflecting economic and political power) was from inner circle to outer and expanding circles, not the reverse, i.e. from a powerful economic centre to a comparatively weaker periphery, and, in linguistic terms, from native speakers of English (NS) to non-native speakers (NNS). Linguistic standards and norms of use were derived from inner-circle countries (particularly Britain and USA) as were ELT materials, methodologies, and teacher supply.

Kennedy also thinks that Kachru's model is now out of date. He uses the work of later authors such as Kirkpatrick and Pennycook to support this opinion, and summarizes their arguments in order to report what they said:

Much has changed since the 1980s when the model was introduced. (At the time the Berlin Wall and the USSR still existed, and CDs and the Macintosh computer had only just been introduced.) The model was never intended to reflect a static state and it is not surprising if global socio-political changes (and a poststructuralist move from macro to more micro concerns on the part of applied linguists) have led to modifications. Some have suggested a different model reflecting a greater linguistic fluidity and hybridity (Kirkpatrick 2007), focusing on language proficiency rather than NS /NNS distinctions. It is true that users of English in Kachru's three circles cannot be as compartmentalized as they might have been (Pennycook 2007). Because of the spread of English, cross-borders migration arising from civil war and economic disparities, and the development of new economic centres, some communities within the inner circle might identify themselves as speakers of English as an additional or international language. Conversely, speakers in the outer and expanding circles may be as proficient in English as speakers in inner circle countries and may indeed regard themselves as native English-speakers.

The above paragraphs give an idea of the many choices a writer must make in order to develop an argument and support his or her opinion. The writer must convince the reader that these choices are valid. First is the decision to identify Kachru's work as important to the topic. The next is to identify the work of Kirkpatrick and Pennycook as also being important to the topic. Finally Kennedy convinces the reader that he agrees with both Kirkpatrick and Pennycook, and thinks that their work is an improvement on Kachru's model.

You will see from the above that expressing an opinion in academic writing is more subtle than saying 'in my opinion' or 'I think'.

Disagreeing with a previous author's work

An important aspect of your written 'voice' is how ready you are to criticize a previous author's work. The written word has a high status in some learning contexts, and some students are unfamiliar with the idea of disagreeing with ideas in academic texts. However, members of academic communities enjoy arguing with each other. Disagreeing with previous authors in your writing shows the reader that you have formed an opinion and can support it. In the example below, the writer summarizes the work of several previous authors and then disagrees with it:

Accounts of conversational turn-taking have often assumed that one person talks at a time (e.g. Sacks et al. 1974). This is not always the case, however, particularly in more informal discussion where there may be considerable amounts of overlapping talk and where speakers frequently complete one another's turns.

Agreeing with a previous author's work

Agreeing with previous authors in your writing also shows the reader that you have formed an opinion and can support it. In the example below, the writer summarizes the work of a previous author and then agrees with it:

There has been widespread uptake of CLT in language teaching worldwide. McKay criticizes this spread of CLT because its emphasis on 'democracy, individuality, creativity and social expression' (McKay 2002: 120–121) fails to respond to local teachers and students' needs and backgrounds. McKay may well have a valid point.

Alternatively the writer can put his or her own idea first, and then use the work of a previous author to support it:

There is a difference between *perceived* and *observed* frequent use, however; a collocation which appears to be used repetitively may not in fact be used repeatedly. Empirical work on collocation has revealed that clichés and idioms are rare in the use of English as a whole (Moon 1998), and that they only appear to be over-used by speakers in particular domains or genres.

The key to developing your own voice is to keep control of the voices of previous authors. Ideas are ordered differently in written texts from how they occur in real life. The writer above read Moon's work before he had his idea about the difference between perceived and observed frequent use. In his text, however, he put his own idea first and then used Moon's work to support it. By putting his own idea first and then supporting it with Moon's work, the writer made sure that his voice was more dominant.

Activity 1

Identifying writers' opinions of previous authors' work

In each extract below, the writer uses the work of one or more previous authors. For each extract decide whether the writer agrees with, disagrees with, or is neutral about the previous author's work. What words or phrases tell you the writer's opinion in each extract? The first extract is done as an example:

1
Waters' warning against a knee-jerk demonizing of all stereotyping needs to be taken seriously. However, while it claims more realism than the cultural chauvinism position, his argument may also be naïve in its lack of belief about how easily the best intentioned people can be taken in, not by the hegemony of political correctness, but by the discoursal power of, in his words, the apparently innocent 'economized' explanations that stereotypes provide.

Previous author: Waters
Writer's opinion: disagrees
Words or phrases: However . . . his argument may also be naïve

2

Much can be learnt here from another branch of Applied Linguistics, that of critical discourse analysis, which shows us how prejudices can easily be hidden in apparently neutral everyday talk, and in institutional, professional and political thinking (e.g. Fairclough 1995). Kumaravadivelu (2007: 52) puts this very well:

> Even people with an egalitarian, non-prejudiced self-image can act prejudicially when interpretive norms guiding a situation are weak. In such a scenario, people easily justify their racially prejudiced acts and beliefs on the basis of some determinant other than race.

3

Kumaravadivelu's view of society, as an inherently racist system, is very different to that of Waters. Waters suggests that an initial, stereotyped understanding may subsequently be modified or abandoned in the light of experience. If we accept Kumaravadivelu's view, however, it is difficult to accept Waters' opinion.

4

Jenkins (2007) takes a similar view to Seidlhofer, arguing that setting phonological ENL norms as targets for learners of English is unnecessary and impractical. She has tried to define a phonological 'common core' based on her research with NNSs that might provide syllabus targets for English as a lingua franca programmes. Her ideas have met with a mixed reception, not least from teachers themselves. As is the case with any innovation, the attitudes and beliefs of users are crucial for successful implementation, and we are only just entering the period of discussion over these issues.

5

The inconvenient arguments from SLA are rejected on the grounds that they are unscientific, or that the work on which they rest is carried out under experimental rather than classroom conditions, or that one study often contradicts another with respect to the details, or that they are too diffuse to offer a firm basis for a teaching programme. But the fact that almost all the research points in the same direction casts doubt on these criticisms.

6

Krashen also argued that [. . .] acquisition is an unconscious process. It is not controlled, and can only occur naturally, as a result of exposure to the language used in a meaningful context. Later research (see, for example, Long 1988; Skehan 1996) suggests that Krashen is mistaken in this, and that conscious processes and a focus on language form can contribute to acquisition. But this does not deny the paradox of knowing but at the same time not knowing.

Introduction to chapter 20

The chapter is the second of those addressing skills used in writing. It focuses on the issue of organizing an essay and making that organization clear to the reader.

Essay organization is not simply a matter of convention. What matters in an essay is the argument that you make, and that argument will be expressed through the way the essay is organized. If the organization is not clear to the reader, then probably the argument will not be clear either. So clear organization is not simply an 'added extra' to a good essay – it is essential to the formation of the argument.

It has often been argued that different cultures have different preferences when it comes to essay organization, and that this can make things difficult if your own background is rather different from that of the university in which you are studying. Most readers of essays are happy to accept conventions that are not their own, but because organization and argument are so closely linked, it can actually be difficult to understand and assess an argument in an essay with an unfamiliar organization. In other words, although some negotiation may be possible, the student really does need to become familiar with how essays are organized in the university where they are studying and to produce essays that more or less conform to this.

As in each of these 'study skills' chapters, we use the practice of our own writers to offer examples of what can be done. The writers of all the first 16 chapters have experienced the difficulties of organizing their contributions, trying to find a way of structuring and expressing their argument so that it makes sense and is convincing. This chapter encourages you to use and learn from their experience.

CHAPTER 20

Organizing an essay

David Oakey

Any piece of academic writing is organized according to the reason why it was written. Research articles in scholarly journals present original work and are written for people researching and teaching in an academic field. Textbook chapters are written by academics in order to help students learn a new subject. Essays are written by students to show their teachers their understanding of issues in their subject; in the field of Applied Linguistics they are the most common means of assessment on Masters courses. While each type of academic writing is different, they all contain similar organizational features. They begin by introducing the reader to the subject, and then signal what the rest of the text will contain. After the main part of the text, there is a final section which summarizes the content.

Readers expect academic writing to be organized in this way, and so understanding how to organize the information in your essay is a very important skill. An essay containing poor work will get a low mark, but an essay containing strong work will also get a low mark if it is poorly organized.

Introductions

Here is the introduction to one of the chapters in this book (the sentences have been numbered):

[1]The concept of grammatical metaphor was introduced into linguistics by Halliday (1985), and it is increasingly recognized that this is a key mechanism by which the resources for the making of meaning in a language can be greatly expanded (see, for example, Ravelli 1988; Martin 1993; Halliday and Martin 1993; Simon-Vandenbergen et al. 2003). [2]It has also been argued that one kind of grammatical metaphor, nominalization, plays a crucial role in the construction of knowledge and thus in education: success in education is seen as, to large extent, associated with ability to understand and use this type of grammatical metaphor (Christie and Martin 1997).

[3]In this chapter I will explore one aspect of this phenomenon, by investigating to what extent mastery of nominalization is associated with academic success in dissertations written by students on MAs in Applied Linguistics and TESOL whose first language is not English. [4]I will look both at the frequency of nominalizations in a small corpus of high-rated dissertations (HRDs) and low-rated dissertations (LRDs), and at the types of nominalizations used. [5]The working hypothesis, based on previous research, is that better dissertations will show higher frequencies of nominalizations, but also, and perhaps more importantly, a more varied range of uses.

The diagram below shows how the sentences in the introduction gradually move from general to specific ideas. The idea in the first sentence (grammatical metaphor) is a large area in linguistics. The idea in the second sentence (nominalization) is one type of grammatical metaphor, and so is more specific. The idea in the third sentence (the relationship between proficiency in nominalization and academic success by non-native speaking MA students) is more specific again. In only three sentences, the writer has moved from talking about a general linguistic feature to talking about that feature in relation to one small set of language users.

The idea in sentence four is even more specific because it refers to the two features of nominalization measured in the study (frequency and type of nominalization in MA dissertations). The idea in the final sentence of the introduction is the most specific of all, and refers to the aim of the research in the text.

Sentence		Meaning
1. the statement covers . . .	grammatical metaphor in general	general
2. the statement covers . . .	a specific type of grammatical metaphor	more specific
3. the statement covers . . .	one aspect of this specific type of grammatical metaphor in one type of writing	more specific
4. the statement covers . . .	the data the writer used in the study in this paper	very specific
5. the statement covers . . .	the specific research goals of the study in this paper	most specific

Figure 20.1

At the end of the introduction here, the reader now has an idea of four things:

- the general topic of the paper (grammatical metaphor)
- the aspect of the topic which was investigated in the study in the paper (nominalization)
- the data used (high- and low-scoring MA dissertations)
- the specific research question the writer hopes to answer.

Some readers will stop reading here if they are not interested in grammatical metaphor. The introduction has told them enough to decide whether to stop or continue reading. If the reader is interested, then at this point he or she will now be expecting to find out two more things:

- do better dissertations contain higher frequencies of nominalizations?
- do better dissertations contain wider uses of nominalizations?

If the rest of the text is not organized according to the reader's expectations, then it will be difficult to read.

Activity 1   Determining the organization of an introduction

Read the introductions below and try to summarize the idea in each part of the introduction. Some ideas may be explained in more than one sentence. Write your summary of example 1 in Figure 20.2 and your summary of example 2 in Figure 20.3.

1

[1]The aim of this chapter is to explore the contribution corpora can make towards the study of spoken language. [2]To this end, examples from the five-million-word Cambridge and Nottingham Corpus of Discourse in English (CANCODE) are examined. [3]The spoken data were recorded in a wide variety of mostly informal settings across the islands of Britain and Ireland and then transcribed and stored in computer-readable form. [4]This chapter focuses on a particular example, the word *like*, in order to illustrate the relationship between language and discourse as it emerges from the corpus data used for this study.

2

[1]Language teachers frequently use the term 'motivation' when they describe successful or unsuccessful learners. [2]This reflects our intuitive belief that during the lengthy and often tedious process of mastering a foreign/second language (L2), the learner's enthusiasm, commitment and persistence are key determinants of success or failure. [3]Indeed, in the vast majority of cases, learners with sufficient motivation *can* achieve a working knowledge of an L2, *regardless of* their language aptitude, whereas without sufficient motivation even the brightest learners are unlikely to persist long enough to attain any really useful language ('you can lead a horse to water, but you can't make it drink').

[4]Because of the central importance attached to it by practitioners and researchers alike, L2 motivation has been the target of a great deal of research in Applied Linguistics during the past decades. [5]In this chapter I describe a major theoretical shift that has recently been transforming the landscape of motivation research: the move from the traditional conceptualization of motivation in terms of an *integrative/instrumental dichotomy* to the

Sentence		Meaning
1. the statement covers . . .		general
2 and 3. the statements cover . . .		more specific
4. the statement covers . . .		most specific

Figure 20.2

Sentence		Meaning
1, 2 & 3. the statements cover. . .		general
4. the statement covers . . .		more specific
5. the statement covers . . .		specific
6. the statement covers . . .		very specific

Figure 20.3

recent conceptualization of motivation as being part of the learner's self system, with the motivation to learn an L2 being closely associated with the learner's *ideal L2 self*. [6]For space limitations I cannot provide a detailed review of the relevant literature (for recent summaries, see Dörnyei 2005, Dörnyei and Ushioda in press); instead, my focus will be on illustrating how such a major paradigm shift has emerged through a combination of theoretical considerations and empirical research findings.

Organizing statements

Most introductions end with a statement of what is to come in the text. This is where the reader can learn how the writer will organize the text. At the end of his introduction Willis makes the following organizing statement:

In this chapter I will argue, taking language description as a starting point, that there are two good reasons why we should recognise that the link between teaching and learning is bound to be indirect. I will then go on to cite Widdowson (1979) to suggest a third reason for this phenomenon.

This statement is the key to the way Willis organizes his paper. The chapter contains the following sections in the same order as he states in the introduction:

Complexity and the grammar of orientation	(the first reason)
Pattern Grammar: Extent and Coverage	(the second reason)
Building a Meaning System	(the third reason)
Conclusions	(a summary of the content of the text)

Similarly, Holliday finishes the introduction to his chapter with statements about how the specific content of his paper is organized:

I shall begin by setting out two basic arguments and then present my own analysis of the way forward. The first argument derives from concerns that cultural descriptions may be chauvinistic and encourage racism. The second is the more popular belief that stereotyping is normal and useful. I shall leave this until second because, against expectations, it is the more complex view and leads to the greatest part of the debate.

Holliday's paper contains the following sections in the same order as he states in the introduction:

The cultural chauvinism argument	(cultural descriptions may be chauvinistic and encourage racism)
The practicality argument	(stereotyping is normal and useful)
Intercultural communication methodologies	(Holliday's own analysis)
Awareness through cultural descriptions	
Awareness through interrogating issues of Self and Other	
Loose ends	(a summary of the content of the text)

You will notice that the writers in these examples refer to themselves in the first person, for example *In this chapter I will argue*... and *I shall begin by*... These are statements of purpose and explain what the writer wants to say in the text. The use of *I* by student writers is debated. Some lecturers prefer students to use impersonal forms when writing statements of purpose, such as making the text the subject of the sentence:

- This essay discusses two approaches to investigating the role of collocation in English vocabulary.

or using a passive verb, such as

- In this essay two approaches to investigating the role of collocation in English vocabulary are discussed.

Activity 2   Matching organizing statements with the content of a text

Below are the organizing statements from chapters in this book. Read the statements and list the ideas you expect to be in the chapter and the order in which the writer will discuss them. Then go to the chapter and check if your expectations were correct.

1 (Swann)
I shall discuss, in turn, conventions for transcribing spoken interaction; the representation of languages, varieties and styles; ways of laying out a transcript; and multimodal transcription.

2 (Oakey)
This chapter describes the insights into collocation which can be obtained using two different methodological approaches, and then discusses where collocation may sit between the conflicting demands of creativity and conformity in English language use, first as a native language and then as an international lingua franca.

3 (Johnson and Woolls)
We will first examine the sort of questions of the 'who wrote this?' type that are asked and how they may be answered. We also examine the effect of the amount of data which is available to assist the linguist as detective in coming to a decision, which is generally, but not always, quite small. And finally we discuss what we mean by two texts being linguistically similar.

VII Editing skills

Introduction to chapter 21

The final two chapters of this book deal with issues that are sometimes called 'mechanical'. This chapter is about how to put references into your essays, both in the essay itself and in the bibliography or list of references.

Referencing systems are largely simply conventional. Each system is no better or worse than any other, and many decisions associated with them are purely arbitrary, but the system has to be followed exactly. (This is a bit like rules for driving a car. It does not matter whether in your country people drive on the left or the right – one is not better or worse than the other – but it matters very much that you follow the rules and drive on the same side as everyone else!)

It is important for students to learn to follow a referencing system, and to follow it exactly, because all academic writers have to do this. When you write for a publisher or for a journal, you will have to follow their rules very exactly, so it is a good idea to get practice in doing this.

Although many aspects of referencing are simply convention, some are driven by common sense. For example, it is important to organize a bibliography in alphabetical order so that your reader can find items in it quickly. To take a rather more complicated example: if you read someone's ideas in a chapter in a book, you need to reference this correctly or else the reader will be confused as to whose ideas are being talked about. For instance, you may wish to talk about the ideas you met in chapter 3 of this book about nominalization and student dissertations. The author of the chapter is Geoff Thompson; the editors of the book are Susan Hunston and David Oakey. It is important that you show in the essay that Thompson is the person with the ideas you are quoting. In the bibliography it is important to show your reader where they can find the paper by Thompson, that is, in this book. There are two things, then, that you need to do:

- In the essay itself, show that Thompson is the source of any ideas that you refer to. For example, you may write:

  It has been suggested that there is a connection between what counts as a good dissertation and the skills involved in using nominalization (Thompson 2009). (The reference is to the writer of the chapter, not the editors of the book.)

- Then, in your bibliography or list of references you need to list Thompson's paper and show where your reader can find it:

  Thompson, G. 2009. 'Grammatical metaphor and success in academic writing'. In S. Hunston and D. Oakey (eds.) *Introducing Applied Linguistics: key concepts and skills.* London: Routledge, 27–34.

The aim of this chapter is to help you to follow conventions and to see in some cases where there is a reason behind them.

CHAPTER 21

Referencing

David Oakey

Each outside source that you use in your text must be mentioned (or cited) twice: once in a short reference in the text and once in a long reference in the bibliography (or list of references). This section looks at features of short and long references as used by the writers of the chapters in this book.

Referring to your sources is an unbreakable rule, but there are variations in the way this rule is applied in different academic subjects. For example, in some academic subjects *bibliography* means 'a list of sources related to a particular topic in the academic literature', and *list of references* means 'a list of only those sources that are referred to in a writer's text'. Some subjects do not make this distinction, and bibliography means the same as list of references.

There are many different sets of referencing conventions: this book uses the 'author–date' (or 'Harvard') system used in many Arts and Social Science fields. When a writer uses an previous author's idea, the author's name and the date of publication must be stated in a short reference in the text at that point:

English is a world language (Graddol 2006).

The writer signals to the reader in the text that the information at that point comes from an outside source.

Because the reader may want to know the full details of the source, the writer must also include a long reference to the source at the end of the text. The long reference contains the full details of the same source:

Graddol, D. (2006). *English Next.* London: British Council.

Because of their number, long references are listed at the end of a text alphabetically by the surname (the family name) of the author.

Short references

Indirect quotation

The author's name and the year of publication are essential, with or without a comma after the author's name:

English is a world language (Graddol 2006)

or

English is a world language (Graddol, 2006).

If the author is the subject of the sentence, the year of publication is in brackets:

> Graddol (2006) claims that English is a world language.

Writers sometimes use more than one source to support the same point. This shows they can make connections between their work and what they have read. The author's names are separated by a semi-colon or comma in the same set of brackets:

> Some silent preparation time will allow each individual to think of how to do the task and what to talk about, which enhances their engagement with the task and generally results in richer interaction (Foster 1996, Djapoura 2005, Ellis 2005: 3–36).

When the writer uses sources by one author which were published in the same year, they are shown with a letter of the alphabet after the year:

> An extension of the practicality argument, which Waters (2007a, 2007b, 2007c) presents in some detail is that the cultural chauvinism argument amounts to an imposition of 'political correctness'.

Direct quotation

When the writer uses the author's words without changing them, they must be shown in inverted commas. The short reference must contain the number of the page from which the words were taken:

> *Da* is a discourse particle, and as Allen et al. remark (1995: 366), 'it is not always possible to provide a literal translation' into English for words of that class.

When a direct quotation is at the end of a sentence, the full stop is usually after the short reference, not after the last word in the quotation.

Short references to secondary sources

A secondary source is a source used by the author of the source which the writer is referring to. The names of both authors need to be included in the short reference. This shows whose work it is and where the writer took it from.

> 'Paradoxically, language is at its best when it matters least; at its worst when it matters most' (Moore and Carling 1988 quoted in Howarth 1996: 13).

Latin abbreviations in short references

To save space in short references, writers often use Latin abbreviations et al., op. cit., and ibid. These are short for *et alii* (and others), *opus citatum* (from the work cited), and *ibidem* (the same place).

Where there are more than two authors, this is shown by *et al.* in the short reference after the first author's name:

> These include turn-taking (Sacks et al. 1974), 'repair', i.e. dealing with dysfluency or misunderstanding (Schegloff et al. 1977) . . .

If the writer uses the same source more than once, this is shown by op. cit. in the short reference after the first author's name:

> One such model, which was developed by Hofstede (op. cit.) in the 1960s and has sustained in popularity, distinguishes between two cultural types.

If the writer uses the same source more than once in succession, this is shown by ibid. in the short reference after the first author's name:

> In his study of CANCODE data McCarthy (1998: 161) finds that 'in the narrative texts in the CANCODE corpus, speech reports are overwhelmingly direct speech, and with reporting verbs in past simple (*said, told*) or historical present *says*.' One of the reasons for this is to add to the 'vividness' and 'real-time staging' (ibid.) of the discourse.

Long references for different types of source

Long references are listed in alphabetical order at the end of a text. They need to contain enough information for the reader to find the source easily.

Long references for books written by one or more people

For books, long references are simple. They contain the author, title, date of publication, and the place of publication.

> Carter, R. (1998). *Vocabulary: Applied Linguistic Perspectives* (2nd edn). London: Routledge.
> Nattinger, J. R., & DeCarrico, J. (1992). *Lexical Phrases and Language Teaching.* Oxford: Oxford University Press.

Long references for edited collections

These are books containing collections of chapters and are edited by one or more people. Long references contain the editor, title, date of publication, the place of publication, and the publisher.

> Baker, P. (Ed.). (2008). *Approaches to Corpus Linguistics.* London: Continuum.
> Hunston, S. E., & Oakey, D. J. (Eds.). (2009). *Introducing Applied Linguistics: Concepts and Skills.* London: Routledge.

Long references for journal articles

Long references for journal articles contain the author, the article's title, date of publication, the journal's title, the volume and issue number, and the pages.

> Timmis, I. (2002). Native-speaker norms and international English: a classroom view. *English Language Teaching Journal, 56*(3), 240–249.
>
> Seidlhofer, B. (2004). Research perspectives on teaching English as a lingua franca. *Annual Review of Applied Linguistics, 24*, 209–239.

Long references for chapters in edited collections

Long references for chapters in edited collections need to contain information about both the chapter and the collection: the chapter author, the chapter title, the editor of the collection, the title of the collection, the date of publication, the pages, the place of publication, and the publisher.

> Koester, A. J. (2009). Conversation Analysis in the language classroom. In S. E. Hunston and D. J. Oakey (Eds.), *Introducing Applied Linguistics: Concepts and Skills* (pp. 67–94). London: Routledge.
>
> Dörnyei, Z. (2009). The L2 motivational self system. In Z. Dörnyei and E. Ushioda (Eds.), *Motivation, Language Identity and the L2 Self* (pp. 1–28). Clevedon: Multilingual Matters.

Long references for online sources

There are many different sources of information on the internet. Many reputable internet sources such as research journals, newspapers and government reports have real-world paper equivalents. In long references to these sources you must include the same information as you would for the paper version, as well as the address of the internet site, and the date you accessed it.

> Graddol, D. (2006). *English Next.* London: British Council. Online. Available from: http://www.britishcouncil.org/learning-research-english-next.pdf (Accessed on 3 September, 2008)
>
> McCarthy, M. (2006). 'Message Understood?' *The Guardian,* 11 April. Online. Available from: http://www.guardian.co.uk/education/2006/apr/11/highereducation.uk1 (Accessed on 5 September, 2008)

Other sources of information only exist online and have no paper equivalent. You will need to consider these sources very carefully before you decide to use them. You will need to include the following information in your long reference: the author, title, the date the source was written, the date you accessed it yourself, and the URL (web address).

If you cannot find this information about the source for its long reference, then you cannot know how much authority the author has on this topic. You also cannot know the quality and reliability of the author's information. If you use a source like this in your own writing, then you are bringing unknown quantities into your own text.

Long references for theses

Unpublished work kept in university libraries must also be given a long reference:

> Katsaridi, A. (2003). The Language of Shop Signs in Greece. Unpublished Masters dissertation, University of Birmingham, Birmingham.
>
> Sakaguchi, T. (2002). Importing Language. Unpublished Masters dissertation, University of Birmingham, Birmingham.

Long reference styles

There are many different styles of writing long references. In published academic writing, the style is decided by the publisher. In academic writing on your university course, your department will tell you which style of references is preferred. The exercises below show how features vary in different styles.

Activity 1   Identifying different long reference styles for a book

Here is the long reference to a book shown in five different styles. What are the differences between each style?

1   Hyland, K. (2006). *English for Academic Purposes* London: Routledge.

2   Hyland, K. (2006). *English for Academic Purposes* Routledge, London.

3   **Hyland, K.** (2006). English for Academic Purposes London: Routledge.

4   Hyland K (2006) 'English for Academic Purposes' Routledge, London

5   Hyland, Ken. <u>English for Academic Purposes</u> London: Routledge, 2006.

Activity 2   Identifying different styles for a book chapter

Here is the long reference to one chapter from this book, shown in the same five styles. What are the differences between each style?

1   Koester, A. J. (2009). Conversation Analysis in the language classroom. In S. E. Hunston & D. J. Oakey (Eds.), *Introducing Applied Linguistics: Concepts and Skills* (pp. 67–94). London: Routledge.

2   Koester, A. J. (2009). 'Conversation Analysis in the language classroom'. Introducing Applied Linguistics: Concepts and Skills, S. E. Hunston and D. J. Oakey, eds., Routledge, London, 67–94.

3   **Koester, A. J.** (2009). Conversation Analysis in the language classroom. In *Introducing Applied Linguistics: Concepts and Skills*, eds. S. E. Hunston and D. J. Oakey, pp. 67–94. London: Routledge.

4   Koester AJ (2009) Conversation Analysis in the language classroom. In: Hunston SE, Oakey DJ (eds) Introducing Applied Linguistics: Concepts and Skills. Routledge, London, pp 67–94

5   Koester, Almut J. 'Conversation Analysis in the Language Classroom.' <u>Introducing</u> <u>Applied Linguistics: Concepts and Skills</u>. Eds. Susan Elizabeth Hunston and David James Oakey. London: Routledge, 2009. 67–94.

Activity 3	Identifying different styles for a journal article

Here are the references to a journal article shown in the same five styles. What are the differences between each style?

1   Timmis, I. (2005). Towards a framework for teaching spoken grammar. *English Language Teaching Journal, 59*(2), 117–125.

2   Timmis, I. (2005). 'Towards a framework for teaching spoken grammar.' *English Language Teaching Journal*, 59(2), 117–125.

3   **Timmis, I.** (2005). Towards a framework for teaching spoken grammar. *English Language Teaching Journal* **59**, 117–125.

4   Timmis I (2005) Towards a framework for teaching spoken grammar. English Language Teaching Journal 59: 117–125

5   Timmis, Ivor. 'Towards a Framework for Teaching Spoken Grammar'. <u>English Language Teaching Journal</u> 59.2 (2005): 117–25.

Whichever style you are required to use, make sure you are consistent. There are several commercial bibliographical software applications available which match your short and long references in your text for you and list them in an appropriate style.

Introduction to chapter 22

This final chapter in this book deals with a skill that is often also called 'mechanical', although in fact it demands a great deal of judgement. We have called this skill 'editing', and it involves getting everything in an essay exactly right: the phrasing, the spelling, the grammar and punctuation. This is something that is a challenge for everyone, whether you are a native speaker of English or not. It is also something that it is difficult to teach – you get better at it through a lot of practice.

You may sometimes want to edit other people's work, but you also need to develop skills in editing your own. To do this, you need to read your own essay as though someone else had written it, without any of the assumptions you had when you wrote it. Here are some questions to ask about your own work:

- Are there any sentences that are not clear, that a reader who is not me would have difficulty in understanding? If so, can I re-write them to make them clearer?
- Are there any sentences that are written in a style that is too colloquial for an academic essay? If so, can I re-write them?
- Does my spell-checker identify any mis-spelled words? If so, am I sure that the spell-checker is correct in each case?
- Are there any spelling mistakes that my spell-checker does not identify; for example, have I written *form* instead of *from*?
- Are there any very long sentences, for example, more than three lines long? If so, am I sure that they are clear and punctuated correctly?
- Am I sure that I have used commas correctly? Should any of my commas be a semi-colon (;) or a full stop (.)? Have I put any commas between a subject and a verb? (An example of this mistake would be: *A very important point to notice, is the correct use of punctuation.* This should be: *A very important point to notice is the correct use of punctuation.*)
- Are there any very long paragraphs, for example, more than half a page long? If so, am I sure they should not be split into two paragraphs?

It is almost impossible not to make any mistakes at all in a very long essay or dissertation. (This is why published books use professional specialists to edit and proofread the final version.) Some mistakes, such as mis-typings, are not too important. But some mistakes, especially odd phrasing, can make it very difficult for your reader to understand what you are saying and must be changed.

Two final pieces of advice:

- If you have difficulty expressing a particular idea or using a piece of terminology, watch out for that idea or terminology in things that you read, and make a note of the phrases other writers use that you might use as well.
- When you write an essay for assessment you will receive feedback on it that will tell you if the language you are using is appropriate and accurate. Read feedback carefully and make sure you know how your next essay can be improved.

CHAPTER 22

Editing your own work

David Oakey

This section contains activities focusing on common errors by student writers. These can be concerned with breaking the conventions of academic writing, such as when using previous authors' work, or including sufficient information in long references. The other area where it is important to edit your own work is the clarity of expression. Academic English contains a lot of information which should be expressed clearly. This primarily involves making sentences simpler and noun phrases more complex.

Activity 1	Editing the use of previous authors' work

What is wrong with the way the writer has reported the work of a previous author or authors in the following sentences?

1 This tendency seems to produce 'speakers of English who can only speak like a book, because their English is modelled on an almost exclusively written version of the English' (McCarthy and Carter 1995).

2 As Carter and McCarthy (2006) point out that the choices of grammar in a teaching syllabus should not only concern written grammar but also the spoken form.

3 Coleman 1997 viewed that the behaviour of students in the countries in his study was generally passive and teacher-centred.

4 Willis and Willis (1996) suggest to use consciousness-raising activities to teach grammar instead of traditional grammar translation exercises.

5 Structural ellipsis is defined that 'a purely structural element is omitted' (Carter and McCarthy 1995: 145).

6 Ellis (1993: 5–6) identifies that 'we can envisage activities that will seek to get a learner to understand a particular feature, how it works, what it consists of and so on, but not to require that learner to actually produce sentences manifesting that particular structure.'

7 The journal *Spoken Grammar: what is it and how can we teach it* of McCarthy and Carter (1995) states the different features of spoken grammar and how they can be taught.

8 Generative grammarians criticize that a corpus is only a sample of language performance and cannot truly be considered as representative of a language (Crystal 1980).

Activity 2   Editing long references

The long references below all use the same referencing style. Each reference contains at least one mistake. Identify each mistake and suggest a correction.

1 Mona Baker (1992). *In Other Words: A Coursebook on Translation*. London: Routledge.

2 Burns, A., & Coffin, C. (Eds.). *Analysing English in a Global Context: A Reader*. London: Routledge. (2001).

3 Candlin, C. N., & Mercer, N. (Eds.). (2001). English Language Teaching in Its Social Context: A Reader. London: Routledge.

4 Carter, R. *Language and Creativity: The Art of Common Talk*. London: Routledge.

5 Coulthard, M. (1994). On Analysing and Evaluating Written Text. In M. Coulthard (Ed.), *Advances in Written Text Analysis*. London: Routledge.

6 Hoey, M. (2005). *Lexical Priming: A New Theory of Words and Language*.

7 Expanding Academic Vocabulary with an Interactive on-Line Database. *Language Learning & Technology, 9*(2), 90–110. http://llt.msu.edu/vol9num2/horst/default.html

8 Schmitt, N., & Carter, R. (2000). Lexical Phrases in Language Learning. http://www.jalt-publications.org/tlt/articles/2000/08/schmitt (Accessed 25 January 2009)

9 Sinclair, J. McH. (1994). *Trust the Text*. In M. Coulthard (Ed.), *Advances in Written Text Analysis*. (pp. 12–25). London: Routledge.

10 Taylor, D. S. (1994). Inauthentic Authenticity or Authentic Inauthenticity? The Pseudo-Problem of Authenticity in the Language Classroom. *TESL-EJ, 1*(2). http://www-writing.berkeley.edu/tesl-ej/ej02/a.1.html

Activity 3   Editing for clarity and precision

Below are extracts from student essays. How can they be improved?

1 The English language learning situation in my country will now be discussed which spends a huge amount of money on the teaching of English.

2 Krashen's approach can be illustrated the example mentioned at the beginning of the previous section.

3 The role of the teacher in the classroom is very important, he or she should aim to help their students to become more fluent and communicative during the follow-up activities.

4 In task based learning, there is one stage which takes place once the main task

has been completed there is one stage which is called the 'post-task' stage.

5   Young learners are extremely inquisitive, and this is a powerful motivating factor. While children's attention or concentration span is much shorter than that of adults.

6   To say conclusively that the significant differences in lexical selection between the groups observed in this study are related to positive and negative politeness is very difficult to say.

7   On the other hand, there is one important limitation of the use of TBT in English classes in elementary schools considering the size of the class which makes teachers hard manage students as it is a too large group to demonstrate the TBT method and monitor the students while students are performing a task.

8   The relationship between the use of language learning strategies to success in learning English as a foreign language, and to gender has been the focus of a growing body of research over the past decade.

9   Despite this long tradition of English language teaching, the methodological approaches used have not been much changed yet as the teaching and learning are seriously concentrated on grammar and reading skills and teachers dominate the classroom.

10 The most obvious difference between learners of English for Specific Purposes and learners of general English is their age. ESP students are normally adults who might have a special reason to learn English for work. On the contrary, the age range of students who intend to study general English is much wider.

Answer key

CHAPTER 17
Activity 1: identifying the head noun in a noun phrase
1. language <u>use</u>
2. language <u>learners</u>
3. <u>users</u> of the language
4. <u>learning</u> a second language
5. the language learning <u>process</u>
6. the <u>role</u> of the language teacher
7. second language learner <u>attitudes</u>
8. second language research <u>projects</u>
9. the <u>importance</u> of spoken language
10. English language learning <u>contexts</u>
11. <u>models</u> of second language learning
12. doing <u>research</u> into spoken language
13. second language acquisition <u>research</u>
14. the <u>psychology</u> of the language learner
15. different <u>varieties</u> of the target language
16. a prestigious standard <u>form</u> of the language
17. language <u>use</u> across varieties and situations
18. the <u>structure</u> of the language of the source text
19. the <u>findings</u> of research into second language acquisition
20. new and different <u>ways</u> of thinking about language teaching
21. individual users' intuitive <u>knowledge</u> of the language system
22. the information processing <u>model</u> of foreign language learning
23. cultural <u>politics</u> within international English language education
24. applied <u>linguistics</u> outside the context of the language classroom
25. theoretical <u>bases</u> of communicative approaches to second language teaching and testing

Activity 2: identifying the head noun in noun phrases containing relative clauses
1. the **topic** <u>being</u> investigated
2. **collocations** <u>marked</u> with a '+'
3. a web **designer** <u>working</u> at home
4. **classes** <u>focusing</u> on speaking skills
5. **texts** and spoken **data** <u>produced</u> by native speakers
6. the 20 semantic **categories** <u>identified</u> by Francis *et al.*
7. the transcript **conventions** <u>discussed</u> earlier in this chapter
8. the **methodology** <u>emerging</u> from the cultural chauvinism argument
9. the **challenges** <u>posed</u> by researching something as ephemeral as speech
10. cross-borders **migration** <u>arising</u> from civil war and economic disparities
11. **controversies** <u>surrounding</u> the introduction of CLT in non-Western countries
12. the **emergence** of new varieties of English <u>associated</u> with communities of English-users

13. **behaviour** <u>considered</u> 'exceptions' to the stereotype in the cultural description methodology
14. a quick **check** of a small sample of applied linguistics articles <u>published</u> in academic journals
15. a **distinction** between societies <u>oriented</u> towards the 'individual' and those that prioritize the 'collective'
16. two necessary **characteristics** of the language learning process <u>relating</u> to the nature of language as system
17. **chapters** <u>dealing</u> with topics in applied linguistics that do not relate directly to language teaching
18. **advertisements** <u>aimed</u> at consumers who speak a first language which is not English and who may in some instances not understand English
19. **research** <u>looking</u> at the effects of an educational intervention designed to encourage primary school children to explore ideas more effectively
20. nominalized **forms** that are standard technical terms <u>associated</u> with different areas of applied linguistics which even the less successful writers use comfortably

Activity 3: making sense of lists of noun phrases
1 The key issues introduced in this chapter are: the characterisation of cultures; critical applied linguistics; and inter-cultural communication.
General noun: *issues;* items in the list: 3
Head nouns of items: *the <u>characterization</u> of cultures* (preposition)
applied <u>linguistics</u> (adjective)
inter-cultural <u>communication</u> (adjective)

2 It discusses three key issues: Communicative Competence, Communication used in classroom teaching, and controversies surrounding the introduction of CLT in non-Western countries.
General noun: *issues;* items in the list: 3
Head nouns of items:
Communicative <u>Competence</u> (adjective)
<u>Communication</u> used in classroom teaching (non-finite relative clause without a relative pronoun)
<u>controversies</u> surrounding the introduction of CLT in non-Western countries (non-finite relative clause without a relative pronoun)

3 There are many factors influencing language learners and teachers: teaching methods, the learners' motivation, the community of the institution in which the learning takes place, and the role of the language being learnt in the community of which teachers and learners are a part.
General noun: *factors;* items in the list: 4
Head nouns of items:
teaching <u>methods</u> (gerund)
the learners' <u>motivation</u> (compound (possessive))
the <u>community</u> of the institution in which the learning takes place (preposition)

the role of the language being learnt in the community of which teachers and learners are a part (preposition)

4 Research outputs based on such corpora of spoken language-in-use are wide-ranging and include, for example, descriptions of spoken versus written lexis and grammar (e.g. Biber et al. 1999; Carter and McCarthy 2006), discourse particles (Aijmer 2002), courtroom talk (Cotterill 2004), media discourse (O'Keeffe 2006) and health care communication (Adolphs et al. 2004). General noun: *outputs;* items in the list: 5 Head nouns of items: *descriptions of spoken versus written lexis and grammar* (preposition) *discourse particles* (compound) *courtroom talk* (compound) *media discourse* (compound) *health care communication* (compound)

5 However, the past two decades have seen major advances in the development of spoken corpora including, for example, the Cambridge and Nottingham Corpus of Discourse in English CANCODE (McCarthy 1998), the Limerick Corpus of Irish English LCIE (Farr et al. 2004), the Hong Kong Corpus of Spoken English HKCSE (see Cheng and Warren 1999, 2000, 2002), the Michigan Corpus of Academic Spoken English MICASE (Simpson et al. 2000), and the Corpus of Spoken Professional American English CSPAE.
General noun: *advances;* items in the list: 5
Head nouns of items:
the Cambridge and Nottingham Corpus of Discourse in English CANCODE (compound, preposition)
the Limerick Corpus of Irish English LCIE (compound, preposition)
the Hong Kong Corpus of Spoken English HKCSE (compound, preposition)
the Michigan Corpus of Academic Spoken English MICASE (compound, preposition)
the Corpus of Spoken Professional American English CSPAE (preposition)

6 Norris (2004) describes a step-by-step process that involves the separate transcription of spoken language, proxemics (distance between speakers), posture, gesture, head movement, gaze, music (i.e. background music that speakers seem to respond to), and print (participants' use of print media), followed by the integration of these dimensions to produce a complete transcript.
General noun: *process;* items in the list: 9
Head nouns of items:
the separate transcription of spoken language (preposition)
proxemics (distance between speakers)
posture
gesture
head movement
gaze
music (i.e. background music that speakers seem to respond to)
print (participants' use of print media)
the integration of these dimensions to produce a complete transcript (preposition)

Activity 4: inventing noun phrases
Possible examples

learners of English
the analysis of writing by learners of English
research focusing on the writing of English language teachers

CHAPTER 18
Activity 1: identifying reporting verbs

The real world dynamics that challenge a stable or context-free definition of communicative competence have given rise to a number of alternative views. For example, Alptekin (2002) argues that Canale and Swain's native speaker grammatical competence is an inappropriate aim in contexts where students are more likely to use English with other non-native speakers. Alptekin suggests that a more appropriate aim is the kind of linguistic competence developed by successful learners of English. Smith (2002) proposes that exploring patterns of communication in social networks can help define communicative competence for groups of individuals. Moreover, Leung suggests that we should go back to the ethnographic bases of Hymes' (1972) original formulation of communicative competence, arguing that language educators should 're-engage with the socially dynamic uses of English and continually re-work the contextual meaning of the concept' (Leung 2005: 138).

Activity 2: identifying patterns of reporting verbs

1. Labov (1972) states that lower middle class women often endorse this type of shift.
Verb: *state*   Pattern: V + *that*   Reports: something the previous author said

2. Willis and Willis (2007) offer ways to generate a varied sequence of tasks arising from a chosen topic.
Verb: *offer*   Pattern: V + noun   Reports: something the previous authors said

3. Edwards and Westgate (1994) suggest that every hour's recording may require 15 hours for transcription.
Verb: *suggest*   Pattern: V + *that*   Reports: something the previous authors said

4. Sakaguchi (2002) investigated the language of drinks cans sold from street kiosks and machines in Japan.
Verb: *investigated*   Pattern: V + noun   Reports: something the previous author did

5. Savignon (1991) defined CLT as involving negotiation, interpretation and expression of meaning in the target language.
Verb: *define*   Pattern: V + noun + *as* + noun   Reports: something the previous author said

6. Halliday and Hasan (1985) use the term 'register' to refer to different kinds of spoken and written language that are found in different contexts.

Verb: *use*   Pattern: V + noun   Reports: something the previous authors said

7. For example, Chilton and Schäffner (1997: 222) point out examples such as *the opposition's claims were shot down in flames*, in articles about politics.
Verb: *point out*   Pattern: V + noun   Reports: something the previous authors said

8. Adolphs (2006: 41) shows the ten most frequent words in the written part of the British National Corpus compared with the spoken CANCODE corpus.
Verb: *show*   Pattern: V + noun   Reports: something the previous author said

9. Kim (2005: 108) also notes that Hofstede's model 'forced a single bipolar dimension of individualism and saw collectivism as an absence of individualism' that was derived from the need to negatively Other 'barbarians'.
Verb: *note*   Pattern: V + *that*   Reports: something the previous author said

10. Kumaravadivelu (2007: 65–9) maintains that cultural stereotypes which are believed to be egalitarian by their users are an influential underpinning of US notions of cultural assimilation which in turn impose ethnocentric cultural viewpoints.
Verb: *maintain*   Pattern: V + *that*   Reports: something the previous author said

Activity 3: the writer's point of view and 'voice'

Activity 4: identifying writers' points of view and 'voice'

1. Some researchers maintain that collocation is central to language production (Sinclair 1991; Hunston and Francis 2000).
Claim: collocation is central to language production
Words in the text: writer's
Writer's opinion of the claim: neutral (*maintain* is the reporting verb)
'Voice' heard by the reader: mostly writer's

2. According to Lamie (2001), for example, one criticism of recording interviews is the uneasiness a participant may feel in response to being recorded.
Claim: one criticism of recording interviews is the uneasiness a participant may feel in response to being recorded
Words in the text: writer's
Writer's opinion of the claim: neutral (the structure is *according to X*)
'Voice' heard by the reader: mostly writer's

3. Table 1 suggests the existence of what Cruse (ibid.) calls 'semi-systematic collocational restrictions' which act on *purse* and other near-synonyms.
Claim: there is a language feature called 'semi-systematic collocational restrictions'
Words in the text: writer's and previous author's
Writer's opinion of the claim: neutral (*calls*)
'Voice' heard by the reader: mostly writer's

4. *Da* is a discourse particle, and as Allen et al. remark

	Statement	words in the text	writer's opinion of the statement	'voice' heard by the reader
1	previous author's	previous author's	neutral (no reporting verb)	previous author (none of the writer's words are used in the sentence)
2	previous author's	previous author's	neutral (*argue*)	previous author more than writer (the previous author's name is at the beginning of the sentence)
3	previous author's	previous author's	agrees (*point out*)	previous author more than writer (the previous author's name is at the beginning of the sentence)
4	previous author's	previous author's	neutral (*claim*); the writer may disagree afterwards	previous author more than writer (the previous author's name is at the beginning of the sentence)
5	previous author's	previous author's	agrees (*as . . . + reporting verb* structure, *point out*)	writer and previous author are equal, due to the *as . . . + reporting verb* structure
6	previous author's	previous author's	neutral (*according to* structure)	writer and previous author are equal, due to the *according to . . .* structure and the use of the previous author's words
7	previous author's	writer's	the reader thinks this is the writer's opinion	totally the writer's
8	previous author's	writer's	neutral (no reporting verb)	more the writer's; the previous author's name is outside the sentence in brackets
9	previous	writer's	neutral	mostly the writer's; the previous author's name is outside the sentence in brackets, and it is the writer's summary of the previous author's statement

(1995: 366), 'it is not always possible to provide a literal translation' into English for words of that class.
Claim: 'it is not always possible to provide a literal translation'
Words in the text: writer's and previous author's
Writer's opinion of the claim: agrees (the structure is *as . . . + reporting verb*)
'Voice' heard by the reader: mostly writer's

5. Chen and Foley (2004) have demonstrated that there is a similar link between higher proficiency in the use of nominalization in the L2 and academic success.
Claim: there is a similar link between higher proficiency in the use of nominalization in the L2 and academic success
Words in the text: writer's
Writer's opinion of the claim: agrees (*demonstrate*)
'Voice' heard by the reader: mostly writer's

6. According to Berg (1995), this is an important step to ensure the suitability of research instruments and to help check for researcher bias in the interview questions.
Claim: this is an important step to ensure the suitability of research instruments and to help check for researcher bias in the interview questions.
Words in the text: writer's
Writer's opinion of the claim: neutral (the structure is *according to X*)
'Voice' heard by the reader: mostly writer's

7. As Bucholtz (2000) argues, transcription therefore requires a degree of reflexivity and an acknowledgement of the affordances and limitations of the particular choices made.
Claim: transcription therefore requires a degree of reflexivity and an acknowledgement of the affordances and limitations of the particular choices made
Words in the text: writer's
Writer's opinion of the claim: agrees (the structure is *as . . . + reporting verb*)
'Voice' heard by the reader: mostly writer's

8. A study of telephone dialogues in a selection of English language textbooks (Wong 2002) revealed that the opening sequences bore little resemblance to those of natural conversations.
Claim: the opening sequences of telephone dialogues bear little resemblance to those of natural conversations.
Words in the text: writer's
Writer's opinion of the claim: agrees (*reveal*)
'Voice' heard by the reader: mostly writer's

9. Seedhouse (2004), who uses CA to investigate classroom language, argues that the classroom has its own 'interactional architecture' which differs from that of language outside the classroom.
Claim: the classroom has its own 'interactional architecture' which differs from that of language outside the classroom.
Words in the text: mostly writer's
Writer's opinion of the claim: neutral (*argue*)
'Voice' heard by the reader: writer's and previous author's (his name begins the sentence)

10. As Bogdan and Biklen (1998) noted, the accuracy with which the transcribing of interviews is done influences how easy it is to work with the reported data from the interview participants.
Claim: the accuracy with which the transcribing of interviews is done influences how easy it is to work with the reported data from the interview participants.
Words in the text: writer's
Writer's opinion of the claim: agrees (the structure is *as . . . + reporting verb*)
'Voice' heard by the reader: mostly writer's

11. In his study of CANCODE data McCarthy (1998: 161) finds that 'in the narrative texts in the CANCODE corpus, speech reports are overwhelmingly direct speech, and with reporting verbs in past simple (*said*, *told*) or historical present *says*.'
Claim: in the narrative texts in the CANCODE corpus, speech reports are overwhelmingly direct speech, and with reporting verbs in past simple (*said*, *told*) or historical present *says*
Words in the text: mostly previous author's
Writer's opinion of the claim: agrees (*find*)
'Voice' heard by the reader: mostly writer's

12. Katsaridi (2003) looked at shop signs in streets in Athens and found that English was used to create a perception in potential Greek customers that the shop sold high-quality goods and that they, the customers, belonged to the social group that would buy such high-quality products.
Claim: English is used to create a perception in potential Greek customers that the shop sold high quality goods . . .
Words in the text: writer's
Writer's opinion of the claim: agrees (*finds*)
'Voice' heard by the reader: mostly writer's

13. As Bucholtz (2000) argues, transcription therefore requires a degree of reflexivity and an acknowledgement of the affordances and limitations of the particular choices made.
Claim: transcription requires a degree of reflexivity and an acknowledgement of the affordances and limitations of the particular choices made
Words in the text: writer's
Writer's opinion of the claim: agrees (the structure is *as . . . + reporting verb*)
'Voice' heard by the reader: mostly writer's

14. Citing the work of social theorist Browne (2006), Waters defines political correctness as a hegemonic force which has become dominant in English-speaking Western society and creates the impression that everyone is either an 'oppressor' or a 'victim' (Waters 2007b: 354).
Claim: political correctness is a hegemonic force which has become dominant in English-speaking Western society and creates the impression that everyone is either an oppressor or a victim
Words in the text: mostly writer's
Writer's opinion of the claim: neutral (*define*)
'Voice' heard by the reader: mostly writer's

CHAPTER 19
Activity 1: identifying writers' opinions of previous authors' work

1
Previous author: Waters
Writer's opinion: disagrees
Words or phrases: *However . . . his argument may also be naïve*

2
Previous author: Kumaravadivelu
Writer's opinion: agrees
Words or phrases: *puts this very well*

3
Previous author: Kumaravadivelu; Waters
Writer's opinion: probably agrees with Kumaravadivelu and disagrees with Waters
Words or phrases: *If we accept X, however, it is difficult to accept Y*

4
Previous author: Jenkins
Writer's opinion: neutral; possibly disagrees
Words or phrases: *her ideas have met with a mixed* (i.e. both good and bad) *reception*

5
Previous author: un-named critics of SLA
Writer's opinion: disagrees
Words or phrases: *casts doubt on*

6
Previous author: Krashen
Writer's opinion: Uses Long and Skehan's work to disagree with Krashen, although a paradox remains
Words or phrases: *suggests that Krashen is mistaken*

CHAPTER 20
Activity 1: determining the organization of an introduction

1

Sentence		Meaning
1. the statement covers . . .	the aim of the chapter	general
2 and 3. the statements cover . . .	the methodology used in conducting the research presented in this chapter	more specific
4. the statement covers . . .	the specific word that is discussed in this chapter	most specific

2

Sentence		Meaning
1, 2 and 3. the statements cover . . .	research issues in the field of motivation in general	general
4. the statement covers . . .	L2 motivation	more specific
5. the statement covers . . .	The specific shift in L2 motivation theory described in this chapter	specific
6. the statement covers . . .	The role of theoretical and research findings in this shift	very specific

Activity 2: matching organizing statements with the content of a text

1 (Swann)
  1. Transcription conventions
  2. Representing languages, varieties and styles
  3. Laying out a transcript
  4. Multimodal transcription

2 (Oakey)
  1. Insights into collocation
       Methodological approaches 1
       Methodological approaches 2
  2 Collocation: creativity and conformity
       Native English language users
       International lingua franca English users

3 (Johnson and Woolls)
  1. Questions of the 'who wrote this?' type
  2. The effect of the small amount of data available
  3. Similarity

CHAPTER 21
Activity 1: identifying different long reference styles for a book

	Name	Year of publication	Title	Place of publication	Publisher
1	surname comma initial of first name full stop	before title in brackets full stop	in italics	before publisher with colon	after place of publication
2	surname comma initial of first name full stop	before title in brackets full stop	in italics	after publisher with comma	before place of publication
3	surname comma initial of first name full stop in bold	before title in brackets full stop	normal	before publisher with colon	after place of publication
4	surname no comma initial of first name no full stop	before title in brackets no full stop	in quotation marks	after publisher with comma	before place of publication
5	surname comma first name in full full stop	after publisher no brackets full stop	underlined	before publisher with colon	after place of publication

Activity 2: identifying different styles for a book chapter

	Writer's name	Year of publication	Chapter title	Link	Book title	Editor's names	Editor-ship	Place of publication	Publisher	Page numbers
1	surname comma initial of first names full stops	before title in brackets full stops	normal	*In*	in italics	initial of first names surname ampersand (&) full stop	(Eds.),	before publisher with colon	after place of publication	after title pp. in brackets
2	surname comma initial of first names full stops	before title in brackets full stop	in quotation marks	none	normal	initial of first names surname *and* full stops	eds.,	after publisher with comma	before place of publication	after place of publication no pp. no brackets
3	surname comma initial of first names full stops in bold	before title in brackets full stop	normal	*In*	in italics	initial of first names surname *and* full stops	eds.	before publisher with colon	after place of publication	after editors pp. no brackets

	Writer's name	Year of publication	Chapter title	Link	Book title	Editor's names	Editor-ship	Place of publication	Publisher	Page numbers
4	surname no comma initial of first names no full stops	before title in brackets no full stop	normal	*In:*	normal	surname initial of first names comma no full stops	(eds.),	after publisher with comma	before place place of publication	after place of publication pp. no brackets
5	surname comma first name in full full stop	after publisher no brackets full stop	in quotation marks	none	under-lined	first names in full surname and full stop	Eds.	before publisher with colon	after place of publication	after year of publication no pp. no brackets

Activity 3: identifying different styles for a journal article

	Writer's name	Year of publication	Article title	Journal title	Volume number	Issue number	Page numbers
1	surname comma initial of first name full stop	before title in brackets	normal	in italics	in italics	in brackets	after issue number
2	surname comma initial of first name full stop	before title in brackets full stop	in quotation marks	in italics	normal	in brackets	after issue number
3	surname comma initial of first name full stop in bold	before title in brackets full stop	normal	in italics	in bold	not used	after volume numbers
4	surname no comma initial of first name no full stops	before title in brackets no full stop	normal	normal	normal with colon	not used	after volume number
5	surname comma first name in full full stop	after issue number in brackets with colon	in quotation marks	underlined	normal with full stop	normal	after year of publication

CHAPTER 22
Activity 1: editing the use of previous authors' work
1. This tendency seems to produce 'speakers of English who can only speak like a book, because their English is modelled on an almost exclusively written version of the English' (McCarthy and Carter 1995).

Because this is a direct quotation of the work of previous authors, the page number from which the words were taken is needed in the short reference.

2. As Carter and McCarthy (2006) point out that the choices of grammar in a teaching syllabus should not only concern written grammar but also the spoken form.

The *as + reporting verb* structure cannot be followed by a *that* clause. This should either be re-written as:
Carter and McCarthy (2006) **point out that** the choices of grammar . . .
or
As Carter and McCarthy (2006) **point out**, the choices of grammar . . .

3. Coleman 1997 viewed that the behaviour of students in the countries in his study was generally passive and teacher-centred.

The year of publication should be in brackets. Also, the reporting verb *view* does not follow the *V + that* pattern; instead it uses *V + noun + as + noun*. This should be re-written as:
Coleman (1997) **viewed** the behaviour of students in the countries in his study **as** generally passive and teacher-centred.

4. Willis and Willis (1996) suggest to use consciousness-raising activities to teach grammar instead of traditional grammar translation exercises.

The reporting verb *suggest* does not follow the *V + to infinitive* pattern; instead it uses either *V + noun* or *V + that*. This should be re-written as:
Willis and Willis (1996) suggest **using** consciousness-raising activities to teach grammar instead of traditional grammar translation exercises.
or
Willis and Willis (1996) **suggest that** consciousness-raising activities **should be used** to teach grammar instead of traditional grammar translation exercises.

5. Structural ellipsis is defined that 'a purely structural element is omitted' (Carter and McCarthy 1995: 145)

The reporting verb *define* does not follow the *V + that* pattern; instead it uses *V + noun + as + noun*. In the passive voice this pattern is *n + be + V-ed as + n*. The clause *a purely structural element is omitted* also does not fit the verb pattern for *define*. It must instead be changed into a noun phrase, *the omission of a purely structural element*. Since this changes the previous authors' original words it is now an indirect quotation, and so the quotation marks can be removed from the sentence. A full stop is also required after the short reference. This sentence should be re-written as:

Structural ellipsis **is defined as** the omission of a purely structural element (Carter and McCarthy 1995: 145).

6. Ellis (1993: 5–6) identifies that 'we can envisage activities that will seek to get a learner to understand a particular feature, how it works, what it consists of and so on, but not to require that learner to actually produce sentences manifesting that particular structure.'

This is a rather long direct quotation of 40 words and should be indented. The reporting verb *identify* does not follow the *V + that* pattern; instead it uses *V + noun + as + noun*. This pattern is not appropriate for the quotation. Use another verb such as *argue* or *claim*, depending on your opinion of Ellis's statement. This sentence could be re-written as:

Ellis (1993: 5–6) argues that
> we can envisage activities that will seek to get a learner to understand a particular feature, how it works, what it consists of and so on, but not to require that learner to actually produce sentences manifesting that particular structure.

7. The journal *Spoken Grammar: what is it and how can we teach it* of McCarthy and Carter (1995) states the different features of spoken grammar and how they can be taught.

The short reference is not short enough. Only the previous authors' names and year of publication are necessary. The verb must agree with the plural subject, so *states* should become *state*. The sentence should be re-written as:

McCarthy and Carter (1995) state the different features of spoken grammar and how they can be taught.

8. Generative grammarians criticize that a corpus is only a sample of language performance and cannot truly be considered as representative of a language (Crystal 1980).

The reporting verb *criticize* does not follow the *V + that* pattern, although it would be very useful if it did! Instead it uses *V + noun*. It is not necessary to use *criticize* in this sentence, however, since the criticism is contained in the statement itself. This sentence could be re-written as:

Generative grammarians argue that a corpus is only a sample of language performance and cannot truly be considered as representative of a language (Crystal 1980).

Activity 2: editing long references
1. Mona Baker (1992). *In Other Words: A Coursebook on Translation*. London: Routledge.
The author's surname needs to come first, followed by the initial of her first name:
Baker, M. (1992). *In Other Words: A Coursebook on Translation*. London: Routledge.

2. Burns, A., & Coffin, C. (Eds.). *Analysing English in a Global Context: A Reader*. London: Routledge. (2001).
The year of publication should come before the title of the book:
Burns, A., & Coffin, C. (Eds.). (2001). *Analysing English in a Global Context: A Reader*. London: Routledge.

3. Candlin, C. N., & Mercer, N. (Eds.). (2001). <u>English Language Teaching in Its Social Context: A Reader</u>. London: Routledge.
The book title should be in italics:
Candlin, C. N., & Mercer, N. (Eds.). (2001). *English Language Teaching in Its Social Context: A Reader*. London: Routledge.

4. Carter, R. *Language and Creativity: The Art of Common Talk*. London: Routledge.
The year of publication is missing:
Carter, R. (2004). *Language and Creativity: The Art of Common Talk*. London: Routledge.

5. Coulthard, M. (1994). On Analysing and Evaluating Written Text. In M. Coulthard (Ed.), *Advances in Written Text Analysis.* London: Routledge.
Chapters in edited books need page numbers; the only words in the chapter title that should have a capital letter are the first word and the names of people, places, organizations, theories and so on:
Coulthard, M. (1994). On analysing and evaluating written text. In M. Coulthard (Ed.), *Advances in Written Text Analysis.* (pp. 1–11). London: Routledge.

6. Hoey, M. (2005). *Lexical Priming: A New Theory of Words and Language.*
The place of publication and publisher are missing:
Hoey, M. (2005). *Lexical Priming: A New Theory of Words and Language.* London: Routledge.

7. Expanding Academic Vocabulary with an Interactive on-Line Database. *Language Learning & Technology, 9*(2), 90-110. http://llt.msu.edu/vol9num2/horst/default.html
The author, year of publication, and the date accessed are missing; the only words in the chapter title that should have a capital letter are the first word and the names of people, places, organizations, theories and so on:
Horst, M., Cobb, T., & Nicolae, I. (2005). Expanding academic vocabulary with an interactive on-line database. *Language Learning & Technology, 9*(2), 90–110. http://llt.msu.edu/vol9num2/horst/default.html (Accessed 25 January 2009)

8. Schmitt, N., & Carter, R. (2000). Lexical Phrases in Language Learning.
http://www.jalt-publications.org/tlt/articles/2000/08/schmitt (Accessed 25 January 2009)
Details of the journal are missing; the only words in the chapter title that should have a capital letter are the first word and the names of people, places, organizations, theories and so on:
Schmitt, N., & Carter, R. (2000). Lexical phrases in language learning. *The Language Teacher Online, 24*(8). http://www.jalt-publications.org/tlt/articles/2000/08/schmitt (Accessed 25 January 2009)

9. Sinclair, J. McH. (1994). *Trust the Text*. In M. Coulthard (Ed.), *Advances in Written Text Analysis.* (pp. 12–25). London: Routledge.
The title of a book chapter should not be in italics; the only words in the chapter title that should have a capital letter are the first word and the names of people, places, organizations, theories and so on:
Sinclair, J. M. (1994). Trust the text. In M. Coulthard (Ed.), *Advances in Written Text Analysis.* (pp. 12–25). London: Routledge.

10. Taylor, D. S. (1994). <u>Inauthentic Authenticity or Authentic Inauthenticity? The Pseudo-Problem of Authenticity in the Language Classroom</u>. *TESL-EJ, 1*(2). http://www-writing.berkeley.edu/tesl-ej/ej02/a.1.html
The article title should not be underlined; the date accessed is missing:
Taylor, D. S. (1994). Inauthentic authenticity or authentic inauthenticity? The pseudo-problem of authenticity in the language classroom. *TESL-EJ, 1*(2). http://www-writing.berkeley.edu/tesl-ej/ej02/a.1.html (Accessed 25 January 2009)

Activity 3: editing for clarity and precision
1. The English language learning situation in my country will now be discussed which spends a huge amount of money on the teaching of English.

The sentence is not clear because the non-defining relative clause adding more information to *country* is detached from the rest of the noun phrase. The sentence could either be re-written as:

The English language learning situation in my country, which spends a huge amount of money on the teaching of English, will now be discussed
or
This essay will now discuss the English language learning situation in my country, which spends a huge amount of money on the teaching of English.

2. Krashen's approach can be illustrated the example mentioned at the beginning of the previous section.

It is not clear what the writer means in this sentence because the use of the passive voice is inaccurate. Can Krashen's approach be illustrated by the example, or can Krashen's approach illustrate the example? The sentence could either be re-written as:

Krashen's approach can illustrate the example mentioned at the beginning of the previous section.
or
Krashen's approach can be illustrated by the example mentioned at the beginning of the previous section.

3. The role of the teacher in the classroom is very important, he or she should aim to help their students to become more fluent and communicative during the follow-up activities.

This is a run-on sentence. It should either be two sentences:
The role of the teacher in the classroom is very important.

He or she should aim to help their students to become more fluent and communicative during the follow-up activities.

or the comma should be a semi-colon.

The role of the teacher in the classroom is very important; he or she should aim to help their students to become more fluent and communicative during the follow-up activities.

In sentences like the one in this example, where the gender of the teacher is not known, you can use gender-neutral pronoun forms such as *he or she*. However it is possible to greatly inflate the number of words required to complete the sentence:

he or she should aim to help **his or her** students to become more fluent and communicative during the follow-up activities.

they/their is also possible because it also does not reveal the gender of the teacher:
they should aim to help **their** students to become more fluent and communicative during the follow-up activities.

It is sometimes considered ungrammatical to refer to a singular teacher with a plural pronoun, however.

4. In task based learning, there is one stage which takes place once the main task has been completed there is one stage which is called the 'post-task' stage.

The writer has used *there is one stage* twice and created a blend of two sentences:

There is one stage which takes place once the main task has been completed.
and
Once the main task has been completed there is one stage which is called the 'post-task' stage.

This should be a single noun phrase:

In task based learning, **the stage which takes place once the main task has been completed** is called the 'post-task' stage.

5. Young learners are extremely inquisitive, and this is a powerful motivating factor. While children's attention or concentration span is much shorter than that of adults.

The second sentence is not a sentence, since *while* joins two clauses in one sentence. The second sentence could be re-written as:
However, children's attention or concentration span is much shorter than that of adults.

6. To say conclusively that the significant differences in lexical selection between the groups observed in this study are related to positive and negative politeness is very difficult to say.

The first noun phrase is too long; the writer also repeats *say*. The information in the sentence can be re-arranged by using a dummy subject such as *it* or *there* so that the writer's opinion comes first:

It is very difficult to say conclusively that the significant differences in lexical selection between the groups observed in this study are related to positive and negative politeness.

or

There is no clear evidence that the significant differences in lexical selection between the groups observed in this study are related to positive and negative politeness.

7. On the other hand, there is one important limitation of the use of TBT in English classes in elementary schools considering the size of the class which makes teachers hard manage students as it is a too large group to demonstrate the TBT method and monitor the students while students are performing a task.

This is a common problem in MA student essay writing; there is too much information for the sentence structure to hold. The grammar here is more like speech, as extra information in added in clauses. Shorter sentences consisting of longer noun phrases will help structure the information. The sentence could be re-written as:

On the other hand, there is one important limitation of the use of TBT in English classes in elementary schools: the size of the class. It is hard for teachers to manage large groups of students using the TBT method and it is difficult to monitor the students while they are performing a task.

8. The relationship between the use of language learning strategies to success in learning English as a foreign language, and to gender has been the focus of a growing body of research over the past decade.

This sentence is not clear because the writer has not been specific enough about whether the relationship is between two things or three things. By reordering the information and starting with a noun phrase about research, the *relationship* noun phrase to be placed towards the end of the sentence. The sentence could be re-written as:

A growing body of research over the past decade has focused on the relationship between the use of language learning strategies, success in learning English as a foreign language, and gender.

9. Despite this long tradition of English language teaching, the methodological approaches used have not been much changed yet as the teaching and learning are seriously concentrated on grammar and reading skills and teachers dominate the classroom.

Again there is too much information for a single sentence to hold. The cause-effect relationship shown with *as* should be divided in two sentences. The idea in the first sentence can be referred to by the pronoun *this* at the beginning of the second sentence. The sentence could be re-written as:

Despite this long tradition of English language teaching, the methodological approaches used have not been much changed yet. **This is because** teaching and learning are seriously concentrated on grammar and reading skills and teachers dominate the classroom.

10. The most obvious difference between learners of English for Specific Purposes and learners of general English is their age. ESP students are normally adults who might have a special reason to learn English for work. On the contrary, the age range of students who intend to study general English is much wider.

The writer is describing the difference between two sets of learners and makes a very common mistake. Sentences describing different features are linked by *in contrast* or *by contrast*. *On the contrary* links one sentence containing a negative idea with a sentence containing a positive idea with an *opposite* (not just different) meaning. The sentence could be re-written as:

The most obvious difference between learners of English for Specific Purposes and learners of general English is their age. ESP students are normally adults who might have a special reason to learn English for work. The age range of students who intend to study general English is **by contrast** much wider.

Index